The
Change Center

By
HOWARD D. BLAZEK

THE CHANGE CENTER
Copyright © 2023 Howard D. Blazek.

No part of this publication may be reproduced, distributed, or transmitted in any form or by any means, including photocopying, recording, or other electronic or mechanical methods, without the prior written permission of the publisher, except in the case of brief quotations embodied in reviews and certain other non-commercial uses permitted by copyright law.

Authorunit
17130 Van Buren Blvd., Ste. 238,
Riverside, CA 92504
877-826-5888
www.authorunit.com

Because of the dynamic nature of the Internet, any web addresses or links contained in this book may have changed since publication and may no longer be valid. The views expressed in the work are solely those of the author and do not necessarily reflect the views of the publisher, and the publisher hereby disclaims any responsibility for them.

Any people depicted in stock imagery provided by Getty images are models, and such images are being used for illustrative purposes only.

ISBN 979-8-89030-018-8 (Paperback)
ISBN 979-8-89030-143-7 (Ebook)
ISBN 979-8-89030-144-4 (Hardcover)

Printed in the United States of America

This book was originally published as *A Week on a Ward* by Vincent Blade Douglas (pen name). It was revised with the appendix added and published as The Change Center under my own name (green cover). This is the fine-tuned current version.

iv

Contents

Preface 1

    Then 1

    and now 2

    disclaimer 2

Introduction 3

    Tripping 7

    Yoga 13

    Mind Control 15

    Linda 21

Getting IN 25

Saturday 45

Sunday 77

Monday 107

Tuesday 141

Wednesday 161

Thursday 179

Friday 193

Getting OUT 209

After Images 217

Final Word 227

Appendix 229

Dead Like Him 231

Epilogue 254

vi

PREFACE

Some 50 years ago, I was introduced to psychedelics and psychic phenomena. It did not end well. Although I only spent a week on a closed psychiatric ward, that one week would drastically affect the rest of my life. It took me at least six months to get the full use of my hands back. I'm not so sure I have ever gotten the full use of my mind back.

This is my story. This is my song. After a lifetime of learning and experience, I thought I would understand what happened to me. I would learn from it and be able to help others. This has not been the case.

The events in this book occurred many years ago. I have chosen to share them at this time in my life.

Then

This book was started while I was still mad. Sheer will power, together with the all-pervading conviction I had something very important to say drove me to its writing. I persevered, despite impaired use of my hands, memory lapses, hallucinations, little energy, and ohmigod, the fear.

I completed the first draft of my story in the six months following my release from the psychiatric ward. Much of it was rewritten in the next couple of years. I was then forced to put it aside. Now, so many years later, an inner need forced me to finish it. The memories are true. The pain was real. Any philosophy, explanations, or rationalizations which have crept in are simply words used to describe something I still don't understand. I had a psychotic flip-out. This is my story.

Preface

and now

The bulk of this ego trip to myself was not touched for years. It was resurrected briefly in the year 2001. It was finished only now. About a year after my ward experience, I was lying in the dead man's yoga position (flat on my back, arms at my side), meditating. Suddenly, it was as though I had been shot in the heart by a long distance rifle. I knew my own mortality and knew with complete knowing that I would die someday. Yes, we all know we will die, but I **_knew_** (or grokked it as used in Heinlein's *The Stranger in a Strange Land*). I broke out of my reverie and begged God to let me live to the year 2000, fully knowing I had a limited time on this planet and all kinds of magical things were going to happen at the turn of the century. And now here I am, still going on, trying to clean up unfinished business and get on with my life. Sharing this experience has been a driving force in my life.

disclaimer

This is a first-person account of a week I spent on a psychiatric ward. I wrote the first draft while I was delusional and still hallucinating. I have made every attempt to tell my story without enhancement, exaggeration, or embellishment. It is as true and as real as I can make it. Names have been changed and identifying items omitted. Also, considerable time has passed

All thoughts and words are mine. Please note that I was hospitalized on a closed psychiatric ward and had some altered perceptions.

INTRODUCTION

This book describes a week I spent on a psychiatric ward. Its writing was triggered by the visit of one of my professors while I was hospitalized. I had begun to become rational and attempted to tell him about my experiences. He suggested it would be meaningful for me to write about them due to my background in psychology.

I began attempting to detail my ward experiences shortly after my release from the hospital. My writing became much more than an attempt to describe a one-week experience. It became my reason to be. It gave purpose and meaning to my struggle to survive and regain my sanity. Writing the first draft of my experiences, done during the six months or so following my release, was one of the most challenging and courageous things I have ever done.

First of all, there was a lack of physical dexterity. For example, a week or two after my release, I had written a one-page letter of thanks to the two professors who had visited me on the ward. I had used a portable typewriter, for goodness sake (the common use of computers and the internet were not yet here). It had taken me an entire afternoon of concentrated effort with many pages thrown away (a word processor would have been helpful). My hands didn't work. Although it was difficult for me to hold rational thoughts for any length of time, my greatest frustration was the inability of my fingers to hit the right keys on the typewriter. Tears formed in my eyes and dripped down my face as I inserted blank page after blank page into the typewriter. I was finally able to type a short, readable letter. My physical difficulties slowly abated over several months.

Introduction

Then there was the fear. As I got into my story, I was telling secrets, chronicling the voyage of an inner space traveler through nightmare country. As such, they came out of the walls, from beyond the veils of my rational mind. Misshapen, vulture-like monsters perched on my shoulder, monitoring my thoughts, ready to control my writing. I ignored them. My story must be told. The hallucinations changed. As I continued to tell my story, typing away, a golden chain formed around my ankle, with one end holding me to the typewriter. I was obviously on to something; the truth must be told, and in its telling I would be set free.

There were the impaired memory processes. I had gone quickly from waking up on the ward with no memory at all to a recall of only my long term memory to a jagged memory filled with quite vivid, complete histories as well as blanks and blurs. In attempting to detail my experiences, I would occasionally blank, not only forgetting what I was trying to say but also what I was doing. Sometimes I would be back in minutes; other times, it would take me hours to resume what I had been doing.

Finally, I was not rational in the truest sense of the word. I could not hold on to a single train of thought, any consistent system of logic, or a sense of purpose. Hindus have compared the mind to a drunken monkey needing to be disciplined. The mind has also been compared to a vast switching unit, with us attending very quickly to now one subject, then another and then another, with an illusion of continuity. As this drunken monkey switched from one thought to another, I would slide into the side pockets of my mind, forgetting where I had started and where I was going. Most of us can concentrate on one thing, ignoring or dismissing irrelevant thoughts. Not me. Not then.

In my weakened, post-ward condition, trying to hold or keep my concentration was difficult, if not impossible for me to do. I would skip from thought to thought and subject to subject with each new entry into my consciousness becoming the main idea. My reasons for writing continually expanded. I was beset by a whole series of existential questions: Who am I? Why am I? What am I? Why did this happen to me? What did I do to deserve this? In addition to trying to answer these

The Change Center

questions, I was determined to expose the apparent absurdities of our hospitals and mental health professionals as well as the pain involved in the healing process. There was also the need to understand the madness and hallucinations which beset me as well as my love affair with Linda, which had taken me beyond the limits of my experiential capability. Was she a goddess? Siva's mistress Kali coming to bedevil me? A saint? Or was she just a decent, nice young woman who happened to fall in love with a jerk? Okay, I really believe it's the latter one.

Anger and determination enabled me to finish the first draft. Rereading it, I was surprised I had used "fuck" about every other word. Fuck me. Fuck the ward. Fuck them. Rewriting it, I would attempt to let go of my anger and create a more objective account of my experience.

On one level, my story is a simple one. I was a bright, idealistic, religious youth who grew up in the Midwest. I was an egghead, geek, nerd, or whatever the current term is for a shy academic. At the age of 17, I sat across from the Dean of Men at a large, Midwestern State University. He told me that based on my high school record and test scores, I could be anything I wanted to be. I could succeed at any academic course of study the university had to offer. All I needed was interest and motivation.

I was only moderately successful in college, having discovered booze, broads, and agnosticism. By my mid-twenties, I had obtained a bachelor's degree in psychology and a master's degree in education, had taught Russian, math and psychology at the high school level, switched to industry and was working as a senior systems analyst. A series of personal crises led me to introspection and a questioning of who I was. Still in my 20s, after all of my gold stars, I found myself balding, growing fat, and smoking and drinking too much. Where had all my promise and idealism gone?

My answer was to return to school and become the teacher and psychologist I had always dreamed of becoming. I was able to obtain a four-year fellowship to a major university in School Psychology. For me, it was a dream come true. I would be able to combine my interest and expertise in the fields of education, psychology, and computers.

Introduction

As it turned out, I would only spend a year in graduate school, returning to my previous job in Chicago with a raise and promotion. Some 15 months later, I would attempt to return to graduate school. Although I had given myself a month to re-acclimate myself to school before winter enrollment, I would meet Linda, with my plans exploding in ecstasy. Two months after meeting Linda, I would find myself weak and broken on a psychiatric ward.

Whether my insanity was the accumulation of bad habits, a magnification of personal faults, a situational psychosis due to pressures pushing and pulling me here and there, the result of emotional overkill with Linda, or simply, the result of drugs as I told the doctors, I do not know.

Although it was probably the result of battling myself, I like to think of my madness as a fall from grace, necessitated by my attaining knowledge of techniques and power far beyond my wisdom and understanding. Whatever the case, in order to understand my story, it is necessary to understand *Magic*. Magic, or rather, altered states of awareness, permeated my existence for some 2 ½ years prior to my breakdown.

The three major techniques, interwoven, which I used were tripping (psychedelics), yoga, and mind control. The psychedelics taught me that the experiential possibilities of any single human being are without limit and for all practical purposes, infinite. Yoga, and at best I was a novice, gave me control, allowing me to pass through mountains, so to speak, and return to my normal state. Mind control opened doorways to the void, allowing me to move through time and space.

Following is an overview of some of my experiences with these techniques, emphasizing the psychic and mystical aspects of my adventure that ended so badly. Although I still meditate, I no longer actively participate in any of these things. I am reminded of Hesse's *Journey to the East*, in which the main character begins telling of an exotic spiritual journey he experienced in his youth that is no longer taking place. He is then led to realize that it is he who has changed and not the voyage. I feel like that. Although my ward experience can be understood in isolation and, indeed, has a number of elements of a classical breakdown, I feel a need to mention these search vehicles as background in order to give set and setting to my ward experience.

Tripping

The world has certainly changed. Drug usage and drug experiences are so very different today as opposed to then. So many books have been written regarding the psychedelic experience that I will just describe what happened to me.

My life has always been cyclical with the highs and lows coming in bunches. As I prepared to return to graduate school, I was on the strongest natural high of my life. My mind had opened with me becoming incredibly productive at work as well as free of the gloomy depression and bothersome illnesses that had dogged me for much of my early life. Perhaps my real problem is that I have never been satisfied; when the good happens in my life, I always look for better.

In this totally open frame of mind, riding the tide of good, even outstanding events, a friend visited me from the west coast. He was doing his guru trip. He had been caught up in the west coast shtick, had turned on, and returned to the Midwest to tell all of his old friends about his new world. He spent a week or two with me in Chicago, talking continually about his new lifestyle. We decided to travel together. We drove down to Florida with me lining up courses and an apartment for the coming semester. We then drove up the east coast to Cape Cod. He would remain there while I flew back to Chicago and then move to Florida.

Ah, what an experience. To that point, I had smoked some marijuana. Although enjoyable, I had done it for purely recreational reasons. He turned me on to Acapulco gold, which at the time was already legendary marijuana in head circles. More importantly, he talked to me about a way of life that promised insights into the wonder of it all. As he said, "I've taken mescaline three times, and after the last trip, I never came down." To him, psychoactive drugs were a gateway into a newly found spirituality and wholeness. He spoke of a way of life and philosophical

Introduction

insights reminiscent of Alan Watts and Timothy Leary. As we talked, he would constantly ask me questions, then wait for answers and listen intently to my responses. Always a latent seeker and a heavy reader, bits and pieces of Lao-tze's *Tao-Te-Ching*, Greek mythology, Zen Buddhist writings and more, spiraled upward from forgotten memory vats into my consciousness. It was as though I gave historical precedent, cognitive background, and verbalization to the lifestyle he had discovered.

As we drove, talked and smoked grass, he turned me on to his version of head philosophy, which was, in effect, a "know thyself" colored by the drug experience. Now, it seems almost blasphemous. Then, it was so very new and different. As one guru out of the East, referring to LSD, had commented, it was so typical of us materialistic westerners to find spirituality through a physical substance like acid.

After constant driving, rapping, and smoking, Rog and I became so in tune with each other that it became eerie. While we've all experienced the "I was just going to say that" phenomenon while talking to a friend, our rapport became continual. I would have a taste for ice cream and he would be turning off the road, driving into the parking lot of an ice cream stand. My mouth would be dry and he would be handing me a breath mint, as I was about to ask for one. He would start to ask me for directions and I would be telling him which way to turn before he could complete his question. This interpersonal sensitivity became so constant that I began babbling about it. He simply shook his head, "Don't you understand? When you talk about it, it isn't happening." Ah, yes, sweet student. There is knowing (experiencing) something and then there is knowing (about) something. If you're there and start talking about being there, you're no longer there, but rather, in a state of being of talking about being there.

My major lesson of the two-week interaction and the key to understanding trip philosophy was simply, to live directly as opposed to the "aboutism" of straight society. With mass communication and the information explosion, we are aware of so many things, with so much of our schooling predicated on learning about things. We have the illusion

The Change Center

of knowing quite a bit. I learned, however, that with regard to certain modes of existence, and experience we know less than a simple savage. Although drugs are a magnifier of certain aspects of experience as well as a source of change, they are not necessary for tripping. Indeed, per head philosophy, each one of us, whether we know it or not, is in on the trip. We are all tripping. Always. Each of us is a traveler. "The only thing constant in nature is change." "Changing is." It is impossible to stand still. Whether our trip is viewed as a journey through life, the life-death process, itself, or as a cyclical sleeping and awakening, it is not possible to stop it, for even death, as Shakespeare noted, may be just another phase.

My interactions with this friend left me both curious and confused. What, exactly, did all of this mean? Live in the present. Live directly. Experience. I spent the fall adjusting to academic life, caught up in new friends and study. Although I had some ego problems (going from a senior analyst playing a small but important role in a multi-million-dollar merger to a first-year graduate student was a little like asking me to sweep the floor when I had been designing buildings), I adjusted well to graduate school, thoroughly enjoying it and loving Florida.

Although I took a modicum of grass with me to graduate school, I stayed straight and had some success. I was still curious and confused about both drugs and the philosophy to which I had been exposed. Over Christmas break, I returned to Chicago and together with another friend drove to the west coast in order to visit my mentor and learn more about this new way of life. There, I met hippies, got involved in endless discussions with strong grass, THC, and a mescaline trip changing my perceptual world. As I prepared to fly home to Chicago, I was still light tripping on the mescaline; I asked my old friend and current guide for some marijuana, as I was not one of the "in" crowd at school. I needed to explore this world more fully.

As a goodbye present, he threw me a quarter pound or so of decent marijuana. When I asked the price, he replied, "The first bag is free." It would take me a whole week before I came completely down from the mescaline. I had a physical release in about three days. The psychological

Introduction

release came at a marathon encounter group a few days later. My fellow graduate students accused me of sitting in the corner like some kind of all-knowing Buddha. This, of course, was what I had been doing, musing in my other world loftiness at their petty this-world concerns.

I spent the winter quarter smoking grass and making new friends. I attempted to understand this alternative culture with its emphasis on living NOW and its lack of concern with materialism and the structures and standards of mainstream American society.

That spring, on my 28th birthday, I took my first acid trip. I no longer had to attempt to understand the NOW or IN society, the alternative culture of peace, love, and happiness freaks. I became one. Tripping and the lifestyle associated with it became my way of life. That spring is perhaps the happiest time of my life. I went from an anxious, balding materialist to being a person I truly loved. Physically, I lost some 30 lb., including 4 inches off of my waist, began walking tall and straight, let my hair grow long (it stopped falling out), and both felt and looked years younger. I stopped smoking cigarettes, stopped drinking alcohol, ate less meat, and generally took good care of myself.

I was in love—with a young woman I met on campus, with myself, and the northern Florida countryside. It was a time of rebirth and rejuvenation, with my life permeated with the discovery of self, others, and nature. I was reborn both emotionally and spiritually. Although I smoked grass and tripped on weekends, it wasn't just the drugs. I also did yoga, became good friends with so many bright, young people, and fell in love with nature.

As all things must change, so did my euphoric state of mind. We had a saying, "Some people have dreams; we live ours." The extended daydream of living simply and lovingly began changing to a world of paranoia and depression. Old concerns began plaguing me. Could I hold on and get that doctorate? What about money, status, and the future? My life was nice, even beautiful, but what about tomorrow? I couldn't sit under a tree for the rest of my life. Could I?

First of all, I fell into depression. The entire world is a game; no game is worth playing. Why bother to do anything? Nothing mattered. From a way of life that had freed up dreams and energy, I fell into lying around wasted and confused. Then, there was the paranoia. At the beginning of the summer, my friends and I had heard about drug busts. Then it was friends and acquaintances who were getting popped. Finally, the people who had been over last night were now in jail. Were we next? It was as though an ever-tightening web was closing in on us. I retreated from my fear and climbed out of my stupor by returning to Chicago. After a year of search and study, I was surprisingly able to return to my former company with both a raise and promotion.

Although I returned straight, I had been exposed to a world of wonder. Both tripping and yoga had blown me away, exposing me to a world I had not even been able to dimly imagine.

Tripping. What is it? So many authors such as Huxley and Watts have written erudite descriptions of it; so many burnouts have told their stories. So many of us have seen friends and loved ones destroy themselves. The world is different now. I am no longer any kind of expert on any kind of drug. Initially, it was very important to me to attempt to analyze and describe the psychedelic experience.

Simply, you take a chemical. This causes chemical changes in the brain and central nervous system leading to a radically changed perceptual world. To me, taking a psychedelic was like having a very intense dream while awake. Anything could happen.

Initially, I could externalize anything my imagination or fantasy life could come up with. Pictures on the wall would begin moving; melting wax on a candle could become an intricate mini-universe and so on. The major difference between the trip experience and certain types of psychosis is that when tripping, one normally knows a dancing tiger moving on a tapestry is just a wall hanging. In very intense trip experiences, there had been built-in warning signals to protect yourself. Supportive friends helped.

Introduction

To me, tripping was an intensification, magnification, narrowing, and centering of experience. Certain aspects are magnified while others are ignored. While tripping can key dreams of the future or memories of the past, one is usually centered in the present due to the intensity of the immediate. Tripping dramatically affected my attention, awareness, sensory perceptions, the concept of time, and internal speed.

I originally viewed psychedelics as a cleansing or toning of experience. As Huxley has pointed out, our bodies actually act as a reducing valve, limiting our experiences for us to survive as an organism. View any sensory input (through our eyes, ears, and so forth) as a tube. Put a screen in the tube. For many of us, our screen is covered with sludge. My mind always came up with the pun that LSD, indeed, acted as acid. At first, it seemed to dissolve the sludge, allowing clearer, sharper perceptions. Over time, as I introspectively watched the effects of the drug on me, the screen, itself, began to disintegrate, resulting in a reduced capability of rationalizing or delimiting my experience, as well as acid nightmares that I was becoming irrevocably changed and not for the better. Not only the screen, but also the channel or tube as well as the rate of input changed.

The concept of easiness stands out. A strong-willed person with a well-developed ego can trip, view it as a sensory experience, either forget about it or perhaps, as some have done, write a treatise or book about the experience. Others would be much easier, tripping into increasingly exotic worlds, with some losing (or finding) it completely. Some were forced to leave the cities and the intense, scattered vibrations one finds in them. Making love to a flower became more important than a raise or promotion to some, while others were tripped into ideas of how to make money.

No longer as easy, I no longer know anyone who trips today. Does anyone still do psychedelics? Or is it all opioids and other types of pain killers? All the heavy trippers I had known have either gone on to other things or are otherwise lost to me. While some former trip heads may view it as an interesting experience, others have changed enough not to know or care or be able to function in any kind of a rational world I can understand. Ambivalent toward the trip experience, I must admit that even now, I occasionally miss the heavens, hells, and happenings of my time of search.

On the other hand, as one of my professors cynically stated, "We use to have to rely on mothers for supplying us with mental patients. Now we have LSD."

Yoga

Although drugs were such a strong stimulus, yoga also played a role in my brief sojourn as a peace, love, and happiness freak. While I had read about yoga in the 1960s and had attempted to do some exercises on my own, I discovered this discipline about a week before my first LSD trip.

A friend had turned me on to some very good smoke. I somehow arrived at my first yoga class, still buzzed. Over the next several hours, doing exercises, chanting, and meditating, I not only stayed stoned, but I also became even more peaceful and relaxed. I knew I was on to something really good. After my first class, I stopped smoking cigarettes. I didn't quit or give them up. I simply spaced into a world where I could no longer smoke tobacco.

It was Kundalini yoga, one of the most powerful yoga's. At best, I was a beginning novice, never really possessing the discipline to fully explore this very powerful technique. Not meaning any disrespect, Kundalini yoga is sort of like a speed freak version of hatha yoga (physical yoga). It stresses certain breathing techniques, including the breath of fire, which, if done correctly while holding an asana or position, has the same power in minutes that would otherwise take the control of hours.

At one level, yoga means "discipline." At another level, it can mean "union." Kundalini yoga is a method aimed at raising the Kundalini nerve coiled at the base of the spine. The goal is to move one's energy upward, sending it to each chakra (a chakra is roughly equivalent to a sensory-motor nerve center).

There are seven major chakras. These centers have physical, psychic, and psychological corollaries. Physically, they are roughly located at the

Introduction

anus, genitals, stomach, heart, throat, forehead, and crown of the head. As one learns this discipline, tremendous power and energy are released with one's subjective world going through step-functions to higher awareness as the Kundalini is raised.

While that spring is perhaps my happiest time, much of the credit must go to this discipline. Although I only did 30-45 minutes of stretching and meditation a day, my habits changed dramatically. I found smoking cigarettes, drinking alcohol, eating heavy foods, or keeping the company of coarse people were all hindrances to my wellbeing. Unfortunately, I misused this discipline, combining it with first grass, and then psychedelics in order to get even higher, ever faster.

Perhaps even more important than the physical changes I went through, was the exposure to a different world view. At the time, I met the Kundalini missionary to the United States. He was a tremendously powerful human being with a thick, black beard, broad shoulders, and strong chest. He emanated strength and did not fit my stereotype of a thin, stoop shouldered, introspective yogi.

He held a lecture in which he demonstrated some breathing techniques. The seating for his lecture was an interesting study in life as it was then. The heads, the peace, love, and happiness freaks, sat cross legged at his feet, attentive and in awe. The straights sat further away in metal, folding chairs. As an indication of my ambivalence and/or schizophrenic tendencies, I sat at the dividing line between the two groups, albeit on the floor. I was not quite a "head," not quite a "straight."

During his lecture, he put down all drugs, including psychedelics and alcohol. The trip heads (peaceful and in the presence of one, who was there) were stunned. One girl stammered, "B-but that's what g-got us here." The trippers sat amazed, mouths open, attempting to assimilate this new information. It was as though they had eaten enormous quantities of bread to see the Buddha. After finally obtaining an audience, they were told that bread was not good for them. There was little protest, only astonishment.

The middle class straights in attendance, sitting on their chairs, were not so easy. One person, in particular, refused to give up arguing and finally stated that even our Lord, Jesus Christ, drank wine. I loved the answer and will never forget it. "No, this I no believe. I do not believe any being so powerful he can raise the dead, could drink alcohol." I was entranced by a worldview that could easily accept that someone could raise the dead, even to the extent of putting restrictions on the habits of one who was able to do so. When I later tried to tell this story to an acidhead, he simply shrugged his head and said, "Hey man, we all have hang-ups."

At the same lecture, a friend had come over and whispered that he had scored what Liam and I had been looking for. I was on the verge of my first acid trip. As my friend left, a young woman I didn't know, gripped my arm, looked deeply into my eyes, and emphatically stated, "Bad vibes." Perhaps.

While Kundalini yoga and the psychedelics were my twin entry into a brief interlude as a hippie, they also opened my perceptual world to several mystical-like experiences. While yoga and meditation can lead to psychic experiences and powers, these are basically put down as hindrances to enlightenment. While tripping, anything can happen. Although I had some mind-boggling trips, I remember the joy and wonder, rather than the disorientation and confusion.

Mind Control

My Eden had been short-lived. Returning to Chicago was an escape to a safe environment. For the remaining year and a half before my breakdown, although I continued to smoke marijuana, I would trip only a couple of times and practice yoga only sporadically. I did become a trained psychic.

I discovered Mind Control through a series of coincidences. I would find out that "coincidences" would permeate the life of a Mind Control graduate as in, "Joe will call in about 20 minutes." As the phone rang

Introduction

some 20 minutes later, there would be a laugh and a wink, "My, what a coincidence."

The course I attended consisted of four, 12-hour days of training accomplished during two consecutive weekends. Techniques used in the class involved self-programming, visualization, and dropping to lower brain waves.

The brain emits many waves, classified according to their rate. Delta waves are the slowest, associated with very deep sleep and the unconscious mind. Theta waves are very slow, associated with the deep subconscious and creative imagery. Alpha waves are associated with the subconscious mind and the dream state. When we sleep and are dreaming, our eyelids flicker; this is REM or rapid eye movement. The predominant brain wave emitted during dreaming sleep is the alpha wave. Beta waves are associated with our awake, conscious self.

In describing mind control, I view the mind as an upside-down pyramid. We live on the surface, emitting beta waves. In a method similar to self-hypnosis, one goes to a deeper, more basic level of mind, the alpha level of slower brain waves and programs one's self. The theory is that what happens at these deeper levels of mind will subsequently affect our normal, awake self.

A simple exercise shows the potential of this self-programming technique. At night, in the reverie between being awake and falling asleep, visualize a clock and set it to the exact time you want to wake up. Picture it clearly and let yourself know this is the exact time you want to wake up, and you will wake up feeling rested and better than ever. While many of us have very good biological clocks, others of us don't. With a little practice, you will be surprised at how easily and accurately you can wake up at any given time. (I can no longer do this very well, so don't feel bad if you can't do it either. At one time, I could consistently wake up to the minute I had pictured in my mind.)

The first half of the course emphasized habit formation, control over the autonomic or involuntary nervous system, and positive reinforcement techniques. It became progressively esoteric, including the idea one could project one's intelligence or awareness to any point in time or space. Think about that for a minute or two. *Any* point in time or space! It ended with one being able to build a mental laboratory at a deep level of mind where one could, among other things, work health cases. The end result of the course was that one could, given a person's name, age, sex, and location, "work" the person, sending energy to aid the person's physical, mental and emotional health.

While the lecture portions of the course were somewhat simplistic, I absorbed them with the proverbial grain of salt. The training was effective. Quite simply, it worked. Perhaps drugs and yoga had opened my mind to "anything can happen." Whatever the case, I very quickly became adept at this new technique. Although I have no evidence whatsoever about any cures I caused or people I healed, the diagnostic capabilities were incredible.

For example, Joe, another student, went into an emotional tirade on the afternoon of the last day of the course. Angrily, he said that although the course had some good parts, it should be sold as an exercise in creative imagery as there was nothing psychic about it. Some four hours later, I would lead him through his first health case. I used my aunt. He went to his level (a semi trancelike state, the alpha state) and started describing what seemed to be a cross between my mother and aunt. With some prompting by myself, he was able to sort out the images and described my aunt accurately, although given her age, sex, and my guidance, this was not especially difficult. He then went into her maladies.

"Huh, gee, I don't know what the name of the disease is, but it's like the red and white blood corpuscles are fighting each other. There's a real heavy purplish color. There are too many red cells. I'll send some help."

My aunt had polycythemia, a blood disease where one has too many red blood cells, resulting in fatigue and dizziness, also diagnosed by Joe. I was hooked. It was amazing. Coincidence? How? He didn't even know what polycythemia was, which I had written on the card.

Introduction

A couple of days later, I worked cases at a graduate meeting with a somewhat flip cohort. His, "yeah, yeah, that's a hit", was not convincing. For example, I had seen a black woman as white. I felt I had come down from a drug trip. It had been a nice dream but come on now, of course, this couldn't work. Two weekends of training, and I became psychic?

My two instructors asked me to show a couple of guests how mind control worked. I ended up working the sister of the wife and was incredibly accurate. I was impressed. I could do this.

Every day, going to and from work on a bus, I would go to my level and work health cases. I did relatives, friends, co-workers, and referrals, sending golden, life-giving energy to anyone who needed it. I realized that rather than a source, it was as though I were acting as a conduit or a relay station that channeled and directed a force that was beyond me. I became quite religious, going to the depths of my mind, saying a prayer of thanks and also, asking that I never be allowed to hurt anyone or to otherwise misuse such a marvelous skill.

Working cases had its humorous side. My boss and our shared secretary had shown some interest, although to be perfectly honest, only my mother and one of her lady friends, who both were going to a Unitarian church at the time, were the only two people who would listen to me without total skepticism. One morning, early at work, as I passed the secretary, I mentioned that her ulcers were in the lower portion of her stomach, and just starting. If she drank more milk and learned to relax, I didn't think she would have any trouble. Returning from my coffee run, she was still frozen in the same position. She stared at me and asked me how I could have possibly known about her ulcers. She had just been to the doctor and discovered she was developing ulcers. I just smiled and said, "After all, I am a trained psychic." We never talked about it again.

I had been working my relatives, just sending love at a deeper level of consciousness (it's impolite to work with someone without their request for many reasons, including knowing too much about them), when I came across my cousin's wife. Her mid-section was spilling forth a strong, whitish-gold light. I knew this meant she was pregnant. On one of my infrequent visits home, I told my mother someone in the family was pregnant. She guessed just about everyone and finally gave up. Smug, I told her about Barbara. "Oh gees. My son, the psychic. She's seven months pregnant, and everyone in the family knows about it."

Working cases had its serious side. Cancer, which shows up as orange-red, proved the most difficult for me. One of my instructors asked me to work his aunt, who was dying from cancer. Although I tried several times, I wasn't so sure I was getting through. After some time, I tried again. She was virtually immersed in a sea of red. I tried to send some help and received a powerful image of her sailing away in a Spanish Galleon. She seemed very at peace and was waving goodbye to some distant shore. Weeks later, when I checked with my instructor, he verified what I had suspected. She had passed away.

Mind Control was not magic. It seemed tied up in wider plan, karma, destiny, call it what you will. Also, not being "clear" (still bothered by my perceptual inadequacies) or fully developed spiritually, my mind would give me cartoons and symbols instead of exact images. The following case illustrates some of this.

A very dear friend of the family was going into the hospital. I decided to work him. I received a clear, strong image of him with a strong orange-red band across his diaphragm. Since one is working on cases in one's mind, one can use any technique which seems suitable to send help. Nothing that I did seemed to work. For example, I tried using a giant eraser to erase the cancer off of my visual screen, but no, that didn't get rid of the red. Finally, in a burst of inspiration, I condensed the orange-red color into a little black pea, plucked it out of his body, and threw it into a wastebasket in my laboratory. Several days later, I found out he had been operated on, and the doctors thought they had gotten all of it. They, however, had operated some 24 hours before I worked the case!

Trying to use psychedelics, Kundalini Yoga, and Mind Control with no real teacher or guide, I was certainly playing Russian roulette with a very loaded gun.

Introduction

But oh, did my mind fill in. I had always been considered bright academically, with the praise of numerous teachers and high scores on standardized tests reinforcing this perception. Hah! My success in school consisted mostly of memorization and facile regurgitation of facts with some isolated stabs at original, creative thinking. I was a whiz at digesting textbooks written about the great thinkers, easily able to comprehend organizational schemes, critiques, and analyses of their ideas. However, studying original works of the masters had left me bedazzled and confused.

Oh, how it turned around. As I became both an explorer and a knower of this huge brain with which most of us are gifted, I became quite arrogant. I found myself reading original works by the great masters, comparing their thoughts to my experiences, separating the chaff from the wheat. At the same time, the "aboutists," those numerous classifiers and arbitrators of knowledge, became almost totally incomprehensible to me.

I think either yoga or mind control with a good teacher would have been okay. I, however, had no guru and also, continued to try psychoactive substances. I began noting some strange things.

For example, about a year after my heyday as a peace, love, and happiness freak, I had a week off and decided to try some LSD. I took two trips, hanging around Lincoln Park and Chicago's lakefront. Later, when I tried to go to my internal laboratory and work health cases, I found my laboratory totally wrecked with green, a predominant color. It would take several sessions of me going to my level before I could reconstruct my laboratory. What did this mean?

I did a reverse guru trip, going out to the west coast to tell my former mentor about mind control. He asked me to help him with his back. The problem is that he immediately got me stoned on stronger grass than I had been used to smoking. When I tried to work him, I got esoteric images. Instead of seeing his back problem as a regular picture (similar to colored x-rays), I saw a huge serpent coiled around his backbone.

What could this possibly mean? Was I just using drug-tinged imagery?

Was my early Christian training coming to the fore?

And then, it all fell through. About six months before my hospitalization, I was doing yoga after smoking some excellent grass. I accidentally did something which popped me through a (the?) Tibetan dorje into a world beyond my imagination. I was tripping for several days. In the middle of this extraordinary experience, I picked up the *Tibetan Book of the Dead* and read a section describing a stage of experiences after a person is dead. It was similar to the world I was living in. I would later find out a man had died in the apartment above me, and his corpse had been rotting there for several days. I sincerely believe I accidentally got caught up in his death vibrations. Whatever the case, my world went tilt and then some as described in the Appendix.

An understanding boss, a loving mother, and a co-worker who did drugs were able to help me return from my walk through whatever had happened to me. I surfaced in a world of hedonism, losing myself in sex, ignoring the perceptual wonders I had been able to experience. This too, turned to ashes. The various trips and psychic experiences had gotten to me. It was time to center, time to take care of my body.

Linda

I decided to return to the beauty of northern Florida. I would be the teacher, the psychologist I had always wanted to be. I would work hard, pay my dues and live a normal, loving life.

Perhaps it would have worked. I don't know. On what was to be my last night in Chicago, a friend came over, bringing Linda with him. He and I had a goodbye trip to Chicago. It may as well have been a goodbye trip to me. It was the first acid I had done in six months since my two trips in June. Something burst in my brain. I heavy tripped for some 30-45 days, not bad for a half a tab of acid.

For the most part, I was just manic and hyper, with everything brighter than normal. One experience stands out, showing some of the far sides of what I was experiencing. Linda worked at a dress shop on State Street just south of Chicago's Loop (downtown Chicago is called the Loop because

Introduction

of the loop the elevated trains make around it). I had visited her, which was a little dicey because of the people and commotion where she worked. Leaving her, I walked north along State Street toward downtown when I realized that I did not hear anything. Startled, I stopped and looked around.

There were people and cars everywhere. It was somewhat crowded due to Christmas shopping with Chicago's downtown a mecca of stores. I stopped and looked around. Across the street, standing in a doorway, was this long hair, a burnt-out hippie who was selling underground newspapers. I had seen him in Old Town (where I lived, a couple of miles north of the Loop) several times. I was surprised that he came this far south. He seemed real. Substantial. He was okay. The rest of the world began turning gray as though I were standing in a cloud or a thick fog. Except for him, my world seemed to be disappearing. I started to freak out.

Disoriented, seeing my world becoming a gray void, I began walking north away from her work. Everything began fading. It was as though my world was being erased. First sound, then color, then it was as though people, places, and things were fading from my existence. I put my head down, just watching my feet and the sidewalk as I continued to walk. I kept saying to myself, "I need a head. I have to find a head. I need a head." I knew what I was saying. I needed to talk to a trip head, someone who had done drugs and could tell me what was going on.

I continued to walk. At the corner, there were a couple of members of the Process. That summer, they had been around Old Town. They seemed to be color-coded and wore different colored robes (I had seen, black, gray, and blue). Today was a dark day, and they were wearing black. They were sort of devil worshipers although the devil was viewed as a personage who executed God's will. I had been to one meeting of the Process. I knew very little about them, and they would be gone shortly, so I never did learn very much about what they believed or practiced. As I understood it, they were devil worshipers, with Satan being a good guy,

The Change Center

the executioner who destroyed the chaff, a necessary complement to the wheat of Christ's kingdom.

A woman dressed in her black robe stopped me and said, "Would you like to read about death?" She thrust an ominous looking glossy booklet in front of me. The front cover was a picture of a large skull. I had found my "head."

"I find death kind of boring."

"What could be more interesting than death?"

"Why, the whole life and death _____." Hysterical laughter. Mine.

She smiled sweetly at me and said, "We're meeting down at the lake at 2:00. Be there."

Although I began meandering toward the lake, I realized my world was substantial once again. Relieved, I made it back home. Coincidence? Searching for a "head" and having a picture of a skull thrust into my face? Sure. Why not? Of course. My whole life has been a coincidence.

I have such regret. I fell so completely in love with Linda. Linda and graduate work in psychology. My two loves. It was a dream that had come true. I had it all. However, my world kept changing. Eventually, it went "pop." This, then, is my story of a week on a ward.

GETTING IN

Sitting on the sofa, blind with rage, I waited for this too to pass. Then I was on my feet, shouting, "Okay, if that's the way that you want it, okay! If that's the way, it has to be, okay. God damn it, okay!" I was shouting at my invisible demons. She hadn't done anything. Or maybe, it was a simple, "I don't care," to me asking, "What do you want to do tonight?" Throwing my jacket on, pulling on my shoes, gaining in anger, rage, and maddening vibes, I knew something had to be done. This had to be over. This must end

I was a wild pinwheel of discordant energy. Linda was a quietly pulsating, comparatively weak orb of life. She was miles away from me, with the two of us separated by a thick, tangible, heavy energy field. It was as if we were both underwater with her a self-contained, satisfied, shielded light source and with me, an enraged, angry, drowning, not knowing which way to swim, not remembering how to float, not content to stay buried, thrashing, wild thing.

Flash. I knew what I had to do. I would drive north, driving until the VW bug gave out. With no money for gas or repairs, I would walk, just walk, walking north, toward home, toward Chicago, skulled out of my mind, putting one foot after the other until it was over. I would keep on going, like a blind insect ever climbing up a wall, zeroed into a single track, unable to stop no matter what obstacles are put in its way.

I could see, sense and feel a feverish me, buried deep in my fur parka, not making it, collapsing in the snow. It would be a fitting end to a dull, dismal, unproductive existence. Let them write: He tried. Not making it, he did try. If they only knew how hard I had tried.

And then, I was outside of the apartment, running quickly. I knew what had to be done, knowing it had to be done and done at once. It had to be done while the anger and rage were still there, done before reason had a chance to return and stop me. This must end.

Remembering: It hadn't been all that bad. Not really. A speeding, zipping, going out of focus me had made it out of the city and had been able to make it back to graduate school. The hassles had been met; getting an advisor, lining up books and classes, finding an apartment. After two weeks of classes, I had flown back to Chicago for my court date.

It had been an absurd bust. After all of the nights and days of paranoia in years past, I had been sitting innocently in Linda's apartment. She shared it with a roommate. Her roommate was going out with a friend of mine. I had met Linda through him. The rumor was that her roommate's ex had done light dealing.

Whether it was because of her former roommate/dealer or the vindictiveness of my friend's separated wife, the police had had a search warrant. There had been a buzz at the door, first a regular, quick buzz, and then an insistent one. As Linda got up to answer it, she said, "This may be something that's going to fuck up our whole evening." A kind of premonition and somewhat of a surprise to me as Linda just plain didn't swear. This was the only time I had ever heard her use the "f" word. Ever. Before, during, or after my week on a ward.

When Linda opened the door, there they were, three narcs with drawn guns. They quickly moved to search the place. I stood up as they rushed into the room and was standing over a small bowl of marijuana. It was some weak grass we had been smoking, pretending to get high. Although Linda's roomie had screamed out that anything they found was hers, they had popped the four of us. My friend, Linda, and I had sat there like the three little monkeys, who neither saw, spoke, nor heard any evil. Waiting for the search to be over, thinking our thoughts, we were quiet and had been told we would be free to go. Her roomie had flipped out, screaming at the cops, following them around as they searched, yelling that she had been through this before, and she knew they would plant something.

They found the bowl of mediocre marijuana on the floor and two pills that looked suspicious. The roomie would later laugh and say that if she had known about the pills, she and my friend would have taken them.

Linda was an almost complete innocent, smoking only rarely. At the time, I smoked about a joint (a dozen or so puffs) a day and had never done any dealing. Except for the psychedelics (taken twice since returning to Chicago and not lolling in the rain forests of northern Florida) and grass, I hadn't gotten into drugs. Three big, old Chicago narcs, with speed and heroin everywhere, busting some kids and myself for some mediocre grass. Busting us took over half their shift and would prove to be a costly mistake for us.

If the bust, itself, was absurd, the court date that I flew back for was an even greater joke. Our lawyer (obtained through connections) thought he was Clarence Darrow ("Look, I know that I can get you off. Look, I can get you off, but this judge, see, it's an election year, and he wants to ride this guy's coat tails, and he's taking a hard line, and look, we got to lay off of this guy. Look, I never lose a case, just stick with me."). Linda was passive. Thinking of the plane fare and the charge (listening to other cases where pounds and garbage cans full of grass were found, it was hard for me to believe anything bad could happen with the four of us popped for a total of much less than an ounce), I wanted to go ahead with the court appearance. My friend and the roomie were adamant about "laying off of this judge." The case was continued. I had flown to Chicago for nothing. Linda and I had found out we needed to be together. We made plans for her to get to Florida the following weekend.

This was my second go-around at graduate study in northern Florida. The first time I had been searching for a Holy Grail, a reason to be. Corny, but true. That first time returning to college in my late 20's, a successful systems analyst, I had had my dream come true. I had received a four-year fellowship to a top graduate school. Aptitude, together with my work in systems, and education had done it. While I did not have spectacular grades and had been out of school for some time, the work was in Computer Assisted Instruction. It was a perfect fit. I left work to

Getting IN

cheers and best wishes. I had made good. To me, it was even more than that. I would get a chance to self-actualize and be all of the things I had ever wanted to be.

Surprise. I was almost immediately shocked at the petty triteness (6 to 7 profs sitting around for hours trying to figure out how to revise a proposed grant in order to get a tape recorder included, while I had just left merger studies where the talk was in the millions), shortsightedness (okay, take all of those person hours spent by first year grad students learning the Core curriculum, an outmoded way of exposing each of us to the assorted facts of a dozen specialties few of us will ever need or use, or how about all of the time spent in writing, individual, narrow theses where do they tie in, what about the option of having everyone work on different aspects of the same thing, using an underlying theory or purpose in order to have some meaning, impact or relevance), the lack of idealism (with me searching for TRUTH and my department head continually saying the Ph.D. is nothing but a union card, do meaningful work at the post-doctoral or career level), and the degree of specialization (holy cow, it takes three months of concentrated effort and study just to understand what these guys are talking about, just to use the same vocabulary). What a shock for this ex-teacher, making it as a senior systems analyst on his way to solid, middle management.

The first quarter, I played the game well (A, A, B, and B), made ripples if not waves, tutored some people, learned my role of "student as low-life," and had more or less adjusted. Christmas break, with a visit to California, THC, and mescaline, together with long head raps with an old friend, who was living high and thoroughly caught up in the west coast shtick of the late 1960's kind of changed my values. The Winter quarter was spent rolling around in the grass with me, receiving all B's and making new friends. School became a distant hassle.

Spring quarter (A, B, B, and C) became a time of search, peace, love, and happiness. The psychedelics had been bridged. Rather than a hassle, school was a, "huh?" My grades were amazing. At mid-term, I had 2 A's, a B+, and a solid B going. It's funny, since I can't remember ever cracking a book. Classes were something to go to if you weren't crashing at the pad or getting high. I held together and saw it through to the end. For finals, I gathered all of my books and papers together, literally thousands of pages, planning to read one line per page. Even this was too much. I took my Personality final crashing from my second psilocybin trip of finals week. With the pages blurring, I finished it in 45 minutes while the other graduate students sweated for two to three hours. It was a solid screw-up, with me receiving my only C in graduate school.

Summer quarter (B) was spent laying around wasted. I had one course and twelve hours of master's thesis, not even being able to develop a topic for my thesis. I had fallen into depression--all the world's a game, and no game's worth playing. I was strung out, almost catatonic, and spent my time staring at walls, wondering how I had gone wrong. Where went the ecstasy, the glimpse (and what a glimpse) at infinity, the highs, and the dreams?

As I look back, it is difficult for me to believe that my great, hippie, trip head experience was only some 3-4 months long as it seemed like years. I crawled back to Chicago, retreating to a lifestyle I could handle. Surprisingly, I returned with a promotion and a major raise. A letter to my former secretary and company need had triggered my return. I had lost 30 pounds, straightened my back, and stopped smoking and drinking. I felt good, except for the cloud over my head. I had caught a glimpse. Yoga and the psychedelics had blown me away. The early 1970s evidenced paranoia and bipolarization of society. I became a double, living in two worlds. Mysticism and long raps with straights who at least smoked grass triggered memories of some of what I had found, while pressures of a 9 to 5 job kept me in the middle-class world.

I lived some 15 months divided against myself. Functioning at work, I was dreaming about what I was missing. The bad habits of cigarettes and alcohol began once again to color my existence. Imbedded in Chicago, not surrounded by rain forests, I found it increasingly difficult to cope, to be happy. Visions were no longer clearly seen, and experiences were no longer mind-blowing ecstasy. I continued on. A delay in a raise at work due to Nixon's wage-price freeze, an aborted attempt to transfer to another department, and management failing to act on a proposal that took me months to prepare, provided the stimulus for me to try school once again. My only dream had been to be a college professor, to be an educated person. "One more time" was my driving force. I no longer did drugs, although I still smoked grass. This time, I would make it. I had learned discipline. I would cope.

I quit work on the last day of November. My boss begged me to stay. Once the freeze was over, he insisted I had a fine future, and I would move right up the corporate ladder. I wouldn't listen. One more time at the merry-go-round, one more try at that elusive doctorate, that life-long dream. It was my dream and my motivation. Was the brass ring still there? Could I still make it?

I planned to leave for Florida immediately. I had horded my shekels (no fellowship now), planned to study for a month, and re-acclimate myself. This time, I would make it. Hah!

My friend came over to say goodbye. He was splitting from his wife and was going to bring over his new girlfriend. Sure. Instead, he brought over her roommate, a girl named Linda. As a goodbye trip to Chicago, he and I split some windowpane acid. Linda declined. After having seen her twice before, we had finally met. We fell in love. My plans exploded in ecstasy. The month of December was an orgy of sight, sound, and sensuality. I had a reason to exist, a will to live. I was in LOVE. Something went "pop!" in my head, and I never came down. I burst into trip consciousness and stayed there day after day after day.

Golden, vibrating energy was in me, through me, and about me. It wasn't just that she loved me, or I loved her or that we loved each other. We were IN LOVE. I used to say yoga could prolong a high for several hours; Linda lasted more than a month. Somehow, I made it to Florida. After returning to Chicago for our absurd court date, we were finally together in Florida. The lack of time and urgency of finding a place had required us to move into a one-bedroom, plastic, efficiency-apartment, one in a cast of hundreds. We were together; it was all that mattered.

The Change Center

Linda had eased into the slow, golden pace of northern Florida like a fish so satisfied at finding its rightful element that it just sits there basking in the filtered sunlight, digging the stationary, non-moving, baby blue quiet. I was still a little scattered from a month plus of almost continual tripping and an orgy of the senses. I continued to try and live a dual life. It didn't work.

Chicago had been firmer. The job was structured; the work was something I was good at. A strong, ordinary environment had tempered the head raps, meditation, and mysticism I had experienced. In Chicago, it was as though I were a messenger, bringing tales of the great beyond; here, I was the newbie. For me, school was the far side of my experience, representing my extremes.

I tried to make it with my head friends. I dropped some orange sunshine (once) and smoked grass. My friends had been structured by school with the trip experiences new and mind-boggling. Now, they seemed adrift. Sharon, an ex-love, had dropped out of school in her last quarter while student teaching ("It's a cage, these kids are kept in a cage!") and was living in a teepee on someone else's land. Bobby had made it through and was hanging around town while working a menial job. Tom had gotten his degree and was working as a garage mechanic. Liam, my true good buddy, after finishing his master's degree with a near "A" average, had voyaged across the country, then followed a guru to Houston, and had resurfaced in northern Florida. He was now hanging out at Bobby's, where he did the cooking.

I tried to get back in tune with these people with whom I had shared some of the most beautiful experiences of my life. I hit the books, trying to regain and remember the endless names and innumerable facts, attempting to interact with the Profs and the other grad students. There had to be some reason for leaving a managerial position moving to good money and a safe, solid, economic future. No longer searching for the Holy Grail of understanding, knowledge, and awareness, there had to be some reason for re-exposing myself to the locked in world of profs and grad students.

While having some difficulty getting in tune with either my old, head friends or with graduate school, there was always the northern Florida countryside. I thought of town and the surrounding area as a woman. The first time around, seeking status, knowledge, and power, while calling it truth, I had been seduced away from small-minded men to this open, sensuous woman. Sitting in her rain forests, basking in her bright but damp sun, soaking up her peace, I had been wooed by this beguiling, always beautiful, knowing yet capricious mistress. Coming down from the north, racing around, full of energy and ideas of mice and men, she had just smiled at me. She waited, knowing I would come to her. And how I did.

Stoned, tripping, blitzed, and just plain high, I had fallen in love with her. Lying in her fields, walking through her forests, swimming in her waters, I had meditated, merging with her. I would get off by myself, smoke a joint, and just lay around, listening to her, feeling her. To a city boy, it was so perfect, so gentle and peaceful.

This time around, I wasn't ready to be seduced. December had been a mind-blowing explosion of essence, a climaxing of body and soul, a disintegration of the barriers of my mind. Rather than falling into the slow, lazy sensuality of northern Florida, I wanted to get it on, pull myself together, get another erection, hit those books, sharpen my intellect, and notch that degree. It hadn't worked before. It didn't work the second time around.

Things started going wrong, or perhaps a right so correct that I couldn't catch up with it all, quite quickly. Scattered, torn by these different aspects of my past and present, I began spiraling ever deeper within myself. I began losing touch with Linda, the marvelous creature with whom I had shared an almost eerie rapport. Liam was the only one I could talk to, and yet, even with him, I found it difficult to talk, to interact. Have you ever become a forest?

Things began happening in multiple dimensions with me getting increasingly frightened. To this day, I still don't know. I still have my regret. There I was, with a second chance at my dream, with the love of

The Change Center

my life at my side. Everything I had ever wanted was right there for me. Perhaps, if I had had the sense to give myself up to it, to just lay quietly in the surrounding fields for a few days and relax completely, perhaps it would have passed. I kept on fighting it, whatever IT was. Golden energy began creeping around my ankles. I could feel and sometimes, even see it. It was as if I were sinking deeper and deeper, slowly but surely. Finally, I was drowning, with only my head above water. Then, I was fully submerged in some kind of thick, heavy, slow moving, palpable energy field. My strength and energy were being sapped with my reason freaking at what only I could see and feel.

Finally, whatever the trigger, although too disoriented to know what to do, strength, together with rage and anger came bubbling up. This must end.

As I ran toward my car, thoughts and images cascaded through my brain. As flashes of the last few weeks entered my consciousness, my resolve tightened.

Outside of the apartment, running quickly in the cool, damp February night, I could hear and feel Linda behind me. A glance behind me: she was running, tugging on her long, brown, suede coat, with her long, thick black hair all disheveled, blowing in the wind. She was yelling, "I'm coming with you." Oh, Linda, how I love you. If only you could have stopped me. Or maybe, if left alone, I would have driven around town, disoriented and freaking, trying to find somewhere that would still the rage bubbling inside of me. Maybe, I would have returned to the hillock, where we (Liam, Sharon, and all those others) had tripped some two years earlier. Perhaps I would have sat in the damp grass, huddled in my parka (a holdover from Chicago and not really needed in northern Florida), and been able to let it all go. Curled in the fetal position, rolling in the mud, perhaps I would have been able to cry and scream and beg forgiveness of a God who must show mercy as justice would destroy so many of us. A good cry, an honest repentance of all of my vain travels and imaginings, and then, maybe then, just maybe, I would have had the sense to see Him in the lightening, in the rain, in those small pines twisting in the wind.

But now, I had a witness, someone to hurt as much as I was hurting myself. Stubborn. I was so stubborn and stupid.

We were in the car. Linda and I were together, yet so many worlds apart. Starting the car, a familiar action, I calmed down, fell in an energy lull, and was almost normal. Linda sat straight, rigid, all tight and apprehensive, like a small girl determined not to show fear as a big, old roller coaster crept up the first, huge hill. She had no idea what was happening, but she would stick by her man. Sure, I had been acting strange, sure she was frightened, but I was her love. She had never tripped or experienced an acid nightmare and she had no idea what to do or say. A bubbling, "Oh Howard, you're so cute when you're flipped out," a screaming, "Stop the car, you mother!" or a gentle, "Hey, let's go get stoned...," may have stopped me even then. She, in her way, had entered my madness. I was determined to play this one out.

Gas pedal held down, I popped the clutch, attempting to gain an illusion of speed and power. We roared out of the parking lot. I used first and second gears and a sharply, turning steering wheel to get the VW to match my rage. A sharp turn, and then we were out on one of the main drags. Bright lights, traffic, motion and commotion surrounded me. Oh my, I was tripping my brains out with the VW, a slow-moving snail, while my mind took off and soared.

Stopped in traffic, going south toward the center of the city, rather than north toward Chicago, I was totally disoriented, completely straight, and fully mad. Everything was bright and strange. Out of the sparkling glitter of town by night, came only determination. This must end. The problem was simple. I hadn't taken anything. I could have understood it if only I had been on something. I hadn't even smoked any grass or had a beer. My metabolism was speeding out of control, but I had not taken anything. If tripping, I could have turned to Linda and forced a laugh, "Weird movies coming down. Sure do feel scattered tonight." No, this was something else. I hadn't taken anything. I held to my strength, to my madness.

The Change Center

Stopped at a light, waiting on one of many hills, clutch held at the friction plate with the engine vibrating due to too much gas, I had an urge to simply let go. Popping the clutch, crashing into the big, old Chevy in front of us, they could come and get me, scraping my essence off of the windshield. No, Linda was there, beside me. No sense in hurting both of us. Hang on.

I suddenly realized that, instinctively, I was driving toward Liam. He was both a friend and a head. He would know. He would be able to help. He could talk me down out of this. We could blow some weed, listen to some sound. It would be okay. Oh hell, Bobby would be there. I hated to have my friends see me so weak and jumbled. It would be okay, though. It had to be.

The car, as if on remote control, moved slowly but steadily toward Liam's and Bobby's apartment. I may have made it. I think I would have, except for the sign. I was at the last stoplight before their apartment. I was moving on, about to make the light, when I saw the sign, a black "Hospital" on a rectangle of white with an arrow pointing to the left. A split-second decision, a quick, skidding turn to the left, and I was lost. Perhaps forever, as even now, so many years later, I still feel diminished.

No longer on one of the main streets, I found myself driving down darkened side streets in a neighborhood that didn't look at all familiar. No longer crawling, the VW raced down those desolate, darkened, foolish streets. Looking back, it was as though I had been climbing up a hill, following a golden path to a safe haven. Then, whoosh! I had taken a side trip to the hidden dark side of the road. It was as though I had been walking on the apex of one of those A-frame roofs and had suddenly fallen to the side. Making my way through a strange forest, I had fallen into a pit, cut off from the sun. Only a few blocks from safety, and now...

I was a confused spectator, watching the VW race down a dark, silent, curved path to whatever?!? Remembering, feeling Linda next to me, I was able to ask her, "Where are we?" I had forgotten where I was, as well as my urgency and need. Anything could have happened. This was a totally new, but not an alien world. Linda was only able to mumble, "I don't know." I must have been terrifying her. Her response served as a cue. I was mad. This must end.

We rounded a curve, and there it was—the hospital. Even now, so many years later, writing this, cold shivers start up my legs and down my back. Why did I have to do it? Why not? You count. I was just a screwed-up druggie who needed a touch of hell. Sure, I had taken all kinds of things. But when was the last time I had taken anything? I was so screwed up I even missed the turn into the parking lot. Oh dear Lord, please let me keep driving. Let it all be a joke. Let this be a happy story. Let me go on and finish graduate school and become a competent, well-functioning psychologist. Let me marry Linda and lead a normal life.

A quick turn-around, and I made the parking lot.

WHY? Why was I doing this to myself? I had so much: comfort, success, an agile mind, a decent body, friends, health, love, hope, and opportunity. So many of us are forced into worlds beyond our control, suffering pain and tragedy, with so many of us crippled and maimed by war and disease. But for me? I had so much. Weeks earlier, a ditty had been going through my mind, over and over, "A boy, so intent on death, met a girl so intent on life, he needed to destroy himself in order to feel worthy." It was more than that, more than some kind of Freudian, death urge.

I had had a dream. In my best moments, it had been a good one. Holding hands with all of mankind, I had realized we're all in this huge, incomprehensible movie **together**. I had seen worlds beyond my imagination, sights and sounds too incredible to verbalize. Coming down from my flights of fancy, I was always amazed by the world to which I returned. How could hate, confusion, and pollution be the real world? Like so many of us who had popped a pill and watched a sunset, I knew better. I had realized we live in a world plagued with **Maya**. Better my dreams and visions, better the symmetry of expanding and contracting energy. Delving ever deeper into myself, I had had the vain yearning of becoming a bodhisattva, a here and now together one who had experienced eternity. I would realize **truth**, find **peace,** and travel with **love**. It had all been so

The Change Center

simple when I first turned on. It had been all so new and so beautiful. Impossible to convey to the straights, let them see if they had eyes, let them hear if they had ears. Somehow, I had lost it all. First, buried in depression, I had run back to Chicago. I had then forgotten the dream, with Linda being the stimulus for an explosion into ecstasy.

Then, somehow, it had all gotten so impossible. Enough was enough.

Jamming to a stop in the hospital parking lot, I only knew it had to be over. Whatever was happening to me must end. Even then, something was tugging at me, trying to stop me. Linda had withdrawn into herself, frightened, unable to figure out what was happening. I was still trying to stop myself; call it a touch of sanity or the self-preservation instinct of a screwed up, jaded me. Perhaps memories of better times and places. Nothing was going to stop me. I was determined. This must end.

In a rush, I was out of the car, slamming the door, running up the steps, bursting into the hospital. I stopped. I had entered a classroom. It was an empty classroom, done in green. I strode to the dark green, portable chalkboard. I stopped, looking over the empty chairs, the kind with the thickened arm for note taking. Me, the former teacher; no matter what I had done or become, my forte was still teaching. Now was my chance at immortality, a chance for some famous last words before falling into insanity so thick and deep that I would never totally recover.

I felt a confused Linda straggle into the classroom behind me. What could I say? Who would understand? I quickly scrawled, "Juice is safer— thus 'quoth' the preacher." Oh well. I had blown it once again. Why couldn't I have written some head logic gem, an obscure Latin phrase, a Russian proverb, or perhaps, a quote from the *Tao-Te-Ching*? Juice is safer. Sure. If you want to run from reality, find it in a bottle. Booze is easier. A sick liver, dulled senses, and a slowly, rotting mind has to better than... Oh well, even now, I don't buy it. It was a shame I needed anything to protect me from the joy of life.

Enough. I ran out of the classroom, bursting into the night air. Linda was somewhere behind me. I stood there, trying to breathe. Waiting.

My attention was caught up in a flickering, neon sign. I headed toward it, jumping a metal guard railing. I stopped. I stood there, reeling, not knowing quite what to do. Linda was forced to come down the steps and walk around the ramp and the railing I had jumped over. Her dimly heard, "I can't follow you," catapulted me into action. At this angle, I could read the neon sign. With a surge of energy and purpose, I headed for the bright yellow of the beckoning, "Emergency Entrance." Linda, some 20 feet behind me, was forgotten.

Once inside, I didn't know what to do. I knew I couldn't discuss drugs with the enemy. I found myself standing in front of a glass, reception window. Several people stood behind the glass, watching me. On the spur of the moment, I drawled, "Ahm drunk, ahm drunk, and I need a place to stay. Ahm really drunk. Ah really am." They just stood there, watching me. One of them perfunctorily asked me a couple of questions. "How much have you had to drink? What have you been drinking?" They were just putting up with me. My act wasn't playing very well. I wasn't coming across. It looked as though they were going to pat me on the head and send me home.

I ignored their questions. Using some of my excess energy, I projected a picture of a drunk standing in front of me. I could see and feel the faint lines of the energy field I had projected. Ah, that was better. Concern crossed their features. I was making it.

There were four of them. Two nurses, an intern, and a cop. The four of them became a portrait, or rather, a still picture. I had gotten their attention; the shutter had clicked and now they were frozen into a picture of concern.

The nurse who was standing there: Wasn't she Mary Evelyn? Mary Evelyn and Ben, were two lovely people, a beautiful, happily married couple. That first time around, believing in the search for knowledge, I had been good friends with Ben. He had had a hang-up with statistics. I had spent hour after hour tutoring him, although he still ended up with a C. Although he received two Cs that first quarter (a third C would have dumped him out of graduate school), he had gone on to become

The Change Center

one of the most successful graduate students in our class. Hard work and perseverance had paid off for him. When I returned to school for my second try at the doctorate, he had haltingly asked me if I would read his thesis on autistic children, as if my interest or approval would mean something. Hah! He and some of the professors had actually remembered my promise, my dreams, and my academic skills that had come so easily. If only they could have understood that this time I was fighting to walk and talk at the same time, caught in a perceptual world I didn't understand.

Mary Evelyn, cute in her nurse's uniform, looked at me with true compassion. It was sweet, this joke I was playing. I was acting just like her son, Todd, and his five year old games. Although she held back her laughter, her eyes had a humorous twinkle. When I had first left graduate school, I had gone over to say goodbye to her and Ben on my next to last night there. After an evening of talking to them and one of the younger professors, he had left, leaving the three of us alone. We had not seen much of each other for the last six months or so, as they were straight and I wasn't. We had stood in a circle hugging each other. They had wished me well. Mary Evelyn had looked at me with love and respect, "Thank you so much for spending this night with us. I know you have so many friends. Thank you so much for taking the time to spend these hours with us." She really meant it. My last night had been spent alone. I had finally gone to a fast-food place with a girl who had been staying with Bobby. My friends had problems of their own, be it finals or head hassles. After a summer spent slightly strung out, if I wanted to return to Chicago, it was fine. Heads only did what was best for them. Everyone was into his or her own thing.

I projected harder. And, of course, it wasn't Mary Evelyn. She could have given me a hot drink and sent for Ben. The three of us could have talked about statistics and autistic children, reminiscing about those first, mind-bending courses. We could have laughed, and joked and then I could have gone home and tried to study. Perhaps, with a good night's rest, I would have awakened as if from a bad dream.

It was a clever picture. It had moving parts. I was led into the emergency room and told to lie down on an examination table. I was told to wait for the doctor. I felt both ashamed and determined. They came in and out, poking and prodding, asking me useless questions. Thorough incompetents, they used large, plastic, play utensils. There was a huge, plastic, blue thermometer; it looked like something out of a small child's, "let's play doctor" game. The whole thing was silly. One of the nurses' kept screwing up. It took her several attempts before she was able to take my blood pressure. This was absurd. Ridiculous. At least they could make it more realistic. If they couldn't play the game any better, if they couldn't use real instruments, why then, someone should call time out and tell me the drunk game, a silly game, to begin with, was over, and I should just go on home.

Worse than their play-acting and incompetence was the fact that I was in an actual emergency room. There were people who really needed help. While I was lying there, a redneck had been brought in, beaten and bloody, staring at me through bloodshot eyes. I began getting upset to my stomach, sick in the fact I wasn't sick. I felt like someone crying over a hangnail, meeting someone with no foot. I was making a fool out of myself. It was time to leave. At the same time, I had a strong urge to see the charade through to the end. Enough was enough. Whatever had been happening to me must end.

The doctor had my father-uncle-grandfather's eyes. Our last names were similar. I knew he knew me, and he knew that I knew that he knew me. Neither of us was letting on. A pat on the head, a few pills and a, "go home, fella," would have sufficed. Instead, he mumbled something and asked me to wait.

Left alone, my shame overcame my determination. I became perfectly straight with no hallucinations or problems. I felt stupid. It was as though a wrathful, must be insane, trip would provide me with a moment of truth, an ultimate confrontation which would let me prove once and for all, that, indeed, I was a man. Let's face it. There was the December of exploding ecstasy when something had popped in my brain. Now,

The Change Center

there was the pressure of having returned to graduate school, with me trying to make it with both my head friends and with the straights who I had known, when I was neither. There was the fear of not knowing or remembering as much as the other graduate students, of not being able to live up to my professors' expectations, especially when they thought I had been such a bright bundle of promise. There was my changing relationship with Linda. Hell, the change in climate, roles, and surroundings had all combined to completely screw up my metabolism. A few nights of solid sleep, some good rest, and some sunshine were all I needed. I was okay, just feeling foolish and ashamed of myself.

I got up to leave. I made it to the open door. Flash. Looking through the doorway into the waiting room, I stopped, totally shocked. It was filled with dull, flat people holding large dolls. I began shaking. Oh no. I had come to the right place. These dull automons were being sent home with fake children. This was some kind of Change Center, some type of reprocessing plant. Those bundled dolls were probably little robots hooked to a central computer. They probably emitted a certain frequency used to control the masses. Trembling, feeling quite ill, I laid back down. I realized I was lost forever. Flash. I was back. I no longer had the resolve to leave.

Later, they led me into the waiting room. It was now empty except for Liam, Bobby, Linda, and myself. Frightened, Linda had called my friends. Liam, with his long, floppy hair, checkered shirt, and tight Levi's, was, as always, together and right on. Bobby stood off to the side, looking austere in his long, brown hair and beard. Liam kept talking to me, looking me in the eye, not afraid of the crazy. Like a complete ass, I kept on saying, "I don't know, man, I just don't know. Ya know what I mean? I just don't know." He told me I just needed to find a handle, and if I could find a handle, everything would be okay. All I needed to do was find a handle, and everything would be okay. My rage and anger were gone. The bubbling madness needing to be satisfied was gone. All I could keep on saying was, "I don't know. I just don't know."

I was so stupid. I was so close to getting out of there. All I had to do was straighten up and say something to Liam like, "Look man, I'm okay. I'm screwed up, but I'm okay. I'm just kind of light tripping–some kind of paranoid, acid residual, or some such. Look, just get me out of here. Tell them I took some bad acid or something. Just get me out of here."

Hell, we could have left, gone back to their place, blown some weed and laughed about my silly hospital trip. It could have become a happening. Hey, you remember when we had to come and get ya? Boy, were you screwed up. Hah. It never happened. All I could do was mutter, "I don't know."

Talking to Liam, with Linda there at my side, I was basically straight. Briefly, I did go altered. Liam, Linda, and I were caught up in an energy circle, caught up in my hospital trip, in my madness. The portion of the room we were standing in started to spin. Bobby, first standing, and then sitting against the wall of the room, was aloof, on stationary ground. He just dispassionately watched us, becoming some kind of an angel or judge. It would be his decision whether or not I could leave. This quickly passed, with the room leveling out. Dizzy, part of me wanted to break away from Liam and Linda, go up to Bobby and say, "Look, Bob, I'm frazzled, but this is stupid. Look, get me out of here." This too would pass.

The last thing I remember is I was given a shot. I was in a new room with two interns. One of them was bent over my outstretched forearm with a hypodermic in his hand. I don't remember leaving my friends. I do remember the insertion of the needle. After that, it's a mystery. I fell away from wherever I had been. Extended white forearm. Hypodermic needle. Thick clouds of oranges and reds, falling away from me in swirling bands of energy. Thick, coagulated blood. Things spun. I was no more.

Much later, I would find out I was given a shot of Thorazine in order to stabilize my metabolism. I guess I had projected being drunk and crazy much better than I had thought. Much better. I woke up in a closed psychiatric ward.

In the 1960s, as a new teacher, I can remember telling my high school psychology class, "Statistics tell us one out of every ten Americans will be hospitalized for mental illness at some time in their lives." Well, only two more in the class of thirty will have to worry about it. The teacher had made it. My quest was over. I woke up totally insane.

44

SATURDAY

I woke up in a hospital bed. Weak but calm, I had no idea where I was or I how I had gotten there. I knew I was in a hospital room. My only thought was *they* had gotten me.

It was a typical hospital room. There were two beds with a metal, nightstand table between them. There were some closets with metallic doors and a sink with a rectangular mirror above it. A partially opened door led to the toilet. Large drapes covered the windows. The room was done in light pastels and was fairly bright. It was a neutral room, even tranquil.

Nearly a decade earlier, as a young, undergraduate student in psychology, I had visited the back ward of a mental hospital in Chicago. One corridor, the furthest back of the back, had been eerie. Each room (or cell, to be more precise) had had a large, metal door with a 3" by 8" slit at eye level. This slit was the room's only ventilation. Each room contained a single, wrought iron bed and a wooden nightstand. The light source was a bare bulb hanging on a frayed cord from the center of the ceiling. The windows were thick, frosted glass. They were frozen shut, and they were barred. There was an abundance of chipped paint and rotting wood. Patients were strapped to their beds (right arm and left leg). My visit had confirmed my worst suspicions of what a mental hospital was like. I had been both amazed and shocked.

My present surroundings were quite different. It was simply a modern hospital room, relatively new, clean, and unemotional.

I was lying there, neither tripping nor freaking on my environment.

Saturday

Not totally realizing, confronting, nor concerned with it, I simply accepted the fact I was in a hospital room.

I was terribly weak. Although uneasy and disorganized, I maintained a certain calm. Thoughts wandered in and out of my head, not staying long enough for me to grab hold of them. THEY had gotten me. My only coherent thought.

Lying there weak and scattered, with my mind acting like a switchboard randomly starting but never completing a myriad of calls coming in and going out, I began with a, "How did I get here?" My mind merry-go-round was momentarily forgotten as I went deeper inside of myself. Oooops. Psychedelic flashes of thick clotted blood falling away from me... Deep orange clouds with circular bands of pulsating energy... White forearm, deep reds, and oranges...

I shivered away from this dizzying pocket of memory. My attention went to my body. I couldn't feel my insides; I couldn't hear my heart. Surprisingly calm, I began trying to hear or feel my insides, my heartbeat. I found myself looking at the wall. I began scanning the physical objects in the room. I remembered I was trying to remember how I had gotten into the room. Oh no. I quickly shied away from even starting to recall the psychedelic remembrance of my injection. I realized my left foot was numb. Concentrating on this, I found myself listening for my heartbeat, which I could not hear. My attention strayed to the wall. Thirty seconds of this went by every hour or two.

I went from weakness to exhaustion. Unable to hold a constant thought, I rolled onto my side and tried to fall asleep. This too, was impossible. After what seemed like hours of trying-to-sleep frustration, I would be back, once again trying to hold a thought, trying to hold my attention to one subject.

My situation may have been similar to someone coming out of deep sedation. Only occasionally would I trip into an altered awareness. I have very dim memories of the baby blue, plastic water jug and the baby blue, plastic bedpan now becoming huge, much like the light blue thermometer of my admittance. When something like this would happen, my mind would delve inward, with me moving toward becoming some small, doll-like figure surrounded by large, play, light blue, plastic objects. Was this some kind of a regression to infancy? Perhaps. Too scattered to retain any thoughts, even paranoid ones, this would be later fuel for my *change* theories.

In this weak, no insides, drifting thoughts, wandering attention state, I had my first interaction with a member of the staff. A black intern/aide came into my room. The nametag on his crisp, white uniform said, "Jerry." He showed me my closet, pointing out that my clothes were in it. He talked and moved quickly, almost choppily. He was of medium height, stocky, and very dark, although his features were not especially Negroid.

He was a bundle of energy, moving this way and that, here and there. He had large eyes, with deep brown pupils set in reddish whites. His eyes darted back and forth, not meeting mine. His speech, with long pauses between phrases, came quickly out of the side of his mouth. His words hung in the air long enough for me to catch their meaning after the fact. (Literally. I could see/feel his words in the air with me reading/listening to them as they disappeared.) It was like listening to a tape recorder, when you're always behind. Due to the pauses between words and sentences, you're able to stay with it, responding to what has previously been heard while trying to listen to what is presently being said. Looking back, he was probably neither hyper nor especially quick. Rather, it was as if my movie had been speeded up. He was reaching me in 1½ or double time.

He asked me how much money I had; informing me that everything over two dollars would have to be kept in the ward safe. At his direction, I groped through the top drawer of the nightstand, finally finding my wallet. I was able to fumble through it, slowly counting out $1.50. While I did this in slow motion, he stood back, similar to a policeman waiting for you to produce your license, but not about to be tricked into looking through your wallet and being accused of theft or bribery. I carefully stated I had less than two dollars. I was pleased with the normalcy of my speech. I could talk. Although my movements were slow, I had been able to keep my hands from shaking. I had been able to count. I waited expectantly, expecting a reward, a pat on the back, or at least an exclamation of wonder at my cleverness. My accomplishments went unnoticed. He simply said, "Okay," and left.

Lying there, I felt as if my first test had been passed. I could still interact with a human being. I lay back, once again attempting to get it together. Horribly weak, my scattered energy sifted through my system. My thoughts ran away from me, much too quick for me to keep up with them. I felt exposed and vulnerable. Unable to figure out what had happened to me or to even complete a single train of thought, I lay there in a total daze. I was terribly uneasy, being so very weak, passive, unthinking, helpless, and dependent. Sleep wouldn't come. Thoughts wouldn't stay. Time passed. Slowly.

My mind was like a spinning roulette wheel. It would stop, but before I could see where it had stopped, it was in motion once more. I tried as hard as I was able to concentrate, think, even meditate. The thought was triggered: Yoga. Mind, body discipline. The spinning wheels of my mind ground to a halt. Yoga. Sweet, blessed yoga. It would work. I would break through or out of this weak stupor. I would be able to gather my strength and control my energy. I now had a purpose, something I could do. No longer just a weak victim, I would once again be able to control my thoughts and direct my body. Yoga. Ah, sweet yoga.

Slowly, shaking slightly, I managed to get out of bed. The blue ward pajamas, although loose-fitting, were too restrictive for my exercises. I struggled out of them, my mind idly wondering where they had come from, how I had gotten into them. The door to the hallway was open; I kept my jockey shorts on for the sake of decorum. I tried to sit on the linoleum floor between the beds. The floor was too hard; I didn't have enough room to stretch. I managed to get back in bed. Much too stiff to assume a half-lotus, I ended up sitting cross-legged in the middle of the bed. The bed was too soft, sagging in the middle. It was like sitting in a shallow hole. It would have to do.

The Change Center

I attempted to do some stretching exercises. Gawd, did it hurt. I was so very stiff and weak. Many times, attempting to do yoga after a long absence, I would be so stiff I would quickly give up. Not this time. Nope. I was determined. Instinctively, I knew I had to do something. Yoga was the only thing I could think of. The stretching and breathing of yoga would settle me, allow me to make it to some familiar reference points. So many times, we forget what we need, what we have to do to get back on the beam, back on focus. I knew I needed to stretch and to breathe, needed to relax and resettle into a more familiar me. I had just started my stretching when Jerry burst in on me.

"What are you doing?!?" all excited, shouting loudly.

"Huh?"

Just what are you doing? There are women and children on this ward. Just what do you think you're doing? Get your clothes back on. You should be ashamed of yourself."

His shouting didn't bother me. It was just excited babble. It was to the wind, to the air, not really directed at me. It was as though Jerry were playing to an invisible audience, perhaps flashing on repeating the incident around coffee. "Ya know what this crazy was doing? No really, he was sitting there nude, ah mean nude an' he had his fingers up his nose or some such thing." He ran to my side, looking like he wanted to grab and shake me. He stood there, open-mouthed, twitching, as if he wanted to jump up and down, needing to release some of his energy.

All of his noise and commotion didn't bother me. He did. He was bright, alive, mobile, and energetic. His eyes were quick, his awareness of self and surroundings together. He was strong and sure of himself. While I was struggling to sit up straight, attempting to clear my head sufficiently just to be able to think, he was able to run around, shout and carry on. He acted superior to me; he was superior to me, much stronger, higher, and more together. I didn't like him. Not a little.

"Stawh! Po-kneemayesh po-rooski?" (What! Do you understand Russian? In Russian.) I began shouting at him in Russian as loudly as I could. Startled, he stopped. No longer shouting, he just stood there with his mouth open. Hah! I had him. I continued yelling at him in Russian. He just stood there, looking confused. My level of awareness began to rise, rising almost to his level. His eyes bulged, confused and wandering.

Wait a minute. He had cocked his head and appeared to be listening to what I was saying, trying to understand what I was shouting. Could it be that he recognized my speech? Did he know Russian? Perhaps I was just speaking too quickly. Was it possible the Russians had a hand in this? Pop. In an instantaneous mind trip, I began to understand the implications of the entire, horrifying plot. The Russians were definitely in on this. Pop. I was back.

Jerry had noticeably slowed in awareness, thought, and movement. My words petered out. My torrent of Russian was over. Jerry, who had been drifting off, started pulling himself together. His startled confusion was replaced by his former sureness, although he did not appear anywhere near as cocky as before.

With a lingering trace of confusion and a tinge of something else (Was that respect I heard in his voice? Did he know that I was part of the real power struggle?), he began again, this time in a normal, even subdued voice. "Uh, sir, excuse me, but we have certain rules. Uh, you'll have to get your clothes back on. We do have women and children on this floor. Come on now. Get your clothes back on."

I complied. Who knows? I didn't want him to become violent, didn't want anyone to get physical with me before I could get to someone in authority. I moved with difficulty, slowly struggling back into my blue, ward clothes. Jerry waited, watching. At last, he seemed satisfied and left without saying anything. He appeared mollified and left shaking his head. My only reaction, "This is going to be more difficult than I thought. No yoga. *They're* not going to let me do any yoga. No yoga. I'll show them. I have a few tricks up my sleeve. I'll show them. They'll see."

The confrontation had actually strengthened me ever so slightly. I still knew some things. I could speak Russian. This would help. I quickly fell

The Change Center

back into weakened exhaustion.

Weakness. All I knew was an all-pervading weakness. Slipping in and out of fantasies, my only real memory is of an all-consuming weakness. The fantasies, themselves, came and went. Each would be perfectly obvious as it happened. A single thought and there I was, with the rest of my mind hurriedly picking up bits and pieces, fragments of a shattered mind, forming them into a history reinforcing whichever fantasy had crossed my mind. Almost instantaneously, I would be in a new fantasy and then another one and so on.

Deep in my head, attempting to figure out what was happening to me, I met and swept through a whole series of basic bipolarities, conflicts, and paranoia. Black-white, male-female, and life-death confrontations... at a more surface level: I was dead, I was a prisoner of war, and I had been caught up in a Change Center... On and on and on...

One of the earliest, strongest, and most persistent fantasies was that I was in a Change Center. Since I was a male, I would be reborn as a female. Changing is. Were these unresolved, homosexual tendencies? Sure. Why not? I had read an article by some psychologists who hypothesized that rather than castration complex in the male or penis envy in the female, a source of many of our basic, sexual problems is womb envy in the male. The male is beset by the desire to return to the womb and is envious of the woman who has one. Hah. I got to live out both fantasies as the ward was my meta-womb, and I would be changed to a female.

My Change theory started innocuously enough. Tired of trying to figure things out, I slowly, cautiously got out of bed. I made my way to the hall door and timidly stood there, looking out into the corridor. I was afraid to leave my room, to interact with anyone, similar to a small boy afraid to meet the new kids in the just-moved-to neighborhood. The corridor was quiet and empty except for one other person. She walked, tall and stately, up and down the corridor, looking neither to the right nor to the left. She wore a flowing blue negligee, a blue housecoat, dark, movie star sunglasses, and a platinum blonde wig. She was quite a picture, this majestic figure, striding up and down, back and forth. I would forget

Saturday

her, and then she would be back in my range of vision. Although she passed my room several times, she paid me no heed. Even though she never turned her head, it was as though she was aware of me, but chose not to acknowledge me. Oh hell. I had her number. She was obviously a male.

Oooops. I was back in a Change Center. I had no feeling in my midsection. The Change was already starting. Standing there in the doorway, not having met or spoken to anyone except Jerry, I tried to face the facts. After some dread, I quickly accepted this new information. I was to be changed.

I rubbed my hand over the stubble on my face. I was in these grungy, ward clothes. Sweat was dripping from my armpits, with my shirt/smock already wet to the waist. I wasn't very pretty. I dropped away and began thinking, "Oh dear, I need new clothes, some make-up, and I just must do something with this hair." I stood there, looking out into the corridor, staring across at the rooms opposite mine. Several doors were open. I could see several hanging negligees. "Oh, how unfair. I have nothing to wear. Here I am, with only these terrible clothes and nothing pretty to wear. I must have some of those." And yes, my imagination came up with this trite, little girl language.

I stood there, unable to move, wanting to race across the hall and grab as many clothes as I could. I could "see" myself snatching a negligee, wrapping myself in it, rolling around on the floor, becoming... I couldn't move. My consciousness shifted. I centered on the fact I was always afraid to do anything, and I was never spontaneous. I was such a coward. My change trip was forgotten as I castigated myself for being such a spineless idiot. I needed to be able to move, to be spontaneous, to stop being so afraid of everything inside and outside of me. Yet, I couldn't cross the hallway, couldn't snatch those clothes. Defeated, I returned to my bed. I had been unable to leave my room and meet the kids in the new neighborhood.

Returning to my bed, ultimately defeated, unable to launch into my transvestite trip, I was totally exhausted. Sleep would not come. I completely spaced out of my Change Center routine. Then it started. A voice began echoing in my brain, "You're afraid, afraid to make a fool out of yourself, afraid to let people laugh at you. You don't bring laughter or joy to anyone." The voice changed. It became cajoling, "Come on, now. Don't be afraid. Come on. Make people laugh. Be a clown. Do something crazy. Come on." The thought of me actually doing something far out, something hilariously crazy and funny, was almost too much. I had spent years disciplining myself to appear sober and serious regardless of what was happening to me. Mustn't let the others know you get high, you know. The voice kept on and on, first reprimanding me, then pleading with me, tempting me, seducing me. I couldn't sleep, couldn't shut the voice off. Finally, I knew it would be over, and I would be able to find rest, if only I could do something really bizarre and funny. Giving in to the voice, I straightened up and got out of bed. I went to the door of my room, firmly resolved to really let go and do it. I would completely flip out, would bring laughter and happiness to others. By making a complete fool out of myself, I would be able to find peace, would be able to shut off the insistent voice. I prepared to jump right into it.

The woman in the room next to mine had beaten me to it. She was a slightly heavy black woman lying on the floor, half in and half out of her room. To my eyes, it looked like she was wearing some kind of green, ballet costume with all of this fluff sticking out at her waist. There was a microsecond of horror. Her features changed ever so slightly. When Linda and I had been popped on that absurd marijuana bust, we had spent the night in jail. Separated from the girls, my buddy and I had spent the night together in a cell. Very early in the morning, we had been handcuffed and herded into a van. There had been this huge, black guy whose wrists were so thick and swollen that they weren't even able to handcuff him. I momentarily flipped out and wondered how he had gotten here. Obviously, all of us hard nuts to crack had been thrown in together for our reconditioning and reprogramming. My Change Center fantasy was gaining depth. Pop. I was back, watching her.

"Ah didn't do nothing wrong, yassir, yassir, ah believe, ah seen Jesus,

Saturday

yassir. Ooooooooohhhhh, Satan, don't you bother me, oh no, oh get away from me devil, ah didn't do nothing, oooh, please." She was screaming and squirming, looking this way and that. The devil, I guess, was only feet away. I couldn't really take her seriously. I didn't feel the devil, or for that matter, anything evil or sinister. There didn't seem to be any discordant vibrations or any bad energy.

I also couldn't feel any pain emanating from her. When our eyes met, hers appeared to be a lot saner than mine (I had caught a glimpse of myself in the mirror in my room a glimpse had been enough, and I had quickly turned away). No, she didn't seem to be in trouble. Rather than worry about her, I was amazed she was doing such a great job of appearing completely foolish. Although a little overawed, I was tempted to get into the act. I came close to trying to help her out. I could have bent over and whispered instructions to her, "A little more saliva, that's it, drool. Ah now, let's see, try looking a little more afraid, hmmm, well, okay..." I held back. She was certainly doing a good job all by herself. I could never have come close.

And then she was looking at me. "Ah know you, Yassir, Yassir, you're the Holy Ghost, Yassir, ah know you, oooh!!!" Her eyes became more real, focusing on mine. She recognized me. Ah hah! Someone knew me. I became quite excited. I gathered myself together and fell right in with her routine. She knew me. I realized I was supposed to do something. I could help her. I could be useful. I could do some good. I waited expectantly, waiting for my cue.

She kept on getting sidetracked, screaming about the devil or about how she hadn't done anything wrong. I kept waiting, all keyed up about getting into the act. I started to get upset. Come on now; let's stick to the script, the one where I have a part. Every once in a while, though, she would get back to me, lower her voice and say, "Ah know you, Yassir, ah knows youse the Holy Ghost." When this would happen, I could feel the energy flow between us. I fell right in with her. She needed me. I could help her. I should do something. Should I bless her, kneel down with her and do some "aums," or should I slug her, or... It was disconcerting as she

The Change Center

would continually leave me, getting into her own thing. I wasn't quick enough. She kept leaping around, doing her writhing and screaming, with me only an occasional part of the scene.

And then Jerry was there. The woman dropped completely back into her original routine, yelling and moaning about the devil. I was completely forgotten by her. Some other people came to help Jerry. He gave me a perturbed, disgusted look; I was in the way. Discouraged, no longer expectant, and excited, I was drearily tired. I went back into my room. Although disappointed and let down, I idly noticed the voice in my head was gone. Lying down, I fell into a deep sleep.

They woke me up for lunch. Everyone ate in the television room or the kitchenette adjacent to it. On the way to lunch, half-asleep, straggling down the hall, I heard one of the aides refer to the television room as the computer room. He was laughing and said something to someone about somebody to the effect of, "We'll settle him down. We'll just get him to sit in the old computer room." Ack. One of my strongest fantasies was thus triggered. Each of us, unique and separate, suffering from scattered vibrations, would be sent to the Computer Room, where we would be mesmerized by the Master Controller. Each of us would be leveled out, brought to the same vibrational frequency by the all-powerful boob tube. It actually seemed to happen. The television set was on a shelf that protruded out of the wall, some eight feet off of the ground. Sitting there, under the television's spell, the strong would get weaker (tired, bored?) while the weak would get stronger (alert, attentive?). To my hypersensitivity, it was evident everyone would get caught up in the television. While our attention was on it, the energy levels of each of us would sift and level out, bringing each of us to relatively the same place.

Those first couple of days, the television was worse than a mere leveler. Occasionally, I would realize it was a two-way device. The characters would come on, observe us, and report our progress, or lack of it, to the Master. Not only would the television modify us, sucking us into its peculiar vibrations, it would also spy on us. Every so often, I would observe television characters (usually those on live talk shows) watching me. I would usually freeze, attempting to remain neutral in thought and action. Very rarely, filmed characters would flash me knowing looks. Were they the captured ones?

My first meal was a strain. While I was weakly putting my tray of food on the table, one of the other patients, a white male in his teens, became manic and began shouting at his food, "Eat me!" He was ignored. As other patients began to eat their food, he began shouting even louder at them, "Go ahead. Eat me. Go ahead. It's okay. Eat me!" Still mostly ignored, a black girl in a heavily sedated, zombie-like state, froze, and stopped eating, only staring at her food. One of the help was at her side, cooing and assisting her. The boy's shouting was obviously disturbing her and starting to get on everyone's nerves. They began quieting him. He started to spin out and then was off, pacing around the ward while the rest of us continued to eat. There was a mumbled "Oh that, Jack. He's always acting up." from one of the other patients. "I know, but he gets on my nerves." from another. And then he was forgotten.

There were three women, the strongest of the patients, who sat together and ate off to the side in the kitchenette. Their lunch was normal, and it could have been in any lunchroom. I was in the television room with a couple of the other patients, including the dark girl who appeared to be only partially aware of her surroundings. I noted these normal-type, strong ladies had broken the spell of the Computer Room and were able to stay out from under its influence.

I was very tired, very exhausted. Still half-asleep, I was too tired to build any fantasies. After I finished my meal, I sat bent over, with my head in my hands, eyes covered. I stayed that way for some time. I became slightly clairvoyant. Even though my eyes were both shut and covered by my hands, I had the illusion I could see everything around me. My reverie was broken by one of the women in the kitchenette. In a loud, knowing voice, she stated, "Humph, he's pretending he can't see!" Startled, I wondered how she could know I could see in this different way. Although I didn't move or acknowledge her comment, a part of me realized how very difficult this would be. *They* could even know about this.

Later, while I was just sitting there, horribly tired, the three women tried to interact with me. They had adjusted well to life on the ward. Elaine appeared immature; she was physically thin with small breasts and had acne. She was the most quiet of the three. Bertha looked a little like a truck driver. Not that bad, but really masculine. She was the most dominant person and the one who knew about my being able to see with my eyes closed. Lillian, the parading blonde of that morning, was always hidden behind sunglasses and wigs. They would all add fuel to my Change theory. Although, I would usually see the three of them as males becoming females, it would occasionally be the other way. Whether going from male to female, or from female to male, it just didn't matter. What was important was that they were being changed.

Lillian and Bertha tried to kid with me, even flirt. I was new meat on the ward. Bertha went so far as to ask me if she could touch me. I was instantly horrified and felt complete panic. If she had touched me, I would have probably screamed. Thankfully, with my glazed eyes and lack of response, she left me alone.

Too dazed and disoriented to interact with them, I made my way back to my room. My interactions with the staff had been a little better than my weak interactions with the patients. My hearing was completely screwed up. I never knew if someone was talking to me or if I was hearing voices. The staff took to calling me, "Mr. Blazek, sir." I wanted to tell them it was okay. They could call me by my first name, but I was never able to get it out. I became, "Mr. Blazek, sir."

On the way back to my room, I knew I was in trouble. My brief interactions with the staff and other patients had only convinced me I was truly in trouble. I needed some kind of handle, something to hold on to, a train of thought that would stay with me for more than a few moments. I needed a rational explanation of what was happening to me. One moment I would be totally blitzed. The next instant I would be fairly straight, wondering how I had gotten into this whole thing. The only constant thing was the incredible weakness. Weakness. Always weakness.

Back in my room, isolated from the staff and other patients (I had no

Saturday

roommate), I made my way to the window. Oooops. The windows on the other side of the corridor, which included those of the television room, kitchenette, and reception desk, looked out on the hospital parking lot. The view on this side of the corridor was a view of an area I had never known. There were thick trees, looking like the edge of a woods, and a water tower. I counted the floors. Ohmigod, I was on the fifth floor. At a very deep level of mind (a near trance state) in Mind Control, I had learned a very powerful, visual mnemonic trick. Numbers were paired with visual images. The letter 5 was paired with *law*. Arggh. Was I being run on Course 5? Of course, why else would I be on the <u>fifth</u> floor?

The world tilted ever so slightly, and I was, indeed, a Prisoner of War. I could see, feel and live it. Weren't those soldiers there? Why else would there be soldiers? Wasn't that really a gun tower? Were these the rain forests of Nam? Tortured prisoners: Couldn't I hear and feel them? Didn't I merge with them?

I pulled away from the window, shaken and exhausted. Back to bed. Back to blur. Back to weakness and frustration at not being able to sleep.

I would slowly orient myself to the ward. The ward itself, consisted of a single corridor. My room was at the far end, away from the large, swinging double-door entrance. The entrance to the ward was kept locked; one could buzz people in from the reception desk, which was about a third of the way down the corridor. Between the entrance and the reception desk, there were, in order, a conference room containing a stereo and some old records, the television/sitting room which served as the major meeting place of staff and patients, and a small kitchenette/supply room. After the reception desk, there was a small passageway leading to a padded observation room and then, a series of double occupancy hospital rooms. On my side of the hall, across from the reception desk, there was a conference room followed by regular rooms. The showers were directly opposite the reception desk. The rest of that side of the corridor was filled with regular rooms. The far end of the corridor, my end, was marked by a large fire exit. It would take me some time (days after my admittance) before I could map the above.

58

Later that afternoon, a cart filled with goodies was buzzed in through the ward entrance. There were all kinds of candy, some magazines, and even a stack of comic books. I excitedly found out I could indeed buy something. I hurried to my room, remembering I had some money on the nightstand. I bought a comic book, the top one on the stack. At last, here was something that would get my mind off of myself. I could forget my problems, stop trying to figure everything out, ignore the mind-blowing trips. I would read a comic book. Sure. It was a mistake.

I have always loved to read. Back in my room, out of deep habit, near normal except for the weakness, I settled into the bed, propping up the pillows, wrapping myself in the sheets and blankets, preparing to get engrossed in my comic. In my ward state of mind, anything could have happened. Have you ever read a comic book after having a case of beer, while taking a roller coaster ride, or just plain stoned out of your gourd? Reading the comic book became very strange, very quickly.

The comic book, itself, was some intricate, science fiction story about a Mr. Atom. He had numerous bizarre adventures, became microscopic, ran into an anti-self, and so on. Whew. I, of course, took everything literally. Concentrating on each word, watching the cartoon figures blur, I went so far as to believe the comic was some secret set of instructions. If I could only follow them, I would be able to space out of the maze in which I found myself. I became totally engrossed in my reading, flipping out several times. Finally, completely exhausted, I attempted to sleep.

As I tried to sleep, I began getting into the comic book. I realized my real fear, my real confrontation, would be with myself. My ultimate challenge, the climax of my existence, would be running into myself. The primal split. In order to get me back together, my two halves would have to meet, merge into a new whole, or attempt to destroy each other, with only one victor. I fell into a feverish, half-sleep, tossing and turning, with psychedelic images of the comic book character and myself confused and swirling.

Saturday

When I woke up, my comic book adventures were forgotten. Once again, I began trying to figure out what was happening to me. Nothing held together. I just spaced back and forth into countless starts at *the solution*. My emphasis changed. From a constant, "How did I get here?" I was consumed with, "How do I get out of here?"

I had already noticed several strange things were happening on the ward. Seeds of the ultimate, conspiracy trip had already been planted. Coming in and out of a daze, I noticed people were continually coming and going, on and off of the ward. It seemed everyone had their own method, their own secret as to how to get on and off the ward. I had started to identify several groups or levels of people. There were the dupes (the permanent staff, most of whom were white) who thought they were in charge but didn't really know what was going on. There were the help (aides and other workers, most of whom were black) who may or may not have been in on things some definitely were. And then there were the patients, with some of them definitely in on it. Everyone, even some of the other patients, seemed to have their own way of leaving the ward. I knew I had to find a key, a handle, a way my way, to get off the ward. Bertha, for example, was quicker than most of the help and intimidated them. I had to find some way to do the same thing. How could I get on top of it, find my own handle, my own way of dealing with the staff? I had to stop being so chicken shit. I must get off of this ward. This obsession held me together; it gave me purpose. I must find a way to get off of the ward.

Not able to dwell on it, I could dimly remember how I had gotten on the ward. No, not the psychedelic injection or emergency room horrors. I had pretended to be drunk. I could remember pretending to be drunk. Hah. The thought dawned. I would get off of the ward the same way I had gotten there. I would simply leave. I got to my feet and went to the closet. I put on my bulky, fur parka. It was a relic from Chicago. Dark green, with a fur-lined hood, out of place in Florida, even in the northern Florida winter. Putting it on, feeling together, I would simply bluff myself off of the ward. I would just tell them I was no longer drunk. Thank you

The Change Center

all very much, but I'm okay. Please buzz me out. Yes, of course, it would work.

Wearing this huge parka, I started walking to the reception desk. It didn't dawn on me that I was still wearing the blue, ward pajamas, and I was barefoot. I took huge breaths, breathing through my nose, calming myself, steeling myself for the bluff of my life.

Danny, a thin, high-yellow male nurse or aide, and Mrs. U., an Asian nurse with whom I was to get emotionally involved, were stationed at the desk. I came spacing along, bundled in the parka, barefoot, with glazed eyes, messy hair, and growing thick stubble on my chin. They didn't hear me coming. I hunched over the counter; still, no reaction. I loudly cleared my voice. Startled, the seated Mrs. U. looked up. Danny, who had been studying some forms, simply stood there, blankly looking at me.

Mrs. U. was the first to recover. In a composed, friendly, even cheerful voice (her eyes were still doubtful), she said, "Oh, Mr. Blazek, we were looking for you. We have to put your nametag on. Danny, please get Mr. Blazek's name tag."

Danny fumbled around, coming up with a thin strip of plastic with my name and date of admittance on it. I shivered. Although it was probably a typical hospital identification band, it was similar to those on newborn babies. Was I indeed to be changed, to be erased, and to be reborn in this place? By this time, I was completely confused and had forgotten why I had gone to the reception desk

Danny, who had still not spoken, kept looking at me ever so strangely. He fitted the plastic band around my wrist. He attempted to punch it closed; this required a small, metal tool. I just stood there, hunched over the counter, completely upset. They weren't going to tag me. I sent energy, tons of it. I could have lifted a car, bent steel bars, and been able to do just about anything. Although I made no overt, physical move (I could have crushed him like a grape), he wasn't able to punch it closed. He kept on trying, looking at me shyly, even apologetically. Finally, he took it off my wrist, trying to punch it closed on the counter top. Mrs. U. tried it. They

Saturday

both tried it. I kept sending energy; no one was going to tag me. I became exasperated watching them and almost snatched it up, doing it for them. Nope. Not that. They weren't going to tag me.

They started trying to make light of it, embarrassingly giggling. The absurd scene went on. Finally, Mrs. U., still giggling, said, "Well, I guess we won't be putting it on just now." Looking grim, with my face set in stone, I just nodded. (I was never tagged. Even after I stopped hallucinating and had some rational recall of my ward experience, I would still think some quirky things had been going on, although most of them were in my own head. Still, the staff were a little weak.)

Satisfied, feeling strong, I walked back to my room in a manner similar to a gunfighter returning from a high noon he had not found to be terribly difficult. Back in my room, discarding the parka, I crawled into bed. Lying in bed, I drifted back into a weak fuzziness. A thought nudged my consciousness: I was still on the ward. My strength and energy totally disappeared, leaving only a weak, tired, defeated shell. I had to get off of this ward. Not angry, manic, or clever, I knew I must get off of the ward. I needed to get outside, needed to get off by myself, and get my thoughts together. Nothing made any sense. I had to get off of this ward, out of this entire situation.

Restless, unable to sleep, I once again got out of bed. I had no plan, no ideas. My only purpose was a deep-seated urge to get off of the ward. I stood at my door. I slowly wandered out into the corridor. I drifted over to the far end of the hallway, the one away from the entrance, the reception desk, and the television room. I found myself staring at a door; it was an emergency exit or fire door. Was it or was it not locked? I had no will, strength, or purpose. I simply stood there, staring at the door. After countless, mind-time of just standing there, a thought broke through. An alarm would probably go off if I pushed open the door. Alarm? My head snapped around, and I found myself staring at a fire alarm.

I had not known it was there. With no conscious volition or purpose, I found myself pulling the alarm. Perhaps I thought that in the resulting confusion, I would slip out of the fire exit. Perhaps I thought the ward would be cleared. I'm not sure what I thought or why I pulled the alarm.

Suddenly, there was an immediate loud clanging and all kinds of commotion. I stood stunned and frozen. As if from a great distance, I watched several doll-like figures running back and forth, crisscrossing from one side of the corridor to the other. My world went sideways. It was as though I were watching all of this running and activity from a great height, perhaps as much as from four or five stories up. Caught up in this unreal, out-of-perspective world, thoroughly entranced by the running figures and all of the commotion caused by the alarm, I completely forgot about slipping through the fire exit. I had become a non-thinking straw dolly. Eventually, I was led back to my room.

Looking back, although seemingly continuous, each of these incidents is like a vignette, a happening out of an eternity of fuzzy, never-ending weakness. Out of this jelly-like weakness, I can recall these isolated incidents quite clearly. The real problem wasn't in these bizarre incidents, but rather, the endless hours of not being able to think or to cope. My predominant state of being was not a series of trippy experiences, but rather, an all-pervading, low energy, impotence. Each time I would get into trying to figure something out, something would happen to sidetrack me into something else. Perhaps a blessing in disguise, as I still had little or no memory and almost no cognitive powers.

After my fire alarm incident, as I was lying in bed, I dropped into a whole new shtick. I realized I was completely worthless. I was haunted by my worthlessness. Everything I had ever tried to do had backfired. I was a worthless fool. A dud. After hours (moments?) of castigating myself, I started to gear myself up. I must shape up. All of these people are waiting on me, taking care of me. Oh no. I must do my part. I had to be worth something. I must do my part.

With a sudden, unexpected burst of energy, I jumped up. I would do my part. Earlier, at the reception desk, I had had some strength. Now was the first time since coming to the ward, that I was able to move, really move. With a manic burst of energy, I ran down the corridor to the television

Saturday

room, to the kitchenette, to the reception desk. I began emptying all of the ashtrays, clearing the tables, dumping my room wastebasket into the larger one at the reception desk, and so on. I was completely hyper, working quickly and efficiently. No longer would people have to wait on me. I would show them; I could do my part. I wasn't worthless. I could help. I was a big guy.

They tried to stop me. "Come on now, come on, you don't have to do that. Come on now." I ignored them. I was doing my part. I worked feverishly. Hah! I would show them. Sweat began dripping from my forehead and armpits as I continued working, all hyper and intent. They continued trying to stop me, trying to reason with me, but not using any physical force.

Very suddenly, my energy petered out. I allowed them to walk me back to my room. I was quite subdued, for you see, a voice was pounding over and over in my head: "You're taking work away from others. This is someone else's job. You're taking work away from others. Find your own work. You're taking work away from others." Exhausted, tired, and defeated once again (When would I be able to do something right?), I allowed them to lead me back to my room. Days later, Lillian would tell me how cute I had been, running around the ward, dumping all of my clothes and belongings into the trash, and so on. Oh well. C'est la vie.

Back in my room, I was half asleep when they came for me. It was Danny and Mrs. U., the dynamic duo. They kind of milled around my room, moving furniture. I finally realized they wanted to move my bed out of the room. Groggily, I tried to get up, wanting to help or at least get out of the way. I tried to tell them I was okay, that I could walk, but I wasn't able to get the words out. Half asleep, with them, completely ignoring me, I became confused and tongue-tied. I tried to show them that I was okay by starting to get out of bed, but they would have none of it. I did manage to get out a half-hearted, "I'm okay. I can walk." Other than a, "No, that's okay." they continued to ignore me completely. Still spaced and disoriented, I simply laid back, relaxing completely, falling into a "whatever happens, happens" head.

They continued to mill around. They were having some real problems. The situation took on a Laurel and Hardy aspect, with them appearing to be incompetent buffoons. Not spun out, but weak and disoriented, I waited patiently, as serious and passive as possible. They continued trying to move the furniture and maneuver my bed out into the hall. The problem was a simple one, requiring them first to move my bed away from the door. After moving the other bed out of the way, they could then move my bed toward and through the door. They could not figure this out and continually tried to squeeze my bed past the one nearer to the door. I'm reminded of an old joke. A guy gets a flat tire outside of an insane asylum. Attempting to change the tire, all of the nuts and bolts he had removed from the flat tire roll down into a sewer. Perplexed, not knowing what to do, he just stands there. A crazy with glazed eyes, standing behind the wrought iron fence of the asylum, tells him to take a nut off each of the other tires and use them to secure the fourth tire temporarily. The motorist looks at him with shocked surprise, "B-but how did you know that?" The inmate answers, "I may be crazy, but I'm not stupid." Although too shattered to have those kinds of thoughts or insights, their actions were similar to someone not being able to figure out how you could use one less bolt for each tire, at least temporarily.

Danny and Mrs. U. finally took to giggling, making much ado out of their ineptness. They finally figured it out. At last, we were in the hall. By this time, I had grown quite bored with the whole thing and was once again half-asleep, lying flat on my back, open and passive. Perhaps Danny was trying to be cute. Maybe he was just trying to be friends. Maybe he was just an idiot. Whatever.

I peered up at him from my highly vulnerable position. He stood at the foot of my bed, out of perspective. Looking at me, he suddenly had an idea; his features changed, taking on a set, determined, even devilish expression. My mind took it further, with his face becoming some kind of devil's head. Leering intently at me, he bent over and began pushing. He pushed as hard and fast as he could, shouting, "Wheeeee!" We raced

Saturday

down the hall with his now grotesque head always staring at me. The walls, rooms, and reception desk went whirling by in blurred swirls.

He put on the brakes. We slid to a stop, coasting to a halt in front of a room halfway between the double door entrance and the reception desk. The room was directly across from the television room. It was the most observable room on the floor. Getting my bed into position was an easy matter as it was to be the one closest to the door. Having positioned my bed, Danny stood there, grinning down at me. It wasn't a malicious grin. Perhaps he was just having fun, goofing around, and trying to have some fun with me. Whatever his intention, the effect had been creepy. In the days to follow, still trying to figure everything out, I would have psychedelic flashes of our trip down the corridor. It would only strengthen my conviction about something strange and wrong happening on the ward. I may not be playing with a full deck, but everything weird wasn't just a product of my imagination.

I guessed they moved me due to the fire alarm incident or because of my Mr. Clean routine. I was now in the hub of activity, surrounded by mirrors and motion. I had a roommate, Jack, another person who bore watching.

Jack was a little strange. In his late teens, perhaps 17 or so, he was a thin, six-footer. He had thick, dark, wavy hair and a pinched, pinkish face. Tremendously immature, he would always be bothering someone and would occasionally throw temper tantrums. The staff and the other patients either put up with him or babied him. He was also the kind of person who had done everything, or rather, had to have you believe he had done everything. His, "oh yeah, I've done that," or his, "sure, I've been into that," were kind of irritating, especially when you knew he didn't know what you were talking about. A nice guy; he was just impossibly immature and childish, with very easy breaking points.

Meeting him my first afternoon on the ward, I was more spun out than he was. He came across as tremendously open and friendly. He had adjusted to life on the ward, having all kinds of entertainments, including a guitar. He told me if I ever wanted to play his guitar or use any of his

The Change Center

things, I should just go ahead and do it. I was disorganized and confused, especially after my ride down the corridor, but felt as though I had arrived at summer camp. Luckily, I had gotten a friendly roomie.

It was right around this time that I would occasionally pop into a Prisoner of War fantasy. Ironically, a simple question by a passing nurse triggered me into this delusion. Having been moved and having met Jack, I was standing in the hall. A nurse, walking by, suddenly stopped and turned, asking me, "You know where you are, don't you?" I just looked at her and said, "Of course. Yes." She nodded and continued on her way.

At the moment, I could have told her I was on a psychiatric ward in a hospital in Florida. I could have told her much more. In our momentary exchange, I had also flashed on my brief, nightmarish glance out of the window, when I had swirled into Prisoner of War. Shivering away from my psychedelic remembrance, my mind quickly built a P.O.W. fantasy, taking isolated facts and fancies, building them into a network supporting that mindset.

For example, Jack was the typical, young G.I., who had cracked early. Some of the young blacks who served as aides and workers were obviously captured soldiers now in the employ of the enemy. Mrs. U., an Asian, and one of *them,* was in on it. Not being rational, my mind would go even further. We were all prisoners, even the doctors, and nurses. These professionals (the dupes) unwittingly served the enemy, not realizing what they were doing. Over the next few days, I would spend endless mind time attempting to figure out who the Master Controller was. My usual guess was a Quasimodo type hidden away in the bowels of the hospital. I would get psychedelic flashes of him moving all of us like chess pieces.

Yes, I could have told her where I was. I even knew what floor we were on, having counted them in my brief glimpse out of the window. I could have probably told her how far we were from my college's campus. At the same time, I knew so much more, including the fact I was a prisoner of war. My P.O.W. trip was instantaneous and at least as real as being able to say I was in a hospital in Florida. Sure, I knew where I was and what was happening, but I wasn't about to let the enemy know that I knew.

Saturday

The ward toilets fit in well with my prisoner of war fantasy. Each hospital room had a small cubicle, containing only a toilet. Showers were in a separate room across from the reception desk. Sinks were in the individual rooms. In the small bathroom (actually a toilet room, I guess), there was a knob on the cubicle wall calling attention to the intercom system by which you could call a nurse if you needed help. The knob was the size of a 50-cent piece and was illuminated by a pulsating, orange light.

Late in the afternoon, I tried to use the toilet. In addition to my mind terror, I also had several physical problems while on the ward, including constipation. So there I was, squatting on the stool in this small, austere, closed-in cubicle with its tiled walls and floor and this ominous, pulsating orange light. Constipated, grunting, the room went tilt. The screen of the intercom waited for my confession. Images of hopelessness filled my head.

Occasionally, I would view the toilets as observation rooms; other times, I would fear gas would be pumped in. I even got into the possibility that they were elevators and I would be taken to a new level of horror. I would always leave the door cracked slightly open so that the elevator wouldn't work. As with everything else, my mind was too melted to maintain a prisoner of war fantasy consistently.

Supper approached. I would try my last escape attempt. A large, steel cabinet containing our dinner was wheeled onto the ward. Trays of drinks were set on top of it, with our food trays on shelves inside. It was a large cabinet, some 3 by 6 feet and about 4 feet high. An aide wheeled it in, plugged it in, and left. Food and drink were dispensed from the cabinet by the regular staff.

As I ate, the thought dawned on me. It would be simple to escape. I could simply pretend I was one of the staff, get buzzed out and just push the cart off of the ward. I would escape this maze of absurdity.

I hurried through my meal and carried my empty tray out to the waiting cabinet. Putting my tray on top of it, I realized no one was around. It would be so simple. I would just unplug it, push it the twenty feet or so to the double-door, entrance to the ward and yell, "Yo!" as the others did. Once the unlocking buzz came, I would push it on through, remembering to take the service and not the passenger elevator. Both elevators were side-by-side, right next to the ward door; I had seen them when they had buzzed the cabinet in. Once out of sight, on the elevator, I would further plan my escape. Once outside, I would run like hell. It seemed simple enough.

I approached the plug. It was a large industrial one and gave off a slight hum. As I bent to unplug it, my world went mad. The slight, electrical hum became a huge roar. The cabinet, itself, became a huge, menacing device with a robot like awareness. Actually, rather than the metallic cabinet becoming huge, it was more as though I became quite small, about two feet tall or so. I saw and heard this device from the perspective of an infant or toddler, a hypersensitive, learning-how-to-walk child. I stopped, completely overcome. As soon as I was able, I got out of there. I returned to my room, completely shaken.

For the rest of my time on the ward, I would approach the cabinet warily, like a puppy approaching a stationary, model train that starts every time the small dog gets close to it. The cabinet never changed on me again. Seeing it in its true size relative to my near six feet, I would vaguely wonder about what had happened. The experience became similar to a bad dream I had had while on the ward, just as the entire ward experience has become an unreal, bad dream to my present self.

The cabinet incident was my last escape attempt on the ward. I would fall into my most predominant thought pattern while confined. Simply, I was lost. It was hopeless. I would be on the ward forever. I would never leave. Ever.

The evening is mostly lost to me. Visiting hours (after dinner, from 6 to 8) are completely lost. Shaken from my cabinet incident, I may have slept through them. I did have some interactions with the other patients after visiting hours were over. They were slowly becoming familiar to me.

Saturday

There were three women, Bertha, Lillian, and Elaine. There was my roommate, Jack. Beth, an impossibly cute, small teenager about 15 or 16, was a little doll, usually showing high energy, and always sweet and cute. There was Cynthia, a black girl of about 14, who sat frozen in her own world, unable or unwilling to communicate with the rest of us. There was the black woman who had thrown the fit outside of the room next to mine, who was rarely seen and usually in the presence of a nurse or aide. There was Martha, a petite woman in her 30's or 40's, who had very fine features.

Martha sat like a porcelain figurine, neither acknowledging nor interacting with the rest of us. Within a day or two, she was released to her family or transferred to another location. There were a few others, some of whom stayed mostly in their own rooms. The ward wasn't very large; it would hold, perhaps, a couple of dozen people, if filled to capacity.

After visiting hours, most patients would gather in the kitchenette or sitting room. There was a natural letdown from the tension generated by the visitors. Although not noticeable to me that first night, it was also the time we would start coming on to our evening medication.

My first night is a blur. My main contribution to the conversation was, "I'm never going to get off of the ward. I'll be here forever." I said it often. Reactions varied. One of the other patients might say virtually anything in response. It didn't matter if their response was a, "No one ever leaves," or a, "I can leave anytime I want to." I knew I was lost. The three women had all kinds of "in" jokes, double meanings, witticisms, and so forth. The conversation would move quickly, up and down, back and forth. I was not able to keep up. I would take everything literally, getting totally lost, while they hurried on to their next statement.

For example, one of them might say something like, "I think I'll just walk right out the door and take a stroll." Flash. I would see an energy door outlined in whitish gold. In my head, I would try and space through it. Failing, I would resurface. I would sit there dumb, not knowing what anyone was talking about. If I did get into the conversation, I would almost immediately be spaced right out of it once more. Occasionally, it would be as if we were on a drug high, the three women and myself. It was as though we were in a circle of vibration. If I could only get in tune, the four of us would be able to space off of the ward on some kind of an energy ledge.

The conversation itself was schizophrenic, with some talk about rocket ships, time warps, and more. I didn't know what was going on, simply sitting there, attempting to interact, with my only contribution an occasional, "I'll never leave the ward." It would be days later when I would find out the three women had been playing with my head. It made little difference, as I had been almost completely gone, and what they were doing didn't make much difference.

Later that night, Jack and I were alone in the television room. One wall was lined with couches with draped windows above them. The couches sat facing the corridor wall holding the mounted television. There were two small, rectangular mirrors, one each on the other two walls. They faced each other. Standing in the middle of the room, I happened to look into one of the mirrors.

My gaze settled on a darkened, shadowy, ghostlike apparition. Due to the placement of the two mirrors, I saw this ghostly caricature of myself reflected in a mirror, reflected in a mirror, reflected in a mirror. growing ever smaller, ad infinitum. My world stopped. For a moment, I was beyond life and death, caught in an endless world of gray mists and ghostly apparitions going on forever, both before me and behind me. Time stood still. Totally spaced out, caught in an endless moment, buried in the senseless, non-ending repetition of my weird, mirror image, I simply stood there.

Hopeless despair. Never-ending regret. Terror beyond time. I was nudged to the side. Call it the Hand of God, or my inability to continue to stand motionless. It was over. No longer between the mirrors, it was over. A shiver passed through me. A convulsive squeezing of the shoulder blades, and I was away from it. It had passed. Thank you, dear Lord. Oh, sweet Jesus, thank you so very much.

Saturday

It must have been late. Jack was pacing around, doing his thing. Not sleepy, I decided to go to bed. Crossing the hall to my room, I ran into Bertha. She wanted to talk. Confused by my mirror episode, I was easily led to a table in the kitchenette. We sat down, hunched over the black, metallic tabletop. It was good to see another human being, good to get my mind off where I had just been. She didn't have anything to say to me. At her suggestion, we began to play some cards.

She taught me a simple card game similar to what I knew as War. It was new to me. She was very nice, even solicitous, treating me like a small child. I had trouble focusing. I dimly remember the tattoo on her arm (did she have one?) went psychedelic with its reds and blues becoming similar to the oranges and reds of my remembrance of the shot of Thorazine. At one point, her face started to change into my dead stepfather's (he was a former Marine and had had a bulldog tattooed on his arm) but it didn't make it.

Weak, tired, and feeling as though I were underwater, I had difficulty understanding the game. Shuffling, dealing, and even holding the cards was a difficult endeavor. My physical coordination had been coming and going all day, mostly going. In both my head and body, I struggled to stay with the game. Flash. I was relatively clear and lucid, feeling good, really good. The simple child's game was just that, a simple child's game. I remembered I loved to play cards. Energy flowed into my fingertips. I felt like speeding up the game, doing some fancy shuffles. Bertha didn't notice my change and continued to mother me, showing me when and how to play, cooing the instructions. She was obviously enjoying her Big Sister role. A portion of me wanted to shout, "Look, this is simple. I know what to do. Let's get on with it." Not wanting to hurt her feelings, I remained quiet.

I held back and continued to play slowly. I waited for her instructions, trying not to win, and, of course, kept on winning. As a child, I used to play dice with my grandmother. It was an Old Country game we had played for pennies. Seemingly, my grandmother would always get the best roll of the dice. She would take to cheating in my favor. If I caught her, I would get tremendously angry. Although I desperately wanted to win, I needed to win fairly. Playing with Bertha, I wanted her to win, but could not misplay or otherwise slant the odds in her favor. She got into the game, concentrating on the cards, making faces when she lost, taking everything very seriously. I began to worry about her, began to worry about my winning hurting her. Over the next week, this would become an obsession with me. I would always be worried about hurting the other patients.

Bertha kind of saved the day. At least, she quickly got me out of any worry or guilt about being a superior card player. Simply, she asked me questions. Trying to answer them opened me to my head and its fuzzy, thoughts and images. My feeble attempts at verbalization quickly dropped me back into, "Huh?" I didn't have to fake anything. Sitting and playing cards, any kind of cards, was an achievement in and of itself.

I dimly remember I tried to explain energy ledges to her. (What in the world is an energy ledge?) I told her if I could only get it together, we could space out of there. Together, on an energy ledge, we could do it. She urged me to try it. Images of her face, large, blocky and masculine, inches from mine, set in concentration, waiting for me to do it. I tried. My effort allowed me to lose it. I lost it almost completely. I was finally able to admit defeat. She leaned back, satisfied I couldn't do it. Did she know? About energy ledges? About moving through time and space? About getting caught between universes? About waking up with no memory on a psychiatric ward? I don't know. Maybe she entered my craziness. Maybe I tapped a vein of fear in her. Perhaps she was just humoring or funning me. She always seemed so strong and so straight. I don't think she knew what I was talking about. Coming so soon after the mirror episode, our entire time of playing cards was surrealistic. Her questions and my efforts at answering them and trying to play cards had totally fatigued me. It was time for bed. Mumbling good night, I left her there.

It must have been quite late. Except for Jack, who had a tendency to be anywhere and everywhere, Bertha and I had been the only two patients who were still awake and out of our rooms. Jack was spacing

Saturday

around the television room, making a little noise. Neither Bertha nor I paid him any attention. Totally exhausted, I straggled back to my room, ready to collapse in sleep. Jack came into the room, also ready to turn in for the night.

I started to strip, getting bare to the waist. Jack looked at me with open-mouthed amazement.

"You're going to sleep like that?"

"Uh, sure."

There were strong energy rushes with the room starting to spin. What was going on? Was he some kind of sexual deviate? I continued stripping, keeping my jockey shorts on. Jack just continued to stare at me. Finally, as if out of some kind of bravado, he also stripped to the waist. He stood there, defiantly looking at me, as if to say, "Hey man, I'm okay. I can strip to the waist too." He just stood there, wavering ever so slightly, looking at me out of his pinched and puckered face. No animosity, just a "look at me, I can do it" expression on his face. I got into bed.

Jack remained standing, still looking at me. He picked up a can of shaving cream, eyes still on me, and began slowly, purposely, smearing it all over himself. He started with his face, got some in his nose and mouth (ohmigod, was he going to eat it?), on his chest, on the back of his head, all over. His look stayed twisted and defiant. At times, he looked as though he wanted to break into some kind of manic laughter.

I almost got into it. I almost got up and grabbed the can from him. I could have stood tall, smeared some in my hair, then had him smear some in his, and then we could have gone back and forth, smearing each other, and then ending our smearing with manic laughter. It almost happened. It didn't.

"Hey, man. C'mon, what are you doing? C'mon now."

"Umpfgh."

It was over as quickly as it began. Some of these other patients must have been traveling through trips as quickly as I was. Without a word, he stopped, put the can down, and washed himself off. He took off his pants and climbed into bed. We were both completely out of the shaving cream trip. An observer, questioning us, may have been surprised that we could hardly remember it had happened, even though only moments had passed.

One of us shut off the lights. Instead of remembering the shaving cream incident or talking about it, we just continued lying in bed, rapping about drugs and other things. It was like getting high with a stranger and finding out you had all kinds of similar experiences. At the time, I was beyond duplicity. I had enough difficulty interacting with a human being, let alone trying to put on a false face. I quickly realized Jack was mostly full of it. No matter what I brought up, and in the comfort of fatigue and talking in the dark, I mentioned all kinds of esoteric happenings, and Jack just kept on saying, "Oh yeah. Yeah, I've been there. Oh yeah, I did that. I know what you mean." It did seem as if he had experienced several things that I had. When I brought up transcendental meditation, which was met with a "yeah, yeah," I finally realized that, for the most part, he didn't know what I was talking about.

While we rapped, with me doing most of the talking and Jack doing a lot of saying "yeah," he would occasionally break into a hyper, singsong burst of slang and whistling. He would make all kinds of weird noises, with it impossible for me to follow him. In addition to not following him, I would be so easy I had trouble remembering what we (I) had been talking about.

I thought Jack was weird. I also liked him a lot. Occasionally, he just got a little too irritating. Otherwise, he was okay. We stopped talking right around transcendental meditation, with him falling off into a restless, turning sleep.

Left alone and still awake, I decided to try and practice it. Perhaps this is what I needed to do to find some peace and begin to figure out what was happening to me. I had never really gotten into transcendental meditation, did not have a mantra, and did not know the technique. As I understood it, the idea was to follow the bubbles of awareness as deeply as possible, with them getting smaller and smaller, until one gets to the

Saturday

source or center of one's thought. This process reportedly results in an expanded awareness and a transcending, "Aha!" experience.

I went deep inside my head, hoping to follow the bubbles of my awareness to a deeper level of consciousness. Uh-huh. Nope. My thoughts were speeding missiles, going helter-skelter. There were no bubbles. Rather, the inside of my head was like a thick, jelly-like mass with gaping holes in it. Bright pockets of memory, still inaccessible to me, were everywhere. It was like standing in the middle of a huge lump of Swiss cheese (made out of jelly) and, at the same time, being in the middle of a crossing or intersection of the most complex subway, train station, or airport in the world. Whew. Nope. I quickly withdrew from inside of my head. Uh-huh. Grand Central Station encased in jelly with trains at their peak, rush hour traffic was not for me.

Lying there, unable to sleep, afraid to get back inside of my head, I didn't know what to do. Jack's shock at my partially, bare body gave me an idea. I would masturbate. By playing with myself, I would be able to get my energy together. The resulting climax, a catharsis of released energy, would clear my head, allow me to sleep, enable me to get some rest. My hand snaked down to my genitals. My breath grew shallow. I felt terribly wicked yet justified. This was necessary. Neither shame nor guilt entered my consciousness.

Nothing. There was no feeling whatsoever. Nothing. Not a thing. My genitals were limp, unfeeling pieces of rubber. They may as well have belonged to a rubber statue or a doll. There was neither life, nor energy nor movement. There was nothing at all, just a growing fear as I wondered if I had already lost my manhood.

My genitals were missing in action. Would I, indeed, become a female? Had it already started? Was it too late for me to salvage my manhood? How would I survive the Change Center? I stopped. I slowly fell asleep, quite afraid.

Thus ended my first day on the ward.

SUNDAY

My head was a bowl of whipped egg whites with gaping holes everywhere. My body was encased in a thick, palpable, immobile sea of Jell-O.

As a child, I had spent a year in bed with tuberculosis. Throughout my life, I have been prone to high fevers and physical breakdowns of short duration. In addition, there had been the depression and bad trips of my late 20's. Nothing I had ever experienced could compare to the weakness and lethargy of those early days on the ward. Helplessness. Total helplessness.

Buried in physical and mental weakness, unable to rationally explain my situation, frustrated in my escape attempts, only occasionally allowed rest from the terror of my external environment (subject to change from the mundane to the mad at any moment) or from the voices and turmoil within, I constantly called on a higher being for help. I would increasingly call on someone or something to save me as *pain*, both mental and physical, was beginning to become the predominant aspect of my life. From weakness to pain, from lethargy to turmoil as I twisted and turned against whatever it was that was crunching my body and mind.

I had been a religious youth and an adult seeker after truth, at least my version of the truth. Confirmed a Lutheran, I had joined a fundamentalist church as a teenager. The Evangelical church forbid drinking and frowned on just about everything else (Billy Graham was okay, but his wife wore makeup). As a young adult, although no longer religious in a church-going sense, I had continued my search for truth and meaning. In addition to my academic studies, this had led me to a heavy reading

Sunday

of Christianity and other religions, including Hinduism, Buddhism, and Taoism. Increasingly, I was led to introspection, yoga and meditation, and long discussions into the night about the meaning of it all. I had a strong desire to figure it all out, to increase my awareness, to understand what all of these philosophers and religious leaders were talking about.

That morning, tossing and turning in my bed, I prayed constantly. It wouldn't hold together. My mind jumped from mystic to saint to Buddha to Christ. I went from this religion to that one to yet another. Going from this method to that belief to this practice to that command, I was unable to hold a thought. I was unable to meditate, unable to concentrate. Even in my cry for help, I was unable to hold to a consistent train of thought.

This went on forever, with a half-asleep, feverish me calling on first, this one and then, that one. I was crying here, struggling there. The inside of my head was similar to my wandering attention state of the previous morning. My head was filled with pain, frustration, and weakness.

Later that morning, I found myself surprisingly alone in the television room on a quiet, Sunday morning. The truth dawned on me. I was cross-programmed. I was praying to a series of entities, attempting to follow a variety of faiths and methods. I must remain constant in my plea for help. I realized I must turn to my source, to my upbringing. I had been, first of all, a Christian. At one time, I had even been a devout, Bible-carrying fundamentalist.

The Lord's Prayer. That's it. The Lord's Prayer. I would repent of all of the bullshit of a wasted life. I would repeat the Lord's Prayer with reverence and sincerity. My faith would set me free. I would repeat it over and over. God would hear me and help me out of my misery. The Lord's Prayer. That would do it.

"Our Father, glory to thy name. Amen." What the...? "Our Father, who art..." Uh? What was going on? I knew the Lord's Prayer. "Our Father, who art in heaven, give us this day our daily bread, forever and ever. Amen." Uh? No, wait a minute. That's not it. "Our Father, our Father, our Father, who..." What's going on here?

I tried. I really tried. I began to cry lightly, salty tears running down my cheeks. Although not realizing it, this was the first time I had tried to remember something from my past while on the ward. "Our Father..." My thoughts continued to run away from me. I couldn't even remember the Lord's Prayer. I kept on blanking. I needed to know the Lord's Prayer.

Defeated, I slowly got up. Shuffling along, like a small, repentant child, I timidly approached one of the black nurses. Not able to get her attention, I stood waiting. She finally noticed me.

"Uh, nurse."

"Yes, honey."

"Uh, do you know the Lord's Prayer?"

Slightly miffed, "Well, uh, do ya mean the 'Our Father' one?"

"Yes."

"Well, let's see..." Turning to another nurse, talking to me, "Gee, it's been so long. Let me just see."

And then there were several nurses around, each giving their comments, trying to remember how the Lord's Prayer went. They were tremendously nice and kind, each one of them trying to figure out how the prayer went. One of them recited it to me, but it didn't sound exactly right. I needed to know **the** Lord's Prayer. No approximation would do. Only by repeating the real one, could I free myself from this pain.

"No-o, I remember it differently."

And then one of the nurses, a thickset, black woman, winked at me. "Just a minute, honey, just a minute. We'll get it for you." And then she was off, holding up a finger for me to wait. The other nurses milled around, waiting for her to return. She was back almost immediately. She had found a Bible. The other nurses wandered off. She stood there, leafing through the Bible, assuring me it would be okay. "Now don't you worry, honey; we'll find it for you." Talking to herself, "Now, let's see, it should be somewhere around here."

With an "Aha, here it is!" she led me back to the television room. Gently sitting me down, she handed me the open Bible.

Sunday

I blankly stared at the pages. The Bible had been opened to St. Matthew, chapter five. The "5" had been circled. My world went, "Oooops." The Master Controller had anticipated me. I was being run on course five. Was there no way back to reality? I shrugged off the growing feeling of loneliness and despair. I nervously began to read. I was no longer sure the Lord's Prayer was *the* answer. (Thankfully, I didn't build a whole philosophy of life on the letter five. Years later, curious, looking it up as I rewrote my ward experience, I would discover the Lord's Prayer was in chapter six, not chapter five.)

This wasn't it. This wasn't it. This wasn't the way I remembered the Lord's Prayer. Then I dimly remembered that there were different versions of the Lord's Prayer. One read, "And forgive us our trespasses as we forgive those who trespass against us," while another version used "debts" and "debtors." In my ward frame of mind, "trespass" conjured up images of cartoon-like people shooting through space, each on their own voyage. To trespass, would be to cut them off, making them slow down or alter their path. The worst form of trespass would be an actual collision. "Debts" had a completely different connotation. As a religious teenager, I had been shocked to discover that there are no **the** Ten Commandments, with Catholics and various Protestant sects having different wordings. On the ward, a minor change in translation was not just a simple change, but a mind-blowing event.

What was *the* Lord's Prayer? How could I be saved? I had to know and repeat the correct one. I drifted into hopelessness. I was never going to be okay. I was never going to leave the ward. My attention drifted away from the Bible in my lap.

The television was going. I passively sat there, idly aware of it spewing forth Sunday morning church music. Eventually, it caught me. I realized the members of the choir, especially those singers on the left, were watching me. Did they know the Lord's Prayer?

There, the tall one on the left, arching his eyebrows at me. Who did he think he was? Did he know the Lord's Prayer? In a moment of bravado, I jumped up and turned off the television. Remembering the nurse's

The Change Center

kindness, I returned the Bible.

With nothing to do, I returned to the "Computer Room." A few other patients started to drift in, sitting here and there. Someone turned the television set back on. Once again, choir music and Bible-thumping Christians telling the world how to be saved filled the air. Did they know the Lord's Prayer?

To shut out the now grown sour taste of religion, I went to the far side of the sitting room and sat perpendicular to the television. Although I could still hear it, I would not be exposed to its rays. There were some magazines on the small table next to my chair. I eagerly picked up a sports magazine. I had always loved sports and followed all of the major spectator sports. It was difficult to read. I still couldn't maintain a train of thought. I began scanning the magazine, flipping through the pages.

Wait a second. What's going on here? The magazine was from the previous fall. The magazine listed the final rankings of college football teams and showed the bowl game winners. Neither the ranked teams nor the bowl game winners rang a bell. I simply didn't remember them. None of them. I didn't remember them! Ongoing pro basketball... how in the world could these teams have these records? Uh-huh. Nope. It couldn't be. The thought dawned: someone had tampered with the magazines. They were gimmicked. It's easy to prove your sanity. Just remember facts. Of course, Ohio State (or was it Michigan?) won the Big Ten. What do you mean? They didn't? It says so right here in this magazine. Doesn't it? But it did, didn't it?

And then I was frightened. It was my first realistic fear while on the ward. With shift changes, there had been a constant coming and going of staff. The only way I knew any of the staff was by reading their nametags. I could not remember their names from moment to moment. What if someone starting changing nametags? It's easy to prove your sanity. Sure, unless someone has changed persons, places, and things on you. All someone would have to do is switch the clock every once in a while, change some nametags, and doctor some magazines. Whoosh, they've got you. There you were, a melted ball of wax, talking to yourself,

Sunday

maybe drooling a little. I could not remember things; my time perception was completely screwed up, and I was on a psychiatric ward. Who would listen to me? Who would vouch for me?

If they wanted to erase my identity or destroy me, it would be a simple matter. My identification, locked in the ward safe for safekeeping, had several different addresses on it. I had lied about Linda being my wife. Many of my closest, straight friends knew I had been getting high. By their standards, I had been acting strange. I had no fair witness, no one who could vouch for me. I was totally helpless. They (whoever they were) could do with me as they will, taking away my identity or pinning theft, treason, or murder on me. I was totally at someone else's mercy.

Even if I were not the victim of some malicious, maddening, diabolical scheme to destroy me, I was still totally helpless. I had no control over the food I ate or over the medication I received. My physical surroundings were severely delimited. I had only partial control over my mind and body, not even controlling my thoughts or memory. From not finding *the* Lord's Prayer, to not remembering sports information to realizing I was helpless, subject to the capricious will of others.

It was too much. I stopped worrying about the sports information, could no longer dwell on my helplessness. I began to do virtually anything to make the time pass. Read, walk, and sleep I would do anything to take up time and have it mercifully pass. Anything to get me off of my situation and let me forget about myself and my situation; I would do anything, just anything.

The morning is virtually lost to me. One microsecond of horror stands out. One of the nurses, maybe an aide, someone I didn't recognize and would not see again, was some seven or eight months pregnant. She was working away at the desk. She seemed pleasant enough. She had short, curly hair and a very pinkish, puckered face. I found myself watching her. Oooops. My world changed. I realized that while she was real, her big stomach was not. It was as though she were growing one of those robot dolls of my emergency room flip-out. This big belly was fake, maybe a robot doll disguised with padding to make it appear as though she were

82

The Change Center

pregnant. I had a momentary urge to go and smash her in the stomach. The thought was neither mean nor malicious. Perhaps I would get a prize for figuring out she wasn't really pregnant. Maybe bells would go off, and a new game would be started, since that puzzle had been solved. Too fatigued to act on my perceptions, the urge to expose the fake pregnancy quickly passed. Whew. Yes. Oh, thank you. Thank you, Lord, for not allowing me to hurt her. Thank you very much. Thank you. Amen.

Later, about noon, I began to very timidly and politely make requests of the nurses. Could I go outside? Could I make a phone call? Could I join the patients who go off of the ward?

No matter what my request, the answer was invariably, "Ask your doctor. Your doctor will answer that. Have you seen your doctor yet?"

"Who is my doctor?"

"Hmm, let's see." The nurse bent over, going through some file cards. "Your doctor is Dr. D."

Arggh. Ack. I had known a "D" in Chicago. He was in his mid-30s, Avant Garde as opposed to hip. In the process of divorcing his second wife, he had been living with a beautiful, young woman with whom I had been briefly involved. He was a moderately, successful intellectual who had begun experimenting with drugs. "D" was difficult to know, always wisecracking and glib. Also, he was a good-looking guy who had won one of my ladies. Well, actually, it was a lady who had chosen him over me. I had been a tripster and he had been married. With his divorce, I had no longer had any chance with her.

The last time I had seen him, we had gotten high together. Together, we had stood looking at a large, modern painting that filled his dining room wall. It was a sunburst, all yellow, orange, and red, with a white background. Momentarily, glib bullshit forgotten, he and I had been together, enjoying the near psychedelic painting. It had been a good moment and the first and only time I had been close to him.

Standing there at the reception desk, I drifted into reverie, seeing the now swirling and ever-deepening sun of that painting.

Sunday

"Have you seen your doctor yet?"

"Huh? No."

Oh my, I had to see "D." What did it mean? Almost immediately, I was back to energy and vibration games. Psychedelic suns began exploding in my head. Yellows, oranges, and reds, images of images, and shadows of my Thorazine shot filled my head. I had to see "D." What did this cryptic message mean? Must I attain a specific vibrational frequency, a particular high to see him? Was that it? What kind of intricate game was this? Was I the only one who was lost, the only one who didn't know the rules? Was that it?

"H-how do I see Dr. D?"

"Hmm, he'll be here in a couple of hours at two o'clock."

With no time perception, whatsoever, and flashing suns in my head, I had to see "D." Not knowing how to reach the correct vibrational frequency, I had been given a clue. Two o'clock. I could not miss two o'clock. Shaken, I didn't trust myself and surely did not trust THEM. I must not miss two o'clock.

I would wander off, returning to the reception desk, first to verify who my doctor was and then find out what time he would be on the ward. I would always check with different staff, hoping they weren't all in on it together. After several verifications, I began returning to the reception desk to check the time. Hours of mind time would pass, but only minutes according to the clock on the wall. I began freaking out. Would the Master Controller allow the big, old clock march ever so slowly to say, 1:45, and then let it jump to three or so? I began hanging out at the reception desk.

And then he was on the ward. Finally, after forever, "D" was on the ward. My doctor had arrived. I could only see him at a distance, as he kept disappearing behind closed doors with different patients. He was using the stereo room for his conferences. It was right next to the ward entrance. My questioning of the staff changed from asking when I could see Dr. D to, "Is Dr. D still here?"

The Change Center

I must not miss "D." I kept an eye on the closed stereo room door, continually watched the clock over the reception desk, listened for the buzzer which would open the ward entrance and allow him to depart without seeing me. Nervous anticipation.

And then it was my turn. Nervous and hyper, with constrictions in my back and neck, I entered the stereo sitting room. It was icy cold. I was fairly together, just totally nervous. This was important. I had to hit him with the right words. Mind racing along, I rehearsed my plan. We sat down together.

He was tired-looking, nearly bald, and had a weak chin. Reds and blues were predominant in his recently shaved face. He was slow and southern. Laconic, with slightly sunken eyes, he reminded me of a lizard. Thankfully, he didn't turn into one. I didn't like him.

"Well, how are you getting along?"

His question triggered my head. How should I play this? What should I tell him? Possibilities raced through my head. Momentarily, I felt rational, energetic, and even sane. Would he wonder why I was there? I had requests. Would I be able to con him into letting me outside? I needed some sympathy for the pain and shock of my ward experiences. Would I get it? I had to show him I needed some help. I couldn't be too open or too honest. If I attempted to tell him about the head terror I was experiencing, I instinctively knew I would fall right back into it. Appearing too intellectual and obviously disoriented, I didn't want a paranoid schizophrenic label. I decided on a middle approach. I would be polite and rely on his authority and benevolence. I would blame it all on drugs. Doctors could understand drugs. I would leave out Mind Control and psychic phenomena. Yes, that's it. Drugs would work.

"Well, uh, I'm, uh, not too sure. I can't really, uh, trust my senses. Like that couch, what would you say the color of that couch is?"

I had it all planned. As soon as he told me the color of the couch (it was brown, red, and green striped), I would tell him I also saw it the same way. I would then try to explain to him how sometimes it would

Sunday

go psychedelic, becoming wavy and blurred, breathing and writhing. As soon as he was able to understand this, I would briefly explain tripping and mention how I was being exposed to temporary hallucinations. He could blame it all on an acid residual. If he could follow me, showed any sympathy, I would then go into self-diagnosis. Maybe, I could even get him to agree to rest, sunshine, and the outside world for me. It just may work.

"I never pay attention to it."

Huh? What the...? He sat there, solid and stolid, unmoving, staring off at the wall. Was he just an automaton, a weak pawn like the rest of us? The stereo was obviously a listening device. Who was in control? Was this just another scheme, just one more plot to break me? My plans and quick thinking were immediately lost in confusion and disorientation. What was going on here?

He mentioned Linda. His features changed ever so slightly. Now I knew who this son of a bitch was. Upon arriving in Florida, Linda had almost immediately found a high-paying job as a cocktail waitress. It was like a miracle, as jobs are always difficult to find in a college town. According to her, she had "just been led to it." Already beginning to spin out, I occasionally thought she was some type of witch (then again, I sometimes thought of myself as a warlock suffering from amnesia). She had started on a Friday night and was to have had her first Saturday night off, as we had tickets for a play. A married couple owned the restaurant lounge where she worked. Linda had been hired by the wife and had been promised the night off. The husband had insisted she work.

It had been a major disappointment. It would have been our celebration night out. Disgusted, I had gotten thoroughly wrecked, arriving to pick her up early. Although I was dressed well, my starting to get long hair and sunken red eyes labeled me as one of those hippie types. Waiting for Linda, I had been hassled by the owners for waiting for Linda inside. I moved to the bar and had a couple of drinks; customers could wait where they pleased.

The Change Center

Getting angrier, I decided to talk with the husband, a Mr. M. Talking to him, he had been polite but cool towards me. I was just about to start my complaints, when his wife and Linda came over. It was quitting time. She could leave. I never did say anything to him about her having to work that night. Instead, he and his wife raved about how well she was working out. His last comment as we left was, "Wait until you see what we make out of your wife. You'll be surprised."

Instant rage. Linda was young and beautiful. She had a sensational wardrobe, having worked in a fashionable clothing store while in Chicago. She had a college education, and was sweet, innocent, and cultured. What was this dumb bigot going to make out of her? Swallowing my rage, Linda and I had mumbled our thanks and left.

A week or two later, spinning out more and more, I had made her quit the job. I didn't like what he was making out of her. On the morning before my hospital entry (how many years ago was it?), totally spun out and disoriented, I had found myself accidentally trying to get a job at the same place. The wife's, "You can't take her place" had led to all kinds of insanity.

Yeah, Dr. D., you phony, I know who you are. Mr. M., Dr. D., a man of a thousand faces, I know who you are. Spoiler of the fresh and innocent. You son of a bitch. If you hurt Linda, if you touch my love, if you...

Bang. Crash. Oooops. It was the first time on the ward I had thought of Linda. Oh nooo. Oh my God! Oh, dear sweet Jesus, what have I done? Oh shit, oh please, oh no. I was on a psychiatric ward! I had left my woman, my love, *alone*!!! I was hopelessly lost, locked away forever. She, a defenseless innocent, was exposed to all of the mesmerizing insanities of an unfair world. I had deserted her. I was on a locked ward. I could neither help her nor myself. This wasn't some intricately, fantastic head game. This wasn't just a bad dream or some mental contest. This was *real*! I was on a closed ward, locked away from my love forever and ever. No. Please no. Oh dear Lord, please no.

Sunday

I began to cry. I cried. I bawled. Tears spilled down my face. I could not stop crying. Apologetically, I tried to smile, tried to stop crying, tried to excuse myself. I cried and cried, unable to stop the tears. This was too much.

Dr. D. allowed me to cry myself out. I was eventually able to stop. Finally, when I was almost settled down, wiping my tears away, we were able to talk.

We agreed I had a drug problem. Doctors did understand drugs. I had no will to attempt to explain I had had about a hit and a half of acid in some three months, with no psychedelics for many months before that. Rather than a drug problem, I felt I had broken something in my brain and fallen through into some world starting as ecstasy with Linda and then changed into an increasingly bizarre hell. I guess I was hyper; Dr. D said something about giving me some medication to bring me down. Linda and Liam (yes, I knew him) would be able to visit me later that day. Thus ended my talk with my doctor. Even with my crying, it had been only a few minutes. I never did get the chance to try to explain my situation or symptoms. I made no requests. All the things I had wanted to ask him were forgotten. It didn't matter anymore.

Liam and Linda were coming. Linda. I would get to see Linda once again. I would get to see my love and my close friend once again. Linda, Linda, Linda, I would get to see Linda. They were coming; they really were. Liam and Linda. Warm sunshine. Linda. Glow. Linda, my sweet Linda was coming.

The afternoon was a haze. Crippled and sick, occasionally hallucinating, I just didn't care. My loved ones were coming to see me. Have you ever seen a freaked squirrel? Oh. Wait. Have you ever seen an unmoving, freaked squirrel? Imagine a freaked squirrel inside of a weak, depressed, unmoving, 180 lb. body, or rather, 180 lb. of freaked, not-able-to-move squirrel. The afternoon was a blur filled with nervous anticipation. I was together. Oh yeah, together like an 18-year-old soldier about to step on a land mine and somehow knowing it but unable to keep from putting his foot down. Still buried in Jell-O, I was sitting on a precipice with rippling energy surging up and down my spine, ripping my insides apart. Linda. Linda and Liam were coming. It took forever.

Then, unexpectedly, they were there. They had arrived. Nervous pacing, uneven waiting, and then they were there. The visit got difficult. It started okay.

Nervously falling over each other, exchanging a babble of forgotten words as we tried to find somewhere to sit, we all kept trying to say hello at the same time. We finally found an empty sitting room. It was across the hall from the stereo room, adjacent to my wardroom. Metallic gray, and it had a tiled floor (off-white mixed with beige), and plastic couches.

We sat down. Linda huddled against me, our hands tightly squeezed together. She was so beautiful. She was dressed hippie-like, with a bright yellow, leather sun sewn on the seat of her jeans. Long, dark, flowing hair framed her clear, innocent, trusting face. Although her face was a mixture of sadness and sympathy, it also glowed with joy at seeing her man once again. I was playing some game she didn't understand, but as soon as I got it together, we could go on being totally in love and happy once more. Liam sat off to the side, to the right of us. He was relaxed and together, wearing blue Levi's and a checkered shirt. His long, floppy, blonde hair was clean and brushed.

Have you ever waited, really waited, for something to happen, and then when it was happening, you were so nervous, tense, and excited, it was almost as though it wasn't happening? That first date, the prom, your first time on stage, the first game of the year, or whatever. So much anticipation and nervous energy you couldn't slow down and enjoy what you had been waiting for. Our visit started like that. There were many hellos with looks of concern mixed with joy at seeing each other again. I waited for the crackling energy to quiet down enough so we could begin to talk. Finally, I began getting into the visit. It was perfect being with these two loved ones.

Just as the three of us began to really talk and share, an elderly, black man came in. Bent over his mop, gray fuzz on his chin, he was cleaning

Sunday

the floor. My two friends and I were center stages, with this old man miles away, part of a distant tableau. Change. Then he was right there, in our energy circle, soaking up our vibrations, monitoring our discussion. With his eyes on the floor, apparently just doing his job and not paying any attention to us, he was listening in. Then, he and I were together, with Linda and Liam dropping to a different level of frequency. I lowered my voice, talking more softly, trying to signal Liam and Linda. They didn't seem to notice him, apparently didn't feel him, and didn't share my perception of what was going on. I began getting agitated. Concern swept their features.

Perhaps it would have been okay, except for the voice pounding inside of my head, rattling my eardrums. "We gave you Liam and Linda. Remember, we gave you Liam and Linda. You owe us. Remember, we gave them to you. You owe us. Don't forget; you owe us. We gave you Liam and Linda." Listening to the voice echoing inside of my head, unable to shut it out, I became increasingly hesitant in my speech. The older man and I were together. Although it wasn't his voice, he knew what was going on. My loved ones remained an unknowing pair.

"Honey, what's wrong, what's the matter with you? Are you okay?" Linda turned toward me, facing me, grasping both of my hands. We sat there, our knees touching, hands clasped, staring at each other. Her face was a mask of love and concern.

Sitting there, with our knees pressed together, our hands so very tightly squeezed together, I looked deep into her eyes. Oh my love, as I look into your eyes, I see... Hah! As I stared into her eyes, I saw two huge, shadowy black devil's heads, one in each eye, staring back at me. They were mirror images of an ominous and foreboding entity. Pictures of me; it was a parody of a parody. Yes, sweet love, as I stare into your eyes, I see... The room went, "*tilt*!" I knew I was in trouble.

Finally, after an interminable time, the elderly black man left. I can remember Liam changing his seat so the old man could mop more easily. I remember Linda and I raising our feet so he could mop underneath our couch. I remember the voice pounding over and over in my head. I

The Change Center

remember hate and determination. I remember thinking they could do whatever they wanted to do with me, but they had better leave my friends alone.

I was back into Change theory. I suspected I owed **them** something, namely Linda and Liam. Oh, gods and devils, do anything to me as you please, but don't, oh don't, mess with the lovely, the beautiful, the innocent, the naive. In that moment, I, the AVENGER, riding to hell and back, with the strength of ten thousand or more, will surely crush and destroy thee." I became impossibly strong, tapping and gathering untold energy and power. No one, nothing, was going to hurt my loved ones. Let them, if they dare, confront me, attempt to destroy me, but never ever touch those deserving of better.

The room leveled out. A nurse began bothering us, insisting it was time for Linda and Liam to leave. We left the room on a scattered note. How could I tell them what I saw, felt, and heard? Liam would understand, but there wasn't time to rap it down. Besides, the enemy was everywhere. As we walked out into the corridor, I was twisted into some kind of all-powerful entity. I blocked the bad vibrations from my friends and cleared an energy trail to the ward entrance/exit. Walking them to the door, I glanced over my shoulder. There were three or four blacks positioned strategically along the corridor. One to the right, one further down on the left and so on. Their black faces stared at me, as if waiting for payment. Wasn't it also a shocked surprise I saw on one of the faces? The voice kept on pounding over and over in my head, "We gave you Liam and Linda. Don't forget; we gave you your friends. You owe us. What are you going to do for us? You owe us." I ignored the voice. The hell with them. My friends, heaven help me, would be safe.

As Liam and Linda were buzzed out, I realized I could follow them. I was in street clothes, having been allowed to dress for the visit. I could make it. Walk tall. Just pretend. Get outside. Burst into fresh air and sunshine. I almost tried it, but I was afraid either Liam or Linda would blow it. If they tried to restrain me, it would get awful. As they left, I had a purpose. I would give the devil his due. This did not mean sacrificing

Sunday

my friends or loved ones. I would die first, if that was my karma.

With Liam and Linda gone, I was suddenly drained of my strength, feeling tired and broken, yet hyper. Once again, I would have to try and get it together. Another fantasy had been born. Sides were being taken. Factions were solidifying. Some force I identified as the master controller was manipulating all of us, even the poor dupes who thought they could trick me into giving them, my friends. He would have to be met. This was, indeed, some kind of Change center, some kind of reconditioning center.

In Mind Control, I had been trained to do health cases (faith healing at a distance), sending love and energy to those in need. At a deep level of mind, while in a near trance, meditative state, I had also been programmed to be a force for good, to send my essence wherever it was needed for the good of mankind. I was, indeed, in the right place. I had fulfilled the purpose drilled into my subconscious. I had managed to get into the world of bad vibrations. Many strange things were happening in this squirrel factory. In the tradition of Achilles and mighty Ulysses, I was charged with action. Time to get it on. Broken on the way, I had better start getting it together to exert a positive influence on my sick environment.

My crusade against the forces of evil would have to wait. The visit had left me shaken and confused. Nervously tired, exhausted, and sticky with sweat, I needed to clean up my act. I was together enough to inquire about a shower. They were available. I could take one. It would be my first real washing in days. This was a good thing as I was beginning to reek of body odor.

Going back to my room to get my things, I ran into Bertha. It was a little awkward. She wanted to talk. Expectant and eager, she blocked my way, looking at me, waiting for what I was going to tell her, as if I had asked for a meeting.

"Uh, I was just going to take a shower. I haven't had one for a while. Uh, probably see you later."

Acting surprised, she reared back her head. It was as though she had withdrawn her head to the far end of some large, vibrational funnel. Her head changed in size, and according to my perspective, it became small and far away. Regarding me from this deep, distant perspective, she suddenly brought her head forward. It came sharply into focus, now looming large at my end of the funnel. Her face had acquired a knowing look.

"Ya already had a shower today."

"Uh, how's that?" I, of course, instantly knew what she meant, replaying the movie of my bawling in my mind.

"Ya know. Earlier. Earlier, ya had a shower." She concluded this with a knowing laugh, cackling over my confusion.

She knew. For goodness' sake, she knew. She knew about my crying episode with Dr. D., about my uncontrollable shower. She knew, just as she had known about my being able to see with my eyes closed. Another subplot. Bertha was in the power hierarchy. She had to be. She could go off of the ward. She knew what when on in my mind. Maybe she did know about energy ledges. Maybe she was just wearing a clever disguise. Who was this person? What was her role in the master controller's Machiavellian plans?

As in most hospitals, doctors and nurses were constantly being paged over the loudspeaker system on the ward. "Dr. Randolph, Dr. Randolph, please report to room 227. Dr. Randolph, please report to room 227." Increasingly, the paging voice would be Bertha's, and the doctor being paged would be Dr. Blazek. There was, of course, no Dr. Blazek in the hospital. Whatever was going on (was she really on the speaker system paging me?), I began suspecting Bertha was one of the real powers behind the phony, superficial power structure.

Standing there in the middle of the hallway, confused by her superior knowing, I had no choice but to walk away from her. I went to my room in order to gather my things. She just stood there, continuing to look at me. Aware of her watching me, I was not up to any kind of confrontation.

Sunday

I have known ecstasy. Taking a hot shower after two days of sweating desperation on a psycho ward is where it is at. Going to the shower room, stripping down, I gingerly poked around, hesitantly stepping onto the cold, tiled, floor of the shower. With no door to lock, I was nervous about someone coming in and seeing my nudity. I was also worried about getting hit with splashing cold. Standing off to the side, I was able to get the shower on. With a minimum of difficulty, I was able to get the water temperature set right. No mean achievement, as my physical coordination would come and go. I moved under the heavy torrent of hot water. It was good, even magnificent.

Basking in the heat, luxuriating in the warmth of the hot water, soaping myself, I felt great. It was my first moment of feeling normal, forgetting I was crazy, that I spent while on the ward. There were no thoughts, no trips, no figuring out, no vibes, no voices, and no fantasies. There was just beautiful hot water and me, coming together in a good, familiar shower. Wow. Double wow. I soaped myself down several times, not wanting to leave the warmth, comfort, and normality of this pleasant, even blissful experience. Finally, after quite some time of peace, I shut off the water and toweled myself down. Even the toweling was a beautiful experience with the towel's rough cloth rubbing against my warm, clean body. I put on some fresh, clean clothes. From Linda? I had dressed in street clothes for my visit with Liam and Linda. They were probably the ones I had worn when I was admitted. I would now wear regular clothes for the rest of my stay. I felt good. I felt great. I stepped back into insanity.

It was difficult to sit around and let time pass. Perceived hours would be only minutes according to the clock. It was too exhausting to keep trying to figure out what was happening to me. Although interactions with the staff and the other patients would pass the time, these brief interludes would often prove to be too disconcerting, even terrifying. A short attention span, tense, bruised nerves, and the fear of an impending trip fantasy led to a boring, jumpy-type existence. I would start to read something (too hard to concentrate, too tiring), go to watch television (oops, starting to get eerie), change my shirt (have to do something), look in the mirror (oops), walk to the kitchenette, sit and listen or talk to someone (hmm, getting kind of crowded and troublesome), space off, try to read (not again) and inadvertently start to think (ouch!). Time passed ever so slowly.

Sunday was the first day I tried to write. Hearing my name being paged, caught in a Change center, realizing my identity was being erased, not wanting to disappear without a trace, I attempted to write down my history. The problem was a simple one. My memory was an empty vacuum with mists and colors sweeping through it, with random rockets coming and going, not stopping long enough for me to recognize them. Sitting, pencil in hand, staring at a sheet of paper, I remembered my name. "My name is Howard Douglas Blazek." Blank. Mist. Swirl. Blinking back the tears, pencil shaking, I swore I would remember. There was an incident with Jerry. Ah, I know Russian. Stop. Blank. Wait. I was being programmed by the television. Ah, I know Alpha Mind Control. I'm acting like a paranoid schizophrenic. Ah, I know psychology. Where did I go to school? Where did I go to school? Ah, I've got it. Slowly, shaking, I put it down on paper in a weak, babyish scrawl.

The worst part of trying to remember was the voice. It was wickedly sarcastic. "Oh, that's so cute, back to pencil and paper. Can't take the movie, huh boy." Over and over, growing stronger and more insistent, the voice was first mocking, then cajoling, and then angry. Echoing continually in my head, the voice both ridiculed and hurt me. Shoot. I knew what it was saying. Spun out in my worlds of esoteric wonder, I had developed whole theories about it. The movie, that is.

Simply and sketchily, one of my many interpretations goes something like this. Visualization is an important key. One can, by being able to hold images in one's head, assume physical positions such as a yoga asana which are normally very difficult to assume. One can direct oneself to numerous paths by being able to hold firm images of oneself getting a promotion, losing weight, and so on. The theory is if one can get a firm picture of what one wants to do or to be, then this image will trigger one's subconscious resources to attain that picture or manifestation of self. The

Sunday

theory is somewhat explicit and can be found in Mind Control, eastern philosophy, and numerous religious writings. I have discovered it in print ranging from newspaper articles to heavy, philosophical tomes.

Acidheads and speed freaks aren't into still pictures, but rather, into movies. Instead of picturing themselves in a certain position, meditating on it, and working toward it, they're into movies. It's a question of speed. This life is a trip, a movie. Shakespeare had his, "All life's a stage with us but actors on it," while the head generation had its movies.

Dopers (grass heads/marijuana users), or so it seemed, heard new things in new ways. Heads saw new things in new ways. It was a matter of speed, with the eye tuned to a much faster vibrational frequency than the ear. The above is the start of what I (we) called a head game.

On the ward, I knew what the voice was saying. No longer a head, no longer into the movie, I was a cop-out. Back to the drawing board, back to cumbersome words, back to pencil and paper, back to slow motion. I managed to get a page or so of history down. It was muddled and an effort. I was torn between my fear of not remembering things and a guilty shame at no longer being in the movie. All in all, my autobiography was not very successful. I would try again.

Liam and Linda had come to see me during late afternoon on a special visit. Normal visiting hours began at six o'clock. As the visitors began pouring in, I felt uncomfortable and out of place. Bertha, bright, alive, and animated, was walking around, arms linked with a dull, placid, tired-looking male automaton. She glanced furtively around and led him to a private sitting room, which Liam, Linda, and I had used, the one adjacent to my and Jack's room. I idly wondered when he would be on the ward. He was obviously marked for ***change***.

Jack's mother was there. She was a tired-looking, physically trim, middle-aged woman with very nice legs. She and Jack went into the stereo sitting room. She was too strong, too dominant for him. He would never be able to trick her into taking his place on the ward. A whole host of black visitors, bright and alive, filled the television room.

The Change Center

Those first few days on the ward, I seemed to be more on a level with the blacks. They appeared to be more relaxed and quicker than the whites. The whites came across as tired, not living in the present, hassled individuals while the blacks seemed a little more with it, more flowing and less uptight. This became increasingly noticeable over the next few days as the regular staff, mostly tired whites, filtered onto the ward. These whites, with noticeable sacks around their eyes and worry lines in their faces seemed to pay only partial attention to their surroundings. The blacks were more involved with their immediate environment. Their faces seemed normal to me, while my super sensitivity picked up and emphasized flaws in the faces of the whites. This was especially true for staff and visitors, as white patients such as Bertha and Jack looked normal to me.

Feeling uncomfortable, with noise and people everywhere, I retreated to my room. I was exhausted as, in many ways, it had been a trying day. Lying down, I attempted to go to sleep. I tossed and turned, falling into a psychedelic half-sleep. Half-awake, half-asleep, I began having a nightmarish illusion of thoughts and vibrations coming through the wall. Too dim and near sleep to adequately verbalize what I felt, I realized I was being fed Bertha's automaton through the wall separating the head of my bed and the neighboring sitting room. I could see, albeit dimly and surrealistically, him lying on a bed, in a trance. He was being linked to me. Too dopily asleep to actively resist it, I highly resented the intrusion into my consciousness. It was as if a tape of Bertha's husband were being run into my brain. Although I was not on top of it or in control, it was as though I was being exposed to his problems and hang-ups.

Looking back, I suspect Bertha and the man I would later find out was her husband, had gone off into the sitting room in order to be alone and to make out. Whatever the reality, experientially I could feel strong emanations coming through the wall. Somehow, I was becoming mixed up with him. It would become increasingly evident that not only was I a helpless victim of my own problems, but I was being exposed to the problems of the other patients. The shell of my being was cracked wide

Sunday

open, allowing the inanities of my environment direct access to a deep level within me.

I was finally able to shiver away from the episode. I tore myself away from it, rising out of my subdued, spaced out, half-asleep, weakened condition. Splashing cold water in my face, I, as with so many of my early ward experiences, quickly forgot what had just happened. I prepared to rejoin the milling patients and visitors once again. Walking around my room, I felt too weak and crawled back into bed.

Depressed, attempting to mull over the day's activities, nothing would hold together. One of the staff came in, a black nurse who I didn't recognize. Seeing my dazed condition, she looked at me and carefully said it was time for my medication. First, she took my temperature and pulse. She then got my pills. There were several of them. Not only was I personally in trouble, I knew I was being confined in a very strange place. I innocently accepted the pills, politely saying, "Thank you." The taking of my temperature had given me an idea. I quickly got the pills under my tongue, pretending to swallow them. The nurse was almost immediately gone.

I now had a problem. It was a delicate one. How would I get rid of these pills? I was in the bed that was closest to the door leading out into the corridor. The door was on my left at the foot of my bed. I was in a direct line with the reception desk. The way my room was positioned, staff at the reception desk could either look at me directly or watch me in the observation mirrors while their backs were turned. The cubicle containing the toilet was directly in front of me. The room sink and the mirror above it were slightly to the right of the door to the toilet. It was obviously a two-way mirror. Hidden cameras and listening devices were everywhere.

I wasn't worried about my thoughts being monitored. They switched often enough that even I had trouble keeping up with them. Just in case, I thought neutral thoughts, not thinking about what I was doing. I slowly got out of bed. I realized my room and the toilet cubicle operated on

The Change Center

different frequencies. As I passed from my room into the john, framed in the doorway, I palmed the medication into my palm.

Sitting on the toilet, I casually dropped the dissolving mess between my legs. I carefully thought about how friendly everyone was while I disposed of the drugs. After attempting to relieve myself, I flushed the toilet while still sitting on it. Even though I was in one of his control booths, I thought I was safe. If the Master Controller could catch me at this, he was only playing with my head and could end me at any time.

Visiting hours were over. As the guests began straggling out, I left my room. Patients milled around in the natural letdown occurring after the visitors left. As usual, a group gathered in the kitchenette, like a coffee clutch, talking down their tensions.

I was often impressed with how kind the other patients were to each other. Everyone was solicitous of each other. Each of the patients, except, possibly, for Jack, appeared to be sensitive to the needs of others. Jack, although a nice guy, was too wrapped up in his own problems to be able to really worry about others. Cigarettes were shared, goodies received from the outside were distributed, and favors were done. We were all in this together.

Jack occasionally tried the god-like acceptance of the other patients. He would become a nuisance. That night, several of us (Beth and the three ladies were there) were sitting around sipping juice or coffee. Some chocolate cake received from a visitor was passed around. Jack went manic, running around, stuffing his face, and doing a, "Umpfgh!" He ruined several cups of coffee, spilling some, sampling others. He bumped into a table, almost hurting another patient. Lillian cringed, saying, "I wish he wouldn't do that." This was answered by Bertha's, "I guess he's kind of tense." Mostly ignored, talked of in the third person, no one became vindictive or confronted him.

With a burst of energy, he ran off to his room. While his, "Look at me!" behavior was boring and irritating, everyone seemed to accept him.

Sunday

Later, when he returned to the group, no one particularly noticed him or brought up his earlier behavior.

Perhaps the attention span of the other patients was as short as mine.

We were sitting around, quietly sipping our drinks, when, "Bzzzzz", the buzzer went off. Elaine's head snapped up, fear clouding her eyes, words, and thoughts forgotten. Other than Lillian watching her to see if she was okay, no one paid any attention. When she was able, Elaine rejoined the conversation as if nothing had happened. Instead of making fun of each other, the patients constantly comforted each other and were almost always gentle and understanding. In my lucid moments, I would be impressed.

The conversation was a blur, although once again, as with the previous evening, all kinds of games were being played. My major contribution was still, "I'll never get better. I'll never leave the ward."

Later in the evening, Beth and Jack began goofing around with each other. They started running back and forth, occasionally bumping into each other, almost wrestling with each other. Their slight physical contact made me cringe. Except for Linda, the thought of any physical contact was abhorrent to me. Also, whenever any of the patients got this closely involved with each other, just as in any kind of serious conversation, there was an underlying current of tension. At any moment, one or both of the participants could flip out. Interacting this strongly was like walking on eggshells or very thin, cracking ice. Anything could happen. Nervous, I sat there, squeezing my arms together.

Jack and Beth were both hyper. Although not completely free (there would be quick stops with glances at both each other and possible observers) and not completely enjoying themselves (at times their behavior was forced), they were able to have some fun, goofing and fooling around with each other. Finally, out of breath, they stopped for a while. A pizza. It would be great to have a pizza. They began to get all hyper and excited again. A pizza would be great.

The Change Center

I was included in the scheme. The three of us would get a pizza. Beth, young, fragile, and so very cute, was incredibly excited. Jack, who took every possible opportunity to act up, was also excited. I couldn't tell if he was enthusiastic about the pizza, or just wanted to jump up and down, letting off energy. More reserved, I also started to get excited about the thought of a pizza. The three of us decided to get one. We split up, going to our rooms to get some money. Beth ran off down the hall, while Jack and I walked to our room.

In our room, Jack and I started to dig around, looking for our money. Searching for my money, I stopped and turned to Jack, asking him if it was okay, if we could get a pizza. He just continued to look through his things, absently mindedly saying, "Sure."

"No, I mean, is it okay, can we get one? Will they let us?" Momentarily rational, I wondered if he knew we were on a closed ward. Did he know we would have to send out for the pizza? Would we be permitted to do that?

He stopped what he was doing. He turned and looked at me, his mouth twisted open in surprise, his eyes large and unblinking. "You know you're the devil. You know you can have anything you want."

Oooops. Moment of stillness. Dark shadows. Psychedelic flashes. My face pulled back in a contour-changing grimace. Swirling mists. Subliminal roar. Voice in my head. Yes, of course, we would have our pizza. In my head, "We shall have our pizza, thus speaketh the lord of the night. The prince of darkness shall have his due." The moment passed.

Back in the hall, the three of us ran up to the reception desk. The nurse on duty was amused. She quickly agreed to our plan and began looking up pizza places in the telephone book. While she made the phone call, Jack, Beth, and I were busy counting out our money, trying to see how much we had. The nurse got the price over the phone. Let's see, now, that means each of us owes so much. Still confused by the devil experience in my room, I had difficulty handling and counting the money. Beth and Jack were equally inadequate. Flash. It was simple. These poor innocents

Sunday

couldn't even count. For the moment, calculus, statistics with its normal curve and analysis of variance, all mathematics, were once again mine. Not wanting to hurt their feelings or butt in and do their counting for them, I continued to fumble with my money. I made sure that the final total and our separate contributions were what they should be.

Waiting for the pizza, we were like three little kids, all excited, talking about how good it was going to be. It was fun.

It was something to do. The hell with all of the head trips, all of the trying to figure out what was happening to me. This was real. We sat around, huddling together, talking about how good the pizza was going to be. Still hyper and disjointed, every once in a while, one of us would jump up and go and do something, just walk or run to our rooms or space around for a while. Eventually, we would all be back together again, talking about the pizza.

When the pizza came, it was exciting. We took it to the kitchenette, opening it as though it were an exceptional birthday or Christmas present. Smelling it, anticipating the taste, we hurriedly opened the cardboard box. We attacked it like three starving animals. It was so good, and it immediately had to be shared. It was too good to keep for just us. "Hey, c'mon, have a piece. It's so good. C'mon now. Are you sure one piece is enough? Hey, help yourself. It's great." It was a great pizza feast. Although it was getting a little late, there were still a few patients around. We all dug in, rapping between bites about how good it was.

All in all, Sunday was one of the haziest and fuzziest days of my ward experience. It was basically spent in waiting, with me spurred to action either by an occasional fantasy trip, severe physical or mental discomfort, or just plain boredom. The big happenings, my visits with Dr. D. and with Liam and Linda had helped the time to pass. Time had been taken up in the actual visits, in anticipation of the visits, and also, in the nervous letdown after the visits were over. The day had not been anywhere near as psychedelic as Saturday had been. There had even been a few moments of near normalcy: taking a shower, sharing a pizza, chatting over coffee.

The Change Center

These were moments when I would forget my situation and function almost normally.

I guess I was getting better. I thought I was getting better. My mind and body were becoming increasingly sensitive to the possibility of pain, however. Increasingly, I would cringe away from the beginnings of pain in either my head or in my body. There were long periods of time when I knew the most blessed thing in the whole world was simply to sleep. How fantastic to be able to turn off, shut down and crawl into a deep, restful, dreamless sleep. To be able to cut off the now constant body aches, to quiet the continuous whir in my head, to be able to just lie down and sleep was all I wanted to do.

But as Shakespeare said, even in the sleep of death, what dreams may come? To be denied peaceful sleep, to be constantly buffeted by physical ache and mental anguish, to awaken scared shitless in the night with my rational ego, my conscious controller too dimmed, tired, and broken to sort things out. To be the victim of a constant, ever-changing, always the same nightmare, grown more believable due to its constancy, to sink further and further into fright and apprehension... Ah yes, sweet Hindus, to be released from this endless cycle of life and death, to be released from the constant wheel of birth, growth, decline, and destruction. To be able to space into the bliss of an all-consuming, ever restful Nirvana seemed the highest good. Perhaps that is where it is at. Sometimes.

I guess I was getting better. First, I would get worse. Jack had been too manic to sleep. He kept spacing around and finally gathered his bedding and took it with him to the stereo sitting room. I was left alone, trying to sleep.

The night was fearsome. Absolutely fearsome. I prayed to Buddha, to Christ, to the kid. The kid. A 14- year-old perfect master, or so they said. He was coming to town. A few days before my ward entry I had attempted to go to a meeting held by one of his forerunners. It had been one of my eeriest, pre-ward experiences. Walking across campus, stoned out of my skull, wearing my Alpha hat, going wherever I was needed, wherever humanity was in danger, I had tried to attend the meeting.

Sunday

The auditorium had become a large, golden womb that acted as a magnet, drawing the robot-like youth of the university. Walking alone, in pairs and in groups, they appeared to be unknowing zombies heeding a call no one else could hear. I still remember walking across campus, being drawn to the meeting, seeing groups of others slowly making their way there. Instead of laughter or movement as in going to a concert or ball game, those drawn to the meeting appeared to be in a trance-like state.

As I entered the lobby of the auditorium, I experienced my first audio hallucinations. Someone seemed to be calling Dr. Blazek although I was only a student. As I slowly made my way into the building, there were several helpers or initiates or whatever, who had red crosses painted on their foreheads. They seemed to be guiding people. Did they really have red crosses on their foreheads? Did they know my name? I don't know anymore. You can keep count.

Inside the building were a handful of steps leading to the actual auditorium. As I walked down the steps, thick, palpable energy rose to my chin. It was golden and appeared to be somewhat substantial. It was almost as though I would be baptized in this golden energy as opposed to the water of Christianity.

I got out of there. It would be a few days before I would sense myself actually drowning in this energy. (Hmm. Let's see. Unable to be reborn in this new religion I didn't trust, with a screwed-up metabolism, I had instinctively turned to a hospital more in tune with my middle-class upbringing. The medicos would shatter me with their Thorazine and other medications, allowing me to be reconstructed. It makes some sense. Sure. Why not?)

Trying to meditate on the kid only triggered these memories of my eerie walk across campus and my inability to attend the meeting with the others who had been drawn there.

Praying, struggling, too jumbled to meditate or to think clearly, I tossed back and forth, sweating and uncomfortable. I began to mumble, "Anything. I'll do anything. I'll do anything to get rid of this pain.

The Change Center

Anything." I fell into Orwell's *1984*. I jumped into the part where the couple who had been having a secret love affair is captured. The male undergoes a number of tortures. Finally, he is confronted with his ultimate, mind-bending dread. He had a lifelong fear of rats. A cage full of rats would be fitted over his face. Faced with terrible panic, he realized the only way to save himself was to sacrifice his love. Let it be her face. Fit the cage of rats over her face. Let her head be torn and maimed by the rats.

As soon as I thought I would do anything to stop my pain entered my head, I realized it was Linda or me. One of us would be destroyed. I had already died a thousand deaths for her. Although the culmination of several trends, a major reason I had so fiercely tried to break out of what was happening to me and had accidentally landed on the ward, was an ever-growing fear I would become violent and do actual physical damage to her.

Linda or me? It was an easy choice. My love was fresh and innocent. I was not. If one of us had to be destroyed, if one of us had to die, it would, of course, be me.

I first curled down under the covers with pillows over my head. I then made a cocoon, covering the pillows and myself with the blankets and sheets. I buried my head under the pillows, tightening the covers around me, attempting to cut off all possible oxygen.

Warning screams sounded deep inside of my head. It was dark. It was lonely. My breath became warm and thick. I started to flip out but held on. The screams inside of my head began becoming somewhat muffled. The darkness, an all-pervading blackness, began becoming comfortable. I buried myself deeper in the coverings. The screams inside of my head stopped.

My breathing, now consisting almost entirely of carbon dioxide, became labored and then easily shallow. I was covered with a deep, feathery caress. It was a gentle, soothing touch. I became impossibly light headed. A growing warm, comfortable feeling sprang up in my head and

Sunday

in my chest. I curled down deeper and more tightly in my bedding.

All pain slowly receded. Everything became blacker and then lighter. My head was filled with a light gray color, almost like a film or television that was turned on but with no picture. Then, as though someone was using a large felt pen, thick black ink slowly filled in my grayish consciousness. I blacked out. Literally.

Thus ended my second day on the ward.

MONDAY

It was so good. I felt all warm and soft, so very weak and helpless. There was no pain or worry. Curled against my pillow, I felt as if an impossibly soft blanket of light awareness covered me. Snuggled deep in my covers, I felt safe and warm. Soft, warm, light, and comfortable, I was dimly aware of a large, gentle something nudging my consciousness.

I was aware of something on my shoulder. A deep voice was cooing, "C'mon honey, c'mon, time to wake up. C'mon, honey." I managed to open my eyes. My field of vision was filled with a giant, white blur. It slowly took form. The whiteness sharpened into a clean, crisp, recently starched nurse's uniform. There was a large, black hand gently shaking me. A large, kindly-looking, black woman filled the uniform. She was softly crooning, rocking back and forth. I felt deep warmth emanating from her. Off to the side, behind her, there was another black nurse, much slimmer, who stood there, abstractly looking at me.

I just wanted to lay curled up in my little ball forever, with this large, friendly, warm being pressed up against me. I wanted to suckle her breast and have her strong, gentle sureness protect me forever and ever. I felt so very good.

Not resisting, a large, blue thermometer was pressed into my mouth, reminiscent of the large blue utensils of my admittance. The nurse was doing something to my arm, taking my blood pressure and feeling my pulse. I liked her warm, strong, thick fingers on my arm. They were so very warm and sure. It was all very beautiful.

"I think we've got him now," the large, close one was talking to the slim, far away one.

Monday

Yes, of course, you've got me. If I would have only known it would feel so good, be so painless, I would have given in sooner. I wouldn't have fought or resisted so hard. I wouldn't have tried to dredge up all of those old memories or continually figure out what was happening to me. I would have simply given in. Yes, of course, you've got me. It was okay. It was more than okay.

The two nurses began laughing and talking with each other. It was as though they were making fun of me. Was it my weak body curled in a fetal position or my stupid, dreamy, silly ass grin? I slowly fought to keep my eyes open. I began to realize I wasn't dead. I began realizing I wasn't a Changed baby girl, but rather, a weak, fuzzy me.

The two nurses must have thought I was cute, lying there all curled up in a ball. They used baby talk with me, while laughing and rapping with each other in loose, singsong voices. I began to get angry, but was far too weak to do anything about it. Damn. I was still on this absurd, inane, hospital ward.

After they were finally able to get me to sit up, the two nurses left. After some time, I was able to struggle into my clothes. Morning cleanup was virtually impossible; I did manage to half-heartedly brush my teeth and splash some cold water on my face. I straggled out into the hall, more asleep than awake. Breakfast was waiting with all of the other patients nearly finished. I was too weak to carry my breakfast tray. Mr. Sam, one of the male aides, carried it for me into the television room.

Thus began my third day on the ward. Monday was to prove to be an event-filled day. I would meet and become acquainted with the regular staff, some of whom had seen weekend duty. In some ways, I would become stronger; in other ways, I would grow weaker. My earlier impressions would only gain depth: there was something strange and wrong with this place.

I finally woke up during breakfast. Still weak and tired, little was happening. After breakfast, I wandered back and forth between my room and the television sitting room. Nothing was going on. More to make the

The Change Center

time pass than for any other reason, I began trying to write.

It was a struggle. I still had little or no memory. One of the nurses came over to see what I was doing. She showed surprise and took my first history to show it to my doctor. It was the ten or so incomplete sentences I had done the previous day. I became totally caught up in my writing, oblivious to all else. I wrote for several hours, or rather, spent several hours trying to write, as I only came up with a page or two. If nothing else, the effort took up time.

Slowly, but surely, the memories came back. Each was resurrected from a deep grave of sludge and slime. More and more easily, I was able to face the swirls and gaping holes of my torn and broken mind without fear of falling into psychedelic panic. I finally had something to do. Not able to figure out what was happening to me, not able to get off of the ward, not able to be worth something, not able to actively resist or go along with the Change, I was still able to do something. I could, with considerable effort and a certain amount of pain, regain my memory. I could not recall or dwell on memories of the ward and recent, pre-ward experiences. These were still lost to me. They were speeding missiles of oddly spliced together film. I would not remember being a Prisoner of War. I would either be a P.O.W., caught up in the fantasy, or I would be something else. I was able to access the still whole, protected in the vaults of my mind memories of my more distant past.

Attempting to write in the television room, I was eyed suspiciously by the other patients. I began feeling uneasy. Both patients and staff would shoot me quick, sidelong glances. Cynthia, a withdrawn, nonverbal black girl in her early teens, blankly stared at me with clouded, unseeing eyes. I began hearing my movie voice once more. I retreated to my room.

In my room, still buried in my work, I would occasionally notice that staff were watching me through the observation mirrors. Although I was sensitive to their observing me, the room did not change into a bugged cell as in my prisoner fantasy. Increasingly nervous and worried, I continued to write. At any time, the patients, the staff, or even I, could fall into a roving reporter game, thinking I was writing about them. I almost

Monday

did get into observing and writing about them. My present, however, was still too shaky and mind-blowing for me to live in it. I delved, instead, into the memories of my distant past, hoping to rebuild a functioning me somehow.

Mrs. H., one of the white day nurses, suddenly burst into my room. Agitated, excited, out of breath from having run down the hall, she burst in on my now calm, totally involved writing. She stood there, pink-faced and distraught, catching her breath. "You'll have to give me that... Oh!?! I'm sorry. It's a pencil." Turning quickly away from me, she began walking back to the reception desk, shaking her head and muttering to herself, "Humph. They said it was a knife." My fears had been justified. Someone was flipping out over my writing.

They had taken yoga away from me. They had taken freedom and sunshine from me. I had been condemned to a room and a corridor filled with broken people and incompetent staff. But, damn, the writing was helping me. They weren't going to take that away. Over the next half hour, taking pains not to be seen, I hid some paper away. I also hid a pencil. To do this, I broke the pencil I had been using in two (Where had I gotten it from?), gnawing the wood away with my teeth to make a second point. I also concealed a note, describing my predicament. I worded it carefully, hoping it would not simply be dismissed as the work of a paranoid schizophrenic. Every time I finished a page, with my total effort of several days resulting in only a very few pages, I also hid that away. I hid everything in a different place. The extra pencil was tucked away under some innocuous articles on the shelf in my closet. The extra paper was buried in a bottom drawer of the nightstand separating the two beds. The note describing my situation was tucked in one of the many pockets of my parka. Completed pages were put in a variety of places, just in case.

Mrs. H. looked incredibly similar to the wife of one of my professors. They had the same last name. Later in the day, gathering my courage, I would timidly ask her about it. She would lightly dismiss me with a, "That's funny. Someone else just asked me about that. Oh well, I'm not." I

The Change Center

wondered why she wouldn't admit she was Sonia. Although Sonia hadn't particularly liked me, the least she could do was admit who she was. Then again, Mrs. H. occasionally reminded me of my professor's little girl, who was about eight or so. Maybe this nurse wasn't Sonia. I thought she had to be at least a relative or one of **them**. It was just one more puzzle to figure out.

That morning, even relative to my other ward experiences, I had one of the most bizarre experiences of my life. I would think about it for hours on end, both there on the ward and afterward. I know I was hearing things. I know I was subject to hallucinations. Trying to figure things out, I was also falling into the web of delusion. Even so, I cannot sort out what was real and what was not. I call it my x-ray trip.

I was lying in bed, still weak from the previous night and exhausted from my efforts at writing. Attempting to sleep, I could only toss and turn in unrest. Although uncomfortable, my pain was not extreme. I began rationalizing my experience. With everything which had happened to me, I began thinking the worst was over. Although weak and underwater, my discomfort in no way approached the pain of the previous night. I could hold on. I could make it.

I began thinking about x-rays. Why would I think about x-rays? "As long as they don't give me any x-rays. Anything but x-rays. If only they don't force me to have x-rays. I'll be okay if they don't make me have x-rays." I use the word "thinking," as opposed to saying I was hearing voices as the voice in my head had my sound and intonation.

I have been distrustful of x-rays for a long time. Due to having had tuberculosis as a child, I have had numerous x-rays throughout my life. As a child going to grammar school in the '50s, I remember the warnings about radiation poisoning in case of a nuclear attack. As a teen, I remember reading about how radiation never leaves us, building up in our tissues throughout our lives. With the increasing use of nuclear energy, I still have some anxiety regarding x-rays. Additionally, as a child, I had read a comic book about a scientist who stepped through a time warp and found himself in a world of intelligent apes. Humans were the lower primates in

Monday

the world. The apes had been amazed he could wiggle his thumbs; they prepared to x-ray him, unknowingly about to use a powerful machine which would inadvertently kill the scientist. The rest of the story traced his escape back to his own world and his own time. I didn't like x-rays. I have a long history of being afraid of them.

Mr. Sam walked in on me. I recognized him from earlier that morning when he had helped me with my breakfast tray. He would become a regular. He was a short, stocky, affable black with grayish-black stubble on his chin. He was friendly, came across as mentally slow, and was the chief instigator of calling me, "Mr. Blazek, sir." In turn, I would always address him as politely as possible, tacking a "sir" on to his name. He came bouncing into my room, looking jovial, laughing, and humming to himself.

"Ah, Mr. Blazek, sir, we going to get you an x-ray. Yes sir, time to get you an x-ray."

Arggh. The enemy could read my thoughts. What can I say? What can you say? What can we say? Coincidence? Sure, why not. What difference does it make? Subliminal hearing? Nurses talking about the need for me to have an x-ray at the desk and good old rabbit ears picking up on their conversation some 40 feet or more away. Maybe yes, and then again, maybe just one more, "Can you believe it?"

Alarm. Terror. The weakened caricature of myself while I was on the ward, simply nodded mutely. Yes, of course, it was time for my x-ray. I was forced to change from my street clothes into my blue, ward pajamas. "Just the rules, Mr. Blazek, sir, just the rules." Finally ready, I managed to get out into the hall. A wheelchair was waiting for me. "Sir, why do I have to sit in a wheelchair? I can walk."

"Just the rules, Mr. Blazek, sir, just the rules."

I obediently sat in the wheelchair. As he pushed me off of the ward and onto the service elevator, I sat there in mute dread. What was happening to me? In my mind's eye, I began getting into Rorschach inkblots.

The Change Center

Prior to my commitment, I had been studying projective techniques used in psychological assessment. Curious, I had self-administered myself a Rorschach inkblot test. It was kind of dumb. It was common knowledge among graduate students: Don't give the inkblot test to someone who has recently tripped. You'll get too many responses. It will be impossible to score. In my increasingly spun-out state, the blots had gone multi-dimensional on me. Each blot is symmetrical with one half the mirror image of the other half. In effect, they had acted as an energy lure to my weakened essence. I had had nightmares of a cartoon-like image of myself falling into the center of these huge energy-pulling blots. On the ward that very first morning, stopped by Jerry from doing yoga, not being able to feel my insides, I had attempted to flash on my innards using the third eye of my mind. Blots. I had only come up with psychedelic inkblots.

A common response to a number of the blots is that they look like x-rays. Huddled in my wheelchair, bent over in fear, being pushed by Mr. Sam toward the great x-ray machine, my head once again became filled with energy-sucking inkblots. I became increasingly helpless.

We reached the first floor. Leaving the service elevator, we entered the main lobby. It was quite busy. Moving slowly down the hall, Mr. Sam and I passed the old, the crippled, and the sick. Shriveled women looked at me out of deep pools of sadness. I was torn between heart rendering sympathy and apprehension. This was obviously a Change Center. Would I be exchanged for one of them?

We passed the main entrance to the hospital. I could see outside. It was sunny. The outside was only a few yards away. I was a doorway away from freedom. I was so very tempted to run for it. The tightness in my gut, together with the weakness in my knees and the fear in my head, kept me from running like hell. We continued past the entrance. Turning in my chair, I took one last look backward at the doorway to freedom. A uniformed guard was sitting there. Where had he come from? (Why would there be a uniformed guard in the lobby of a hospital?) I would have been caught even before I could get outside. Oh well.

Monday

As we approached our destination, it was like approaching the edge of the Grand Canyon. I began feeling this was it. The policeman, wasn't he there the night I had been committed? The nurse. Surely, she had been there. This then, would be the climax of my entire hospital trip. It was as though everyone had been gathered, all waiting in anticipation. I had thought the worst was over, that I was getting better, but now!?!

We finally reached our destination. Mr. Sam left me sitting in my wheelchair in the middle of the corridor. There was a waiting room filled with people off to the side. Left alone, too weak to run, I got up and went into the waiting room, walking stiffly and slowly. No one said anything to me. The seated people just looked at me oddly. I was dimly aware of how I must look to them. I had been too weak to shave that morning, I was back in the ward pajamas, and I had deep, sunken eyes (only momentarily glimpsed when I would accidentally look into a mirror). I wanted to warn them. I almost went hysterical. In my mind's eye, I could see myself shouting to them that sure I was crazy, but "Ohmigod. Run for your lives. This is a terrible, evil place. Get out while you can. Please, oh please, believe me. Run for your lives." In my mind's eye, I could also see myself breaking down and crying hysterically. I knew I would go completely out of control, if I tried to warn them. I held my tongue. I went back out into the corridor and sat defeated in my wheelchair.

I began hearing voices. Mr. Sam was off somewhere, probably making arrangements for my x-ray. I could hear his voice in my head talking to someone, "Ah don't know, ah don't know why he didn't run. Ah don't know as we went by the doorway real slow. Ah don't know. He could have run. Do ah still get one?" The hell with them! No, I wouldn't run. It wouldn't be any two-for-one nonsense. Let them do their thing. I'm not cracking. I instantly knew what this was all about. **They** were trying to collect and annihilate all of the undesirable aspects of me. They were the ones who decided what was undesirable. If I had attempted to run, they would have gotten one for me, the crazy, and also, one for me, the attempted escapee. Mr. Sam was worried about getting at least one for me, as their plan hadn't worked.

The Change Center

When I was finally led into the x-ray room, this all passed. The new horror was too strong and too immediate. A black nurse met me. She was slim, alert, and alive. Her eyes met mine; she seemed to know me. She was incredibly beautiful. I had a strong, masochistic urge to be dominated by her. There was also a young white nurse or nurse's aide there. She appeared to be completely dazed and stupid looking, with her light, blue eyes and pink nose going out of focus as she stared at me in a confused and befuddled manner. It was as though the black nurse and I were standing in the center of a very strong, stationary energy field, the edges of which were rotating in a large circle. The white aide was outside of our energy field; she had trouble staying with us. Her features blurred to one side, similar to how a spectator would look seen from a very fast merry-go-round.

It happened then. I know I was confused. I know I was hallucinating. Okay, I was a totally psychotic, paranoid schizophrenic. Who cares? After hours of pondering, I still don't know what really happened. I can even rationalize Mr. Sam walking in on me during my fear of being given an x-ray as subliminal hearing on my part. They had probably been talking about me getting an x-ray, with me overhearing the conversation without being consciously aware of it. I have no idea, whatsoever, about what really happened in the x-ray room.

The black nurse, calm and competent, got an x-ray plate and positioned it on the platform used for taking pictures from above. She placed my right hand and arm on the x-ray plate. Why? I was supposed to be getting a chest x-ray. Why would she be x-raying my arm? Next to my arm, she carefully positioned what looked like a huge, light blue mitten. It was large and insulated, looking similar to what a person wears to take something out of the oven. It was a good 10 to 12 inches long. Docile, I complied with the nurse's wishes, keeping still as instructed, in order not to ruin the x-ray. She seemed very pleased. Stepping behind the radiation screen, she gave me a big smile and said, "We're going to make a model patient out of you." She flipped the switch, taking a picture of my right hand and arm.

Monday

Ohmigod! My hand. It was the right hand and my right arm. It was the power arm. My strength. What was going on here? I had missing insides, or so it seemed my first morning on the ward. And then there were the inkblots, swirling and consuming my consciousness. They were going to make me into a *model* patient. I would be photographed, duplicated, and replaced with magnetic controls. I would become a stupid robot, totally under the control of some unknown entity.

Frozen, I stayed where I was, bent over with my hand and arm on the x-ray plate. The black nurse came and took the plate away, very confident and happy over my cooperation. While she was positioning a plate for my chest x-ray, I straightened up and began wandering around the room, as if in a daze. Through my now tear-filled eyes, I took a look at my x-ray order sheet. It blurred. I saw an order for x-ray # lebbenty-lebben. I was truly lost. Having fallen through a time warp, they were x-raying me over and over again, until finally, I would be totally and inexorably destroyed. The mesmerized white nurse just stood there, looking confused, probably an innocent dupe in this terrible game.

The black nurse positioned me for my chest x-ray. I weakly let her. Having had dozens of chest x-rays, I knew the routine. I could only think, "The hell with them." It wasn't as easy as all of that. At precisely the moment she pulled the switch, I purposely moved. Let the Master Controller figure that out. They could blow away my head with their terrible drugs, take away my power with their confinement and secret doings, but they weren't going to mess with my heart.

Finished, I was led back out into the corridor, helped into my wheelchair. Mr. Sam began pushing me back to my room, back to that god-awful corridor. Shaken and terrified, I had to do something. I had to get out of there. This was just too much. Duplicating my arm? Replacing my insides? Whatever was going on, it had to end.

I began pitching Mr. Sam, "Sir, please, oh please sir, just let me see the outside. Just let me sit in the sun for a minute. Oh, please, sir, please. Just let me smell some fresh air and feel some sunshine on my face. Oh please. Please, sir, just for a minute."

The Change Center

"Uh, Ahm sorry, Mr. Blazek, sir, Ahm really sorry, but it's against the rules."

He was blanking, growing confused, and feeling sorry for me. I must be free. Once outside, I would run like hell. Let them shoot me and feed me to the dogs. I must be free. I continued pleading with Mr. Sam, hoping to con him into giving me the chance to be free. He seemed to be wavering. I was getting through to him.

"Poor, poor boy," clucked an elderly nurse, overhearing my begging. She was walking by us with some difficulty as she was wearing high, black, buttoned, therapeutic-looking shoes. The spell was broken. Mr. Sam came back to earth. Shaking his head, clearing it, he squared his shoulders and took on a firmer disposition. There was no longer a chance for me to trick him.

It really didn't make any difference. My resolve had been broken. Linda's roommate had had superman comics all over the bathroom wall in their apartment. One strip had had a futuristic setting. Criminals were forced to wear special shoes which dropped them to a lower, slower vibration frequency. Ordinary people who were able to move much more quickly had been able to recognize, avoid and censor these criminals. This matron, obviously an authority figure in the hospital, was just another captive, another dupe, like all of the rest. She had been forced to wear the special shoes, forced to move slowly. She still thought she was in control, but she wasn't close. Where was it to end? How could I, one frightened little absurdity, have any chance against Quasimodo and all of his insidious devices and hypnotized dupes. How could I ever hope to be free? Something was very wrong with this place.

By the time we got back to the ward, I was totally freaked. Weak and tired, I retreated to my bed. In a weakened, dreamlike state, eyes closed, I began getting flashes of a deliciously beautiful, slim, black nurse bent over a partially hidden object in the brightly tiled basement of the hospital. In amazement, I watched this movie going on in my head. Flash. It became ungodly real, as vivid as my world with my eyes open. I looked on in

Monday

amazement. This beautiful creature was playing with some small doll-like figure. As she manipulated the doll, my world changed.

I was forced to act. I sat up and got out of bed. The movie was forgotten. I had a constriction and magnetic tugging in my stomach. I needed to move. I was being pulled and tugged around the ward, feeling this strong force in my stomach. I let it happen, confused and amazed.

It changed. As a child, I had played with Scotty dog magnets. I had had two small magnets with plastic dogs (one black, one white) glued on top of the magnets. Using a thin surface such as a piece of paper, one could move the top one by moving the one underneath the paper. It was like that. I became a huge magnet, tugged this way and that through my neutral surroundings by some incredible force. Similar to skating without moving one's legs, I was being pulled around the ward.

Certain paths or routes felt better than others. If I went in the wrong direction, the pain would rack my insides. Turning, going in another direction, if it was the right one, I would only feel a slight tugging, now in my stomach, now in my feet. I first moved only when it was necessary to stop the pain. Then, not fighting it, I gave myself up to it, moving whenever I felt a slight pull. I would occasionally catch psychedelic flashes of a beautiful black woman manipulating some small object in the bowels of the hospital. I was led, pulled, and pushed this way and that around the ward.

I was finally led to the shower room. Shuffling past the showers, I began feeling a glowing force just ahead. Although I still had no feelings, whatsoever, in my genitals, I began getting almost sexually excited with warmth in my chest, head, and hands. An aware, rational portion of my mind just kept watching me, not attempting to censor my actions. Walking around, behind the showers, I came upon a bathtub. It was filled with incredibly dirty, grayish water. I stopped. Standing there, it seemed right. Was this to be a baptism of death with me crawling into this filth? I began feeling drawn to the water. My fingers idly wandered to my shirt buttons. Part of me wanted to get rid of my clothes and crawl into this stagnant pool of gray.

118

I jumped. Someone was coming. I quickly came together, bursting into a sweaty nervousness, similar to a young male surprised in the early stages of masturbation. Sweating, feeling guilty, I turned around and started to get out of there. A black nurse, one of the nicer ones, was leading a black woman to her bath. The patient was the woman who had flipped out on my first day on the ward. The one who had cried out about the devil and the Holy Ghost. Seeing me, not noticing my confusion and guilt, the black nurse crooned, "Oh my, Mrs. X, someone else may be ahead of us. We just might have to take our bath later?" With this, she looked questioningly at me. I managed to mumble a, "No-o." I got out of there.

Back in my room, my magnet trip was still not over. Jack walked in. We looked at each other. We both started to laugh. It was a burst of compulsive, hysterical laughter. Uncontrollable. Flash. Zip. We were two magnets with opposite polarity, existing in the same horizontal plane. We were bound together in some very strong, electro-magnetic field. Polarities would switch. We would be drawn together and then pushed or repulsed apart. We were somehow tied together on a horizontal plane, with me also controlled on a vertical one.

We both seemed to know what was going on. Then again, Jack would play anyone's game as long as he got the chance to act up and get rid of some of his manic energy. We tried to talk, but could only laugh and laugh. Momentarily able to stop laughing, a glance at each other, and we would be off into riotous laughter once more. If I remained stationary, Jack was forced to move. If he came to a halt, I would be catapulted into action.

With considerable effort, fighting the rising laughter and magnetic tugging, I was able to get out, "Uh, Jack, uh, it's as if we're, uh..." Hysterical, mind-blowing laughter. Grasping a thread of strength, "Huh, I can't stop laughing when I'm near you." Laughter. Space. Movement.

"I know," was his only reply, and then he was off running around the ward.

Monday

For the next twenty minutes or so, we were similar to some kind of vaudeville act or a skit at an ice show. We were like two clowns skating around, trying to avoid each other, but inadvertently running into each other with a bang. For example, I would be lying in bed, aware of Jack spacing around the kitchenette. I would be aware of him in both a head and a body sense. I would be drawn to the television room. So would Jack. Entering by different doors, he would see me and be propelled backward. Occasionally drawn together and then repelled apart. Continually, one or both of us would break out in manic laughter.

Finally, saying the hell with it, I decided to break the programming. I remained in bed, resisting the tugs and pulls. The pain was unbelievable. I doubled up, gasping, first biting my blanket and then stuffing the pillow in my mouth. I grabbed my gut, digging my fingers into my stomach. I would have done anything to stop the incredible pain.

For the rest of the morning, I had a truly magnetic persona. I don't know the cause. Perhaps it was my radiating fear and the metal wheelchair. It was probably just my head. On Sunday, I had used Jack's electric shaver. Now, trying to plug it in, I almost zapped myself. Just getting the plug next to the wall socket had produced a violent reaction of electric shock.

Bertha, who had been across the hall, was instantly standing beside me. I guess I skipped time frames as she seemingly made 20 feet in about a tenth of a second. She had been off of the ward and had brought me a gift of cigarettes. Maternally, she took the shaver from me and plugged it in with no difficulty. She gave me a superior but friendly smirk as she handed it to me. Standing away from the wall socket, I carefully took the shaver, mumbling my thanks. Gingerly holding its plastic cover, I was able to shave, although I continued to get slight electric shocks along my chin, neck, and cheeks.

Things became conductors or receivers for me. As a fledgling hippie, I had turned people on to wood and metal. Wood is a symbol of life and, in the Hindu system, the fifth element to earth, fire, air, and water. If you're tired, weak, or depressed, go hug a tree. If relaxed and sensitive to it, you'll be able to feel a faint but vibrant life force. Conversely, if you have all kinds of excess, scattered, nervous energy, use a large metal object that's grounded, such as a hot water radiator or metal lamp post, to drain off scattered energy. Relax, imagining your excess energy draining off into the metal. It seemed to work. On the ward, I was too scattered to attempt this, although I would have loved to have been able to hug a tree.

I had long been sensitive to vibrations but never before anything like this. I was truly electromagnetic, with all kinds of positive and negative poles attracting and repulsing me. There were sparks and slight shocks. The experience was probably similar to how someone would feel who had built up static electricity by rubbing his or her feet on a thick carpet on a damp day. It was so very intense. My electric personality lasted several hours.

Increasingly, I was falling into either of two mindsets. On the one hand, I was a prisoner in a Change center, subject to some diabolical scheme. On a more realistic level, this would translate to a restricted environment and a perceived strangeness in some of the staff. I was hurting the other patients. Although I was getting better, I was like some kind of a bull in a china shop or an odd-sized piece in a puzzle. I didn't know how to play the games of the other patients. I was hurting them.

Getting over my magnet episode, I was lying down in my room, feeling sorry for myself. I was hurting other people. I couldn't play their games. My writing was bothering the other patients. I had ended the magnet game with Jack. I had also ended another game. I had found a calendar. Gone was the metaphysical mind-boggling of Saturday and Sunday.

A calendar. Wandering around the ward, I had found a calendar. It was tacked to the wall next to the reception desk. It was clear. I could read it. It was February. Days were crossed out. It was Monday. I had been on the ward for 2 ½ days!!! Amazing. If somebody had asked me how long I had been on the ward, I would have answered, "forever." If pressed, I would have continued to say forever, flashing on the thought that a part of me was always on the ward as a portion of me was always insane. If someone could have gotten me to real time, I don't know what I would

Monday

have said. A month? A year? Weeks? Subjectively, it had been a very, very long time. This brief description of my stay on the ward does not do justice to the incredible amount of mind time I spent there. Not even three days! Difficult to believe. It would take several more days before the reality would start to set in. I had only been on the ward for 2 ½ days. It was absolutely amazing.

In those first couple of days, there had been a number of riddled, trippy, not really remembered interactions with Bertha, Lillian, and Elaine. They were the chief instigators, taking the rest of us for a ride. It hadn't been malicious. It was more like grownups playing with children. Sitting around, having coffee, we were in a rocket ship. Vavoom, going to a different time. I don't really remember what it was all about. I took everything very literally. A, "for ages," meant exactly that, not just a few weeks but a very long time.

Although I can't remember the content, I know a game was being played. Later in the week, Lillian would start in on me about something to do with time. I would tell her I knew what day it was. I had found a calendar. She would be very surprised and answer with a, "Oh, then you know we were only funning, that we weren't serious." I was unable to analyze the situation on Monday. It would only be Lillian's surprise later in the week, which would allow me to hazily remember the three women playing with my head. The information that I had only been on the ward for a couple of days was enough. To be able to think, "Well, then, that means...," was still beyond me. I sat amazed. A couple of days!?!

Sitting alone in my room, I became increasingly sad. I couldn't play the games of the others; I didn't know the rules. I didn't want to hurt anyone, but I didn't really know any games we could play. Despondent, I picked up Jack's guitar and began plucking the strings. Hah! A warm, soft glow covered me. I would sing and be happy and entertain the others. I would start with myself, for if each of us isn't happy, we really can't bring happiness to others. That was it. By being happy, I would bring happiness to others. Excited, I picked a Bob Dylan song out of Jack's songbook. I began playing and singing. I can't read music, don't know how to play the

The Change Center

guitar, and have a voice that couldn't hold a note if my life depended on it. It didn't matter. No one would mind. I would be happy, sing well, and spread my joy to all. I began to lose myself, playing and singing one song over and over. I just stroked the strings, letting my voice do its thing. It was a moment of lightness and joy. I was a traveling minstrel, spreading good tidings across the land. It was a good time.

I felt someone standing behind me. There was nothing sinister about it, just someone standing there. I stopped playing and turned to see who it was.

She jumped. "Oh, I thought it was Jack who was playing."

Reading the nametag on her nurse's uniform, "Hello, Mrs. U. How are you?" (I had no idea who she was. It wasn't until searching my memory to write about my ward experiences that I realized this was the Mrs. U. of Saturday. The nurse who had helped Danny to move my bed.)

She broke into a big, bright, happy smile and started shouting in a joyous, laughing, surprised voice, "He knows me, he knows me; he's getting better!" With that, she was off, running down the hall to the reception desk with her legs going from side to side in the deliciously, provocative way of running women have. Other than noticing her rump (pleasant) and her legs (sexy), my only thought was that some strange things were going on around here.

Her "getting better" bumped me into Mind Control. In a near trance (the alpha state), I had been programmed to repeat and believe, "Each and every day in each and every way, I'm getting better, better and better." Seemingly an innocuous, beneficial way to achieve a more positive mental attitude, I was excited by the possibilities of self-programming. On the ward, however, the "getting better" phrase bumped me into memories of psychic experiences and the heavies. Guitar and singing were forgotten. I lay down and once again began trying to figure everything out. I not only wasn't able to function in the normal waking state, I also wasn't able to use slower brain waves indicative of a meditative state or the "third eye"

Monday

of yoga. Attempting to go inside of my head brought the same swirls, fear, and dismay as before.

Ah, though, I was learning. I could think of Mrs. U. and her not unpleasing Asian face, her naiveté, and her sexy legs and posterior. When I had first met Jack, thinking of him as a fellow prisoner and a bunkmate at summer camp all at once, Mrs. U. had walked by. With a knowing leer, he had said, "That's yours." A portion of me had taken this to mean it was my job to infiltrate, con, and defeat this Asian authority figure. Part of me had also caught the obvious meaning. She was an attractive lady.

Watching her undulating hips and white stockinged legs, I had wanted her very much. If I were ever lured into one of those secret rooms to hurry the Change, it would be with Mrs. U. I truly desired her.

Later Monday afternoon, I stopped Mrs. U. in the hall. We talked together for quite some time. In a male-female sense, she appeared to be both gullible and easy. She had an innocent, trusting, interested (really interested), pleasant manner about her. Together with her trying-to-understand openness, she had a body that exuded strong sexuality. She reminded me of the type of woman, who, resisting sexual advances, would quickly be fighting her own body and her own body juices. She had a nicely rounded, sensual appearance. Standing there, talking with her with our bodies ever so close, she entranced me. My body could feel her warmth. Although I still didn't have any feeling in my groin and would not be able to have an erection until quite some time after I got off of the ward, I lusted after Mrs. U.

Mrs. U. didn't seem to notice my desire and would have probably been shocked at my thoughts. It didn't matter. Just talking to her, standing close to her, was enough. Our discussion was a fantastic tonic for my shattered personality. Standing there, leaning against the wall, physically close to her, I began telling her about different eastern philosophies, about Buddhism, and about the third eye. She listened attentively, not showing any shock or dismay at my words, commenting that she had a grandfather who had been a Buddhist priest, so she knew something of these matters, although not in any depth. She asked me what I saw in the third eye.

The Change Center

Looking at her, now with love, I spaced. Using the third eye, I flashed and focused on a remembered poster of a small, Asian girl that a friend of mine had had hanging in his apartment. With love and tenderness, I told her, "I see a young Chinese girl, about three, very beautiful, running down a city street amidst falling leaves. She is very happy. She is very beautiful."

Mrs. U. seemed to space with me. Then, with her Asian face set in concentration, she replied, "Yes, then you know what is going on. You know where you are."

"Yes, of course."

Maybe she hadn't been listening to me. Perhaps she was humoring me. Whatever the case, I was gone. I instantly knew about traveling through time and space, about projecting one's essence through the use of mental images, about the need to obtain coordinates and reference points to be able to be accurate. I knew so much more. Thoughts swirled through my head, "Hah! Have you had enough clues? Of course, I know what's going on. Who do you think you're messing around with, anyway? You think you are part of the power elite. You think you and the Chicoms are behind all of this. You don't even know that you're all puppets in Quasimodo's intricate game."

I was suddenly filled with worry. My thoughts changed. Had I given too much away? Did I have enough knowledge, enough aces up my sleeve, to bridge the next level of control? First, the blacks had tried to control me with their silly voodoo dolls and superstitious trust. Now, I was trying to bridge another level of control, another gap in the mystery of the ward. It was exciting. Almost.

Mrs. U. left me standing there and went back to the reception desk, now assured I was okay. She started talking to one of the black nurses. She began pointing to her forehead. They both started to laugh while sneaking glances at me. Oh, Mrs. U., how could you forsake my love and my trust? How could you make fun of me when I had tried so hard to tell you what was happening to me? I knew she was just putting the

Monday

black woman on. Mrs. U. would tell the true story with all of its sinister implications to her superior. Things would start to get interesting.

That afternoon, Jack, Beth, Cynthia and I were taken to physical therapy. Mr. Sam and a large, heavy black nurse escorted us. On the elevator ride down to the therapy room, Jack and Beth, especially Beth, talked about how they hated physical therapy. Jack, as usual, just seemed to be going along with whatever was happening. Beth seemed to have some real misgivings about the impending exercises. Cynthia stood mute and withdrawn in a corner of the elevator. At my deepest, most crippled state, our eyes had met. I had almost been able to communicate with her. She was weak, disoriented, and withdrawn. I don't remember her ever talking. I didn't get into Jack's carping, Beth's fear, or Cynthia's withdrawal. The elevator ride did not match my anxiety of that morning. If nothing else, I was just glad to get off of the ward.

The six of us, a weird group, to be sure, made our way through the maze of corridors on the first floor. I noticed hallways, blind alleys, and exits as we turned here and there. I needed to get oriented to the hospital and its layout. I had no real urge to break and run; that morning had squirreled my nerve. I was also starting to get involved with the intricacies of the situation, and I was lasting whole minutes as some kind of psychic secret agent. I kept alert. If the opportunity ever presented itself, I knew I had to be prepared. I was convinced I was doomed to the ward forever. My only hope would be to escape.

The physical therapy room was a scene out of a health club ad. Brightly lit and modern, it was filled with intricate devices. There was a plethora of equipment. Several sets of springs, similar to what boxers use in training, hung from the walls. There was a large wheel that could be turned with a crank, foot and leg devices used to lift weights, levers to pull and squeeze. There was a large, elevated ramp on one side of the room. It was a couple of feet high and had a metal railing.

Mr. Sam spaced off. The black nurse positioned herself on the ramp and hunched over the railing, looking down at us. As instructed, the other patients and I were lying on the floor. A late middle-aged, physically

The Change Center

trim, authoritarian nurse led us through a variety of stretching exercises. Stiff and weak, it was a little difficult for me to do the exercises. I wasn't complaining, as the diversion was welcome.

Oooops. The room went in and out of focus and changed. I fell into a dimly remembered science fiction movie. Humans had been turned into pigs and other animals in a subterranean torture chamber. It all fit. There was the room with its intricate devices, the gloating pig-like overseer on the ramp (literal, as the features of this heavy black woman, had changed), and us, helpless on our backs on the floor. After a moment of alarm, the room changed back into a this-reality focus.

Facing us, leading us in calisthenics, the physical therapist kept looking over her shoulder into another room which adjoined the therapy room. A green screen hid her view from us. I had caught a glimpse inside this other room when we had come into the therapy room. It contained an elderly woman who appeared to be quite ill. She was in bed being fed intravenously. As I did the exercises, I could feel energy waves leaving me and flowing to this old woman. I was being drained. Oh sure. I understood what was happening. From the young and strong to the old and weak. Good old Change theory. I allowed it to happen, not bothering to try and resist. It was beginning not to make very much difference to me. I had no control over any of this and may as well suffer through it.

I was so very stiff. I enjoyed doing the exercises. Everyone seemed to get into them. Even Cynthia, mute and withdrawn, although she was almost always out of step, several beats behind the rest of us. There didn't seem to be any reason for Beth's worry and Jack's antics. I began feeling things would be quite different if I weren't there. Perhaps there would have been a party or a real reason for Beth being so hesitant about coming to do physical therapy. Something was wrong. I could feel it. It was as if the entire exercise session was a show for my benefit. As I slowly surfaced while on the ward, this would become an increasingly predominant theme. Things would be different when I the observer, was not there.

As we finished the exercises and prepared to leave, I tried to catch a glimpse of the old woman. I expected her to be much younger and

Monday

stronger looking. She would have gotten a lot of good stuff from our group. With Mr. Sam's return, I lost my train of thought and forgot about trying to see whether or not the elderly woman had been rejuvenated. We returned to the fifth floor without incident. No one was letting on. No one was giving away the joke.

Back on the ward, I was in a neutral, near-normal frame of mind. The diversion, itself, as well as the physical movement involved in the exercises, had been good for me. I was told Dr. D. was waiting to see me. I was led to the stereo sitting room. With no opportunity to build anticipatory anxiety, I was only slightly nervous as I entered the room.

Not too surprisingly, Mrs. U. was there. I had bridged the next level of control. My face remained expressionless as her eyes met mine. Dr. D. paid me little attention. His eyes were on the first page of notes I had written.

"Hmm, I see here that you've been doing some writing."

"Yes, sir."

And then, very quickly, looking directly at me, he asked, "Po-knee-ma-yesh po-roose-ki?" ("Do you understand Russian?" in Russian.)

"Un peu." Without thinking, I inadvertently answered, "A little," but in French.

Dr. D., with a smug look on his face, simply nodded. He flashed a knowing look at Mrs. U. It was a look of superior knowledge, a look of "Aha! We've got him." Her Asian face impassive, she nodded. I couldn't figure out if she controlled him, if he controlled her, or if they were both on the same team, controlled by someone else. For better or worse, I had cracked the Russian/Chicom bloc.

Compared to the first interchange, the rest of our session was bland. Dr. D. looked tired and acted bored. Mrs. U. remained attentive and silent. Dr. D. asked me to verify the contents of my letter. I was able to amplify some of it, explaining, for example, that I had taught. He asked me why I thought I was hurting other patients on the ward. I shivered. This was too close for comfort. I mumbled something about not being able to understand or interact with the other patients. Dr. D. remained tired looking, seemingly neither interested nor impressed.

Stumbling in my speech, I knew I was coming across as a little shaky. There was nothing I could do about it. I hoped Dr. D. would see me as a normal intelligent person, who had had a brief psychotic episode or drug flip-out and was getting better quickly. After that first meeting on Sunday, I had no desire to try and explain my condition to him. The hallucinations, psychic experiences, physical discomfort, fears and disorientation remained with me. All I wanted to do was to please him enough so I could get off of the ward. In my brief encounters with him, I was always nervous and uncomfortable. I had no faith in him and was always wary of stepping on his professional toes or southern ego. My numerous requests were always forgotten and went unasked during our brief sessions.

Our meeting was over quickly. Dr. D. and Mrs. U. seemed satisfied. They had only been into that very first encounter, testing my knowledge, seeing what I knew. Not yet recovered enough to be into duplicity, I had automatically fallen into a subservient patient role. As I left, I began flashing on the intricacies of the situation. I wondered what new shocks were in store for me.

I spent the rest of the afternoon waiting for Linda and Liam. I kept on reflecting on what was happening to me. I could almost hold a train of thought. Although I would continually slip into and out of things, I could remember things I had been thinking about. I kept on rehearsing a script of what was going on.

On a paranoid level: There were various factions. It was like coming to a new schoolyard. Instead of one gang, there were several. Each group vied for your submission and allegiance. First of all, there were the black staff, who were promised control if they would perform certain duties. I suspected they weren't allowed to leave the premises and were forced to live in crowded dwellings hidden away in the bowels of the hospital. They had to get a certain number of replacements to leave the complex. At first, I had been controlled by the blacks with their voodoo dolls and

Monday

superstitious trust. It seemed the blacks mentally tried to get me to do things. I had heard them talking about me, "He just doesn't listen; he doesn't obey." Some secret power had promised them complete control if only they followed certain secret formulae. I was always totally polite to them and did whatever they said, as long as they met me straight on and called me by name. They could not control me mentally, though they seemed to try.

Then there were the white "in" patients, such as Bertha, Elaine, Lillian, and Jack, although Jack kept on screwing up. They had to lure new initiates onto the ward, acting as bait for friends and relatives. They did this to obtain certain privileges and the promise of eventual release. The strong ones, such as Bertha, actually acted as ward bosses, intimidating both staff and patients.

Then there were the dupes. Mostly white staff with a couple of blacks, who thought they were in control. They were definitely allowed to leave the premises and return to their homes. They really didn't know what was going on. They had probably been hypnotized to serve ungodly ends. Perhaps each morning, they would report for their daily mesmerizing.

On the bottom rung, there were the newbies. These were the patients, such as myself, who did not yet serve any faction. We had not been let in on the game.

The entire hospital was some kind of Change center, sucking in the sick and the disoriented, together with their families and friends as well as concerned, but unknowing professionals. All of us were being used for some hidden purpose. Perhaps the sick were being used as lures with the well ones duplicated; perhaps the hospital was a great leveler with all of us being brought to some hypothetical average. My perception and interpretations changed constantly. In the misguided battle for supremacy, I was being battled over by the caretaker, black staff, and by the "in" patients, with the professional staff unaware. Certain factions, such as Dr. D. and Mrs. U. may know more than the others and think they were part of the power structure, but this was only a delusion on their part. They were still only pawns in the puppet master's incredibly, intricate

The Change Center

game. My conscious mind would continually note facts and incidents reinforcing all of the above.

On a relatively straight level: I was sick. I was tripping. I had diminished control over my head and my body. I was scattered, delving both into my own fear and paranoia, but also, into other people's nightmares. I was picking up and getting into the terror of the other patients. In my weakened condition, I was exposed to both my own hells and the hells of other patients.

Either way, I was lost. I was too exposed and too fragile. The staff were too unknowing. I would never ever leave the ward.

Tired and disoriented, I began wandering around the ward. It was too difficult, trying to keep all of these complex thoughts in my head, although I knew I needed to tell Liam about what was happening. He would understand. I wandered by Beth's room. She was asleep, curled in a ball. She looked quite ill. Her features had changed. She was much darker and looked East Indian. I was fearful. That afternoon, an elderly black man had been wheeled onto the ward on a stretcher. Seen only that one time, he had been crippled and in obvious pain. He had white hair and looked to be in his 90s. His skin was a mottled, light brown or tan; he looked as if he had been much darker but lightly bleached.

I instantly knew what was happening with the images of Beth and the old man merging in my head. This was just another case of vibrational vampirism. Beth's health was being drained into him with his color going to her, just as the tape of Bertha's husband had been read into me. From the young to the old and from the strong to the weak; this refrain rang through my head. He was obviously in the room next to Beth's, the one with the closed door. Wheeled in for his fix, couldn't they see it was destroying her! I shivered, blanching at both my impotence and the injustice of it all. The innocents such as Beth and Linda should be protected. If *they* wanted to play their hideous games, let them try someone like me. Leave the weak and the innocent alone. Shaken, worried by what was happening to Beth, I continued on my way.

Monday

Waiting. I was caught up in endless waiting, with only fear and fantasy to break the boredom and the now continual pain. Supper came and went. And then it was six o'clock. Liam and Linda were among the first visitors.

I was prepared. I was rehearsed. First, there were the hugs and joy at seeing each other again. It was so fantastic seeing them again. Linda had brought me a bag of goodies, including cigarettes, candy, and more of my regular clothes. Surprise and joy quickly registered. Then, almost immediately, holding Linda's hand for dear life, I started in, "I'm never going to get well. I'm never going to get off of this ward. I'm never going to leave here."

In unison, they immediately responded with, "Oh no. Come on now. You look much better. You'll be okay." They would have none of my talk, but I couldn't stop. Small tears started in Linda's eyes.

I kept on about how I would never leave the ward. By now, I sincerely believed I was lost forever. In a distant sort of way, I was even beginning to accept it. I went so far as to suggest that Liam and Linda would be good for each other. I was about to suggest that he should live and sleep with her. Before I could get into that, Liam immediately cut me off at my, "You'd be good for each other." I desperately tried to get Liam into my paranoia and conspiracy theory. I told him about the Russian/French incident, the inept staff, some of the bizarre things happening.

Liam was beautiful. They both were. Linda held on to me, squeezing a "no" into my hand every time I got into my "I'll never leave this place" rap. Tears filled her eyes with her voice coming out in heavy, emotional whispers. Liam was prepared to blow me out of my delusions.

He listened to me. Totally relaxed and involved, he sat opposite me, looking straight into my eyes, not off to the side like Dr. D. or with his head cocked in quizzical amazement like Mrs. U. He had no judgments or ego analyses to make. He stayed with me. Not only listening to me, but also able to hear me.

132

When I told him about answering Dr. D's Russian in French, without him saying anything about it, Liam immediately came back with, "Yeah, so what, we both know he's kind of squirrelly. Look, man, every time I try to talk to him about you, he just cuts me off and says you've been on drugs for a real long time. We both know that's not true."

"Yeah, well, I kind of told him I took drugs." Liam's face just wrinkled up, but he let it pass.

When I would start giving him some paranoid explanations of what was happening to me, his face would just wrinkle up in a, "Who are you trying to kid? Hey, brother, this is Liam, come on, we've been there together."

I couldn't really con him. Hell, he certainly had been there. We had both been there, living through some heavy experiences together. He simply stayed with me, listening, not spacing off, not rehearsing what he wanted to say, and just waiting for me to say something that made some sense or conversely, something that didn't make any sense. He had no value judgments, just a "be straight with me" attitude. Gawd, what a therapist Liam would have made. He's so honest, open, straight on, and together. If a crazy happened to say something new to Liam, no matter how totally bizarre, he would probably stop him and say something like, "Hey, whew, hang on. Let's get into that. I think I understand what you're talking about, but let's…"

I wasn't able to amaze, snow, shock, or frighten him. I desperately began trying to hit on an honest approach to let him know about the hopelessness of my situation. I sat facing him, staring into his eyes, watching for a reaction to my words. If he started to wrinkle up his features, it meant I was spilling forth bullshit. If he looked at me askance, it meant I wasn't getting through. I finally thought of a way to explain my situation that he could understand. "Hey man, look, you know about scattered vibes. Look, I'm scattered, apart, not in control. I can't do yoga or meditate or get off by myself. They give me pills that weaken me and affect me in ways I don't understand. I don't know their effects or how to cope with them. Sick people surround me. I'm being caught in their

Monday

dreams, in their bad vibes." I went on and on. Liam knew what I was talking about. Dreams and vibes. We had both been there. I didn't have to convince him or worry about whether or not he thought I was crazy as we had both experienced some incredible things while on psychedelics. We had a common frame of reference.

As I told him about some of the things happening to me, his initial response was, "Are you digging it?" It's simple. You take this little pill, and your world turns funny. No matter how crazy, wild, or bizarre your perceptions, it is okay if you're able to dig it. If you're sensing people, places, or things through walls or across distances, it's fine as long as you're enjoying it. If you're not, then you simply pass on it. Rationalize, switch tracks, shut down, think about something else, and get into the music or whatever. We had all kinds of sayings, techniques, and logic to aid us to get higher than kites; we also had all kinds of methods to help us get back down. We had been the explorers of our minds, attempting to see what we could see while covered in this veil of illusion.

When I explained to Liam that it wasn't cool, that I had no control over what was happening to me, and I was in pain, he registered surprise. He was used to having fun during his trips. He told me I had to hang in there, hold on, relax, and slowly but surely get a handle on what was happening to me.

I continued to pour out all of the nonsense about what was happening to me. He simply accepted it, continued to listen, and occasionally hit me with the right words, words I needed to be able to live through what I was experiencing. The gist of his advice was that I was tripping, and I might as well enjoy the movie. If I couldn't enjoy it, I needed to hold on and wait until it got better. Although I never got to it, telling Liam about the science fiction horror of the physical therapy room would have only produced envy or a joke. "Oh wow. No kidding? Hey, remember when we had to drop a half tab for that to happen? Hey, what other movies are you into? Are you digging it?"

Eventually, Liam got me to laugh at myself. Then, the three of us were laughing at all of the bad numbers I was doing to myself. In a moment

The Change Center

of levity, I even let slip how I dumped my medication in the toilet. I told them how I had thought I was a prisoner of war and had snuck into the john with it, holding it under my tongue. I would find out later that Liam would squeal on me. Although I received medication several times a day and only remember dumping it that one time, I would never have to worry about whether or not to take it again as I would be closely watched for the rest of my stay. Rapping down the bullshit with Liam, holding Linda's hand, laughing, I began to feel pretty good and also, pretty silly. Maybe, just maybe, I was going to get out of this god-forsaken place. During those couple of hours, I had my first glimmer of hope. Weak and distant, it was hope, nonetheless.

As visiting hours drew to a close and they were getting ready to leave, I spaced into some of my most serious paranoia. Not only were they concerned about me, I was worried about them. I kept on asking them if they were okay. Laughing, they mentioned the day before they had gotten lost, and they had to be shown the way out of the hospital. I began to know fear. Was it possible? Was I, indeed, the lure with the two of them some new victims? Could they have been taken down into the basement and placed in front of the swirling wheel of lights? Were they in the first stage of the treatment leading to their total disintegration? Probably not. Hopefully not. Liam seemed too together, and Linda was too warm, soft, and just plain herself. I voiced my fears and kept warning them. They had the sense to reassure me, rather than just dismissing my fears.

They were perfect. They told me that they would be taking my Volkswagen bug. Liam had gotten the car keys from the desk. Yes, they were sure they could make it outside okay. No, I shouldn't worry. They led me to the windows in the sitting room. They pointed out my car. They told me to stand there and watch them leave with it. They even explained to me how they would leave the hospital, what turns they had to take, and so on. Walking them to the ward entrance, I was filled with love and trust. What a pair! They were obviously worried about me, but not too concerned about my being crazy. Their love showed through. There were no judgments or analysis. I was simply a loved one in trouble. With

Monday

friends like them, half of our mental patients could probably go home tomorrow.

They left. I went straight to the window and stood waiting for them. Time started to stretch into forever. I held on, overcoming my short attention span, remembering I needed to wait and see them. Then they were there. At the car, they remembered to stop, turn, flash me the peace sign and vigorously wave. Linda blew me a kiss. They drove off. Whew. They had made it. But wait, a VW van, full of hippies, wasn't it following them out of the parking lot? I felt a brief spasm of fear, but smiled it away. Liam and Linda would be okay.

The ward after visiting hours was always a letdown. Monday had been the start of the regular ward routine. The weekday staff had started their shifts. The staff, some of them having worked over the weekend, began becoming recognizable to me. Most patients, especially those who had received visitors, would continue to hang around the sitting room, unwilling to retreat to their rooms. We all received our medication during visiting hours; some were on heavy tranquilizers so we would all get a contact high. Each day, everything would slowly but surely become more mundane and less mind-blowing.

Bojangles was at our coffee clutch. He was a large, light-colored, black aide with a huge, protruding stomach. Balding, with the hair on the sides of his head sticking straight out, he looked like a fat Clarabelle the Clown (or do my readers not remember the Howdy Doody show of the 1950s?). He would dance around, impossibly light on his feet for all of his bulk. Although sensitive and deeply serious, he was always laughing and making jokes, bouncing here and there. Woo, I'm the Bojangles man. Jack, particularly, seemed to like him and always joked around with him.

Bojangles seemed nice enough, although I didn't trust him. He came across as phony to me, seemingly always putting on a show but not really into his antics. He would quickly shift from a big, old clown to a quietly serious hulk. He always seemed to be conning someone. That night I began picking up on a new phenomenon. It was the most evident with Bojangles.

Simply, the "in" patients were quicker and probably more intelligent than the caretaker staff. As mentioned before, they had all kinds of "in" jokes and sayings. They would put both the other patients and the staff on, with the aides not knowing when they were being kidded. By this time, I was caught in between. I began getting some of the jokes and understanding some of what was going on. I was still too slow with too short an attention span to really interact or be an "in" member. If one of the patients pretended to flip out to get a favor or just to play with someone's head, Bojangles would start to joke, waver, then get worried. I was too slow to pretend. Bojangles and some of the other staff began watching me to see what my reactions were. If I laughed, they would laugh; otherwise, they would start to take the patient seriously. If one of the staff started to bulldoze, and they would, I would be there, a second conscience staring hard. It became confusing, as no one knew whose side I was on, including me.

Observing the coffee clutch, I began building a theory regarding laughter. Simply, you could tell where a person was at by what they were able to laugh at. This would be amplified. I also realized a number of the patients both conned and intimidated certain of the staff. It is well documented that there is a tendency for confined people to identify with their captors, serving in some cases as better guards than the actual guards. I never went so far as to try and police the other patients. I always identified with them, although after those first few days of complete disorientation, I was perhaps the most well-behaved, subservient patient on the ward.

Becoming fatigued, I left the coffee clutch. It had been a fairly normal event with Bojangles running around, making jokes while the patients became involved in animated conversation. Danny had come on duty and had done a swish routine. I idly noted both he and Bojangles were a little effeminate and probably gay. I did not, however, drop into any mind-boggling Change theory.

The visit with Liam and Linda had been a revelation. The normal coffee clutch had reinforced the normalcy of their visit. For the first time

Monday

since landing on the ward, the thought dawned on me that maybe, just maybe, I wouldn't be there for the rest of my life. For the first time, I thought about the possibility of being allowed outside, of going home again, of living once more. My entire will had been consumed with trying to figure out what was happening to me while trying to still my head and body terror and regain my memory. This new shtick of actually leaving the ward and going home was too good to be true. It was too much hope for me. Of necessity, I spaced away from thinking about it.

I turned in early. Trying to go to sleep, I felt indescribably shaky. Nervous. Jumpy. Still my weakened, semi-depressed self, a new dimension had been added. The jumpiness seemed to be coming from within my bones. Sleep would not come.

Jack was too hyper to lay down. He kept on spacing around, doing this and that, with me dimly aware of him. He eventually gathered his things and went off to the stereo sitting room. I continued to try and fall asleep.

My head began filling with strange images. Colored mists and dimly heard voices swirled through my head. Tossing and turning, I fell into a half-sleep. I began fixating on trying to figure out what was happening to me. What was going on? Who was in control? I needed to get to a level of mind where I was not subject to this ever-changing swirl of color and sound. A clear, strong voice sounded in my head, "Alpha, alpha, go to alpha. We are in control of ourselves at all levels of mind. Go to alpha." I tried to relax, attempted to go to a deeper level of mind, attempted to reach the alpha state, tried to meditate. Nothing worked. Tossing and turning, with a melted head and impaired hearing while an eerie shakiness came from deep within my bones, I fell back into being an impotent victim.

I began getting psychedelic flashes in my head. In my mind's eye, they were more real than real. I began seeing shadowy figures disappearing down a corridor to the right of the reception desk, going down concealed steps deep into the bowels of the hospital.

The Change Center

The Master Controller resided there. Whoever was rattling my mind and body, whoever was playing with me as though I were a toy; they must be met. God only knows what they wanted of me. Enough was enough. This must end. In the style of mighty Ulysses and the Avenger of Sunday's fantasies, I got out of bed. I was very shaky and physically weak. The hell with it. This must end.

The ward was darkened and deserted except for Danny sitting behind the reception desk. As I moved out into the corridor, he gave me an odd look and then went back to his reading. I began pacing back and forth in the darkened area between the reception desk and the ward entrance. The only light was at the reception desk. I kept to the shadows, hesitant to break into the small, lighted area in front of the desk. I began pacing faster and faster, still afraid to dart past the reception desk, afraid to enter the psychedelically seen corridor to the far side of the reception desk.

I would later find out that the corridor, rather than leading to a stairway which enabled one to get to the hospital basement, actually led to a padded, observation room. It would have been quite a joke if I had raced past Danny and ran down the corridor, only to find myself in a padded room. Real funny. Sort of like dropped babies.

Danny distractedly glanced at me. He muttered to himself that it was going to be a long night. Under my breath, I said, "Yeah, a real long night." Determined to get to the bottom of this once and for all, I kept on pacing, building up anger and courage. I began having trouble walking. The magnetic pains of the morning returned. They stabbed my insides. Angry, confused, and totally pissed, I struggled against the pain. Tired of being a weakling, buffeted by and helpless against all of the nonsense and paranoia of my days on the ward, I gritted my teeth in determination. Doubled up in agony, I continued to walk against the pain, turning in ever-tighter circles. I began getting external flashes of light, seeing energy doors. They would occur in front of and in back of me. They were fiery, neon outlines of doors, rectangular bands of fire, and sparks going on and off.

Monday

Arggh. Oh no. Turning quickly, I had run into one of them. My left hand was hit with electricity. Ohmigod, the pain. Clutching my left hand, doubled over in pain, I managed to get back to my room. Glancing over my shoulder, I caught Danny sneering at me. This was not going to be as easy as I had thought.

Sleep came, but not quickly. Thus ended my third day on the ward.

TUESDAY

black nurse woke me up early in the morning. She was slim, competent, and attractive. She must have been one of the night staff; this is the only time I remember seeing her. She gave me my medication in a no-nonsense fashion and watched while I docilely took it. She remained waiting, making sure I swallowed it. I felt good, almost normal. In retrospect, the medicine would tear me apart. Each day, I would become increasingly normal.

After breakfast, I found out I could obtain and use a razor. Under Mr. Sam's watchful eye (don't let the crazy alone with that thing), I gave myself my first close shave since coming to the ward. I scraped myself several times under the chin line. This has been a habitual problem with me; it usually happens every time I use a fresh blade. The exciting thing about the shave is when I looked in the mirror, I only saw myself. It was a haggard, tired me with dark, sunken eyes, but a person I recognized nonetheless. When borrowing Jack's electric shaver, I had not been able to use a mirror, but rather, shaved by touch. Now, even a bleeding me elicited no psychedelic flashes or mind fright. A couple of black nurses, standing in the hall, started clucking about my bleeding and urged me to use a wet compress to halt the flow of blood. I simply nodded in agreement as I was used to it, needing to use a washcloth or tissue paper almost every time I used a new blade.

Jack came into the room. He started to blanch at the blood and was ready to launch into one of his manic episodes. I paid him little attention. I just smiled and cut off his antics with a curt, "Hey man, I just cut myself, that's all, it's cool. It'll stop." Seeing that no one wanted to play his "freak out at the blood" game, he spaced out of it and went about

Tuesday

his business. He was becoming irritating. His immaturity and constant willingness to act up were starting to get to me.

After shaving, I took another shower. Feeling relatively good, normal and together, the shower wasn't the bliss of Sunday's happening, but rather, a good, natural, ordinary act. Putting on clean clothes, I felt good. Things were looking up.

Returning to my room, I noticed my bed still wasn't made. I asked Mrs. H., one of the day nurses, the one who looked like my prof's wife, if it was okay if I made up my bed. She looked at me with some surprise and answered, "Of course. The patients are supposed to make their own beds." Too new to being normal to analyze the situation, I began noticing how slipshod things were. This was my fourth day on the ward. I had taken two showers at my own initiative. I had first borrowed Jack's shaver and then a razor from the desk. What was going on, here? If I had remained unshaven and reeking, would anyone have noticed? I let it go.

We had our first group therapy meeting that morning. It was held in the conference room next to Jack's and my room, the room where I had first met with Linda and Liam. Altogether, there was quite a crew of us: Dr. D., Mrs. S., the head floor nurse who was rarely seen, a black nurse who shepherded Mrs. X around the ward, and about 8-10 patients. It was quite subdued, although it had a promising beginning.

We sat down with most of us, wondering what to do. There were some new patients, including myself. The other new patients seemed as spun out and disoriented as I was. Almost immediately, before we were all settled down, Mrs. X, the black patient who had rolled around on the floor yelling about the devil, made a request, something about clothes or visitors. Dr. D., who was preparing to get into the session, absent-mindedly agreed to her request. He began giving out instructions to the group. The black woman was on her feet, arms stretched out, and shouting, "Oh thank you, sir. Thank you!" She was quickly across the room, grabbing him in a bear hug, trying to kiss him. He froze, his face a momentary mask of disgust, not wanting her to touch him but also, not wanting to freak her further. He kept his aversion fairly well hidden, turning his face away from her. The black nurse, who had been sitting beside Mrs. X, was immediately on her feet and quickly next to her. She firmly, but tenderly, took the woman in her arms. Cooing to her, she was able to get the black patient to let go of Dr. D. Continuing to hold her firmly, but with compassion, she was able to get the woman back across the room and into her seat. Mrs. X was quiet almost immediately. Dr. D. sat red-faced.

It had become ominously quiet. The black patient had spaced, staring off into nothingness. The nurse started to apologize for Mrs. X, but was cut off by Dr. D., who had regained his composure. "Well now," he began, "Does anyone have anything to share with the group?"

Quiet. Stillness. This was my chance. After having blown it in two brief sessions with Dr. D., I could now get in one of my numerous requests. I could finally ask him a question. "Huh, sir, I was wondering if it would be okay if I could use the phone. I was..."

"Let's not bring up personal requests. Let's talk about things we can share with the group." I had blown it once again. I was too late with my request. Mrs. X had beaten me to it.

Silence. Stillness. The patients sat like statues. A number of us started to fidget. Dr. D., after a long pause, said, "Well now, this certainly isn't like Friday. Doesn't anyone have any problems today?" Hmm, Friday, the day before I was on the ward. Sitting there, in this subdued, uncommunicative group, I began feeling things would be quite different if I weren't there. Similar to the way I had felt in the physical therapy room, I began thinking something very strange was going on here. Everything would be different if I weren't there. I was the outsider. I didn't belong.

A few idle comments were made. There was restless movement. The silence became uncomfortable. Mrs. X returned from wherever she had been. She launched into, "Ah just want to work, ah just want to go home, ah just want to do my work, ah want to work..." She went on and on, repeating herself. In a brief lull in her speech, while pausing for breath,

Tuesday

Dr. D. jumped in and agreed this was a worthy goal. With an "oooh"," she was back on her feet, arms outstretched, moving toward him.

The black nurse was quicker this time and caught her before she reached him. This time the nurse's cooing and tender restraint were not enough to quiet Mrs. X. After several minutes of trying to quiet her down, the black nurse was forced to leave with her. On her way out of the door, the nurse looked at Dr. D. with her face wrinkled into an "I'm sorry" gaze. She seemed very mollified by her ward's behavior. The nurse started to apologize for Mrs. X, but was cut off by Dr. D.

We were back where we started. Ominously quiet once again. I was too uncomfortable just to sit there. I had to say something. "I feel much better, ah, I think I'm getting well. Anyway, uh, much better." No response. "I, ah, hear things though." There was still no interest. "Like I keep on hearing a Dr. Blazek being paged." With this comment, I shot a sidelong glance at Bertha. Did she know I knew it was her voice on the intercom that was continually paging me? Did she know I knew she was part of the power structure? Hah! I was learning to take chances. Let Quasimodo try and figure this out. Who did they think they were messing around with, anyway? "Of course, ah, I, ah, know there's no Dr. Blazek, so I, ah, must be hearing things." While verbalizing this, I flashed on the fact I was working on a doctorate, although admittedly, not a medical doctor. I idly wondered if I was jumping time frames. Perhaps I would be the doctor who cured me. This new possibility so intrigued me that I only half-listened while Dr. D. more or less repeated what I had said. I abstractly agreed with him that I, indeed, was hearing things.

My sojourn into verbalization started several "I'm getting better, but..." speeches. Dr. D. began looking disappointed. The head nurse kept on looking at her watch. It seemed as though they were waiting for some outstanding stories, something intimate. It never happened. Occasionally, Dr. D. would look at Beth, so young and pretty. He even touched her once. At one point, his face even twisted into a psychedelic mask of lust. I was tempted to censor him, but was not able to move or say anything.

The Change Center

The session finally ended with little or no rapport ever reached. Both the patients and the staff seemed disappointed. Jack had sat in the corner, hunched over, asleep throughout the entire session. I had a notion to do something bizarre to liven things up. I had wanted to jump up, announce I was a CIA agent, and everyone was under arrest for not complying with the Confession II Act. I was afraid the staff might take me seriously, and I wouldn't be able to pull it off as a joke. I was even more afraid that I, myself, would fall into it and then, I would be in real trouble. I simply bit my tongue and suffered through the drawn-out session.

Later, wandering around the ward, I found myself watching Mrs. H. vigorously clean the kitchenette. She never paid me much attention, reminding me once again of my professor's wife. Muttering to herself, maybe to me, "Humph. I don't know why I'm cleaning this up when the patients are supposed to be doing it?" The thought flashed, "You're doing it because you're being controlled, you dummy." I let it pass. She seemed too together and just a little bitchy to be a total dupe. Although I would have been more of a hindrance than a helper, I would have enjoyed helping her. She was young and attractive. A pat on the head and her thanks would have done wonders for my ego. I was a little surprised at her needing to clean up. Bertha and Lillian, and to a lesser extent, Elaine, enjoyed making coffee and supervising our evening coffee clutches. They also took quiet pride in cleaning up afterwards, emptying the ashtrays, cleaning the cups, and wiping off the tabletops. I guess they were only on night duty.

I continued wandering around the ward. For the first time since my room had been changed, I walked to the far end of the corridor. On my way, I passed an open door of a room with no patients. It may have been my former room. Mrs. S., the head floor nurse, sat there, staring straight ahead, looking hypnotized. A tape recorder was going. An animated black nurse, the one who was always with Mrs. X, was walking back and forth, gesturing. I shivered with trepidation. We had used a tape recorder in Mind Control. Mrs. S. was obviously one of the controlled ones. Another white nurse looked on, slightly dazed. Would she be next? I managed

Tuesday

to go by without them seeing me. I thought I was okay. I wouldn't be forced to sit in front of the circle of whirling lights, with them force feeding thoughts into my brain through their insidious taping machine. I wondered, almost aloud, "When would this end?"

Back in my room, any feelings I had had about being together were quickly being dissipated. Bored, not having anything to do, left alone with my thoughts, trying to figure things out, was still a dangerous endeavor. Walking around, eating, shaving, taking a shower, and talking were all becoming commonplace. My attention span was still horribly short. Worse, in addition to my weakened depression, I was becoming very shaky, twitchy, and nervous.

A social worker came to visit me. It was a welcome diversion. She was young and pretty with long, light brown hair and academic-looking glasses. She had on a fuzzy, red sweater and a tight, black skirt. High heels set off her long, shapely legs. Somewhat nervously, she introduced herself and said she would like to talk to me. I immediately liked her. We set off for the stereo sitting room. As we walked to the room, Jack saw us, giving her a leer while winking at me. I was having none of it and ignored him. My lust was reserved for Mrs. U. and my love for Linda. This was just a very pretty girl-woman.

We sat down in the stereo sitting room and began talking. She was trying very hard to be competent, objective, interested, and, best of all, helpful. She was very intent on doing everything right; I must have been one of her first cases. I began liking her even more.

At first, I was a little bit shaky. I had a difficult time talking. As I realized this wasn't going to be one of those five-minute quickies as with Dr. D., I became quite verbose. I felt superior to this young woman in an academic, professional sense. I began confidently talking about myself in analytical, schoolbook terms. I painted myself as an intellectual graduate student, succumbing to various pressures, eventually experiencing several brief but intense psychotic episodes. I lightly touched on my paranoid schizophrenic tendencies. I enjoy talking about myself and got into the whole thing. It was exciting. She was a good listener. She let me talk. She

The Change Center

seemed concerned as well as interested in what I was saying. During my discourse, I mentioned that several of the patients seemed more normal than some of the staff. To this day, for example, I would prefer Bertha and Lillian to Bojangles and Danny.

She interrupted me, "But you can tell the difference between the patients and the staff?" She was deeply concerned, probably recalling symptoms encountered in the classroom. Cynically flashing on all of the hidden conspiracies, I replied, "Yeah, I can tell them apart. The staff, it's easy to tell who they are. They're the ones who wear name tags."

Very serious and very worried, she countered, "But I don't wear a name tag, and you know I'm not a patient. Or do you?"

"Huh? Oh yeah, sure, you're too pretty to be a patient." Ah, Mr. Smooth may be making a comeback.

Laughter. How I liked this serious, trying-to-do-everything right, young woman. We talked and laughed for over an hour. She explained that she would act as my liaison with the outside world and if I ever needed anything, I should ask for her by name. I think I impressed her, and she probably wondered why I was in there. We had an excellent discussion. It had been a tremendous release for me, dredging up my symptoms and talking about them in graduate school jargon.

I had stayed normal, lucid, intelligent, and perhaps even sophisticated throughout our entire meeting. I never let on. She never knew. Straight people are so very easy, so very unaware. A little over halfway through our meeting, I had felt the vibrations coming through the wall. They had been extremely strong. They encircled, caught up, and drained the social worker. Talking, releasing some of my mind rot, I had become stronger, more sure of myself. The social worker, upon entering the room, had stood tall and straight. Although new at the game and a little nervous, she had appeared sure of herself.

As we left the room, she was stooped and tired looking. I felt strong and really together. Our heights, or so it seemed, had changed in relationship to each other, with me having grown a foot or so. I actually bent over,

Tuesday

hoping she wouldn't notice the new difference in our heights. As we passed the television room immediately adjacent to the stereo sitting room, I saw that my guess had been correct. Cynthia lay there, curled up on a couch against the wall, some 10 feet directly behind where the social worker had been sitting. She was in a deep, heavy sleep or trance state. Cynthia had caught the social worker in an energy drain.

Recalling the nurse in black, therapeutic shoes on the way back from getting an x-ray, remembering the easily duped staff, and rerunning the movie of Mrs. S. being mesmerized after the group therapy session, I had no real hope for this woman. I hoped they wouldn't hurt her, as she was so very nice. She, of course, would be of no help to me.

The day passed very slowly, with me popping into and out of a near normality. One moment, I would be relatively clear and lucid; the next instant, I would be back into confusion and disorientation. By this time, I was just plain tired. Having had a sickly childhood, I was used to the feeling. I was sick and tired of being sick and tired. I did not feel at all well physically. I began feeling very sorry for myself. Having nothing better to do, I began trying to write once again. Even this did not hold together. I began repeating myself.

Those first couple of days, I had been hallucinating so continually that I had been forced to live in the present. Now, I started to broaden my time frame. Not able to adequately verbalize it, it was as though I were on some kind of roller coaster I couldn't get off.

Bored, troubled, and in pain, unable to take the ups and downs any longer, unable to rationalize my ward experiences, I just wanted it over. After the brief hope of Liam's and Linda's visit of the night before and the near normalcy and strength of this morning, I simply could no longer handle it. The pain, the weakness, and the occasional tripping were just plain getting to me. It was as if my mind and body had declared, "Hurray! Ohmigod, I'm getting better!" and then here I was, getting worse.

The pain was unbelievable. It was totally out of any of my previous experiences. The pain came from my very innards, from the depths of my being. My bones to the very marrow were being crushed like nuts in a nutcracker. Then, they would become all rubbery with an impossibly strong, sickly weakness emanating from within me. I couldn't stand it. Nothing I did seemed to work or lessen the pain.

It was early afternoon. I lay in bed, tossing and turning in pain. Completely helpless, racked with a pain I didn't understand, I simply moaned, crying to myself. Already overly sensitive to pain, this weakness in the limbs and god-awful pain coming from the inside out was too much for me. My insides were like crunching teeth.

(Dear Medicos: Did it ever dawn on you that your medicine hurts? Did it ever dawn on you that humans could endure almost any pain if they know why and for how long? Can painkillers and tranquilizers be paired with your anti-psychotic medicine? You say I never told you about my pain? Did it ever dawn on you I was crazy? That I was locked up on a closed ward? That I was completely disoriented and scared shitless? I hope you never know my fear and agony.)

I began praying, to anyone who would listen. I prayed to every God I could think of, even to the Kid, the perfect master who had been the subject of the meeting held a few days before my commitment. I prayed for sleep, for rest, for a lull, for anything to make the pain go away. I began hallucinating.

With images floating through my head, I finally realized what was happening. I was being set up as the cosmic lure, the trap for masters. My mind twisted the old joke about the guy, who by continually baiting fish hooks, became the master baiter (masturbator). I was the bait, the lure. I was the worm on the hook. I had developed good karma through Mind Control, yoga, and sending love and trying to be a nice guy. I was now serving as a lure for the bad guys to get the good guys. Or was it for the good guys to get the bad guys? I was cross-programmed at all levels of mind. I had used Mind Control to break the negative programming of my childhood and in turn, used drugs to get behind the Mind Control programming to see the real truth. I was and was not a mind control devotee, a Christian, a newbie yoga student, a nice guy, a carouser, and

Tuesday

more. I attempted to drift (the "flowing is" of my acidhead days) in order to allow the most powerful one to win, whether it was a force, idea, belief, or entity. I kept on running into myself, with each version of me a microcosm of the macrocosm. In this war against myself, I realized no one could win, as I was cross-programmed. I dimly realized that my real confrontation would be with myself, with my two polarized selves meeting in confrontation or merging back into the unity of the ONE. In this completely frazzled state, I didn't care who would win. I didn't care about myself, as long as the pain would end.

Throughout this twisting and turning pain, this calling out to the gods, one thought held me together: Linda and Liam. Before I gave myself up to complete chaos and utter destruction, I would hold on and see them one last time. Linda, my love, I will see you one more time. Liam, good buddy, I can last one more time. I had to see them one more time. I began chanting to myself, "Linda, oh Linda, my love, one more time. I'll wait. I'll hold on. One more time." I became obsessed with the desire to see Liam and Linda. I had to hold on. I just had to see them.

The pain changed. It grew more intense. I began crying. I couldn't stop the pain. Finally, I began shouting in my head, "Linda, oh my god, I'm so sorry. I'm so sorry. I just can't stand it any longer. Oh my god, I'm sorry." The pain changed again. It was as though I was being beaten with a cat of nine tails. I could see and feel the welts opening up across my body. It was too much.

Giving in, giving up, twisted in aching unreason, on the edge of complete chaos, I staggered to the reception desk. Little Miss Glasses sat there. She was a new nurse's aide; it was her first day on the ward. She was white, very young, had blond hair, and wore thick glasses. Her slightly crossed eyes appeared huge through her thick lenses. She was stocky with thick legs. I had briefly met her that morning. She seemed nice enough, although a little slow. Thankfully, Bojangles was also there.

I addressed him. "Look, I can't stand it anymore. I can't wait any longer. I know what's happening, and I can't stand it anymore. Please give me something to stop the pain. Please!"

The Change Center

I heard little Miss Glasses way off in the distance as if she were miles away. She was very precise, not having looked up or having noticed my condition. "The doctor says that you're not to receive any additional medication." Although new, she knew the rules.

Staring in desperation at Bo, he just looked at me. He seemed to want to start laughing. Was this just another patient con, another joke? He was easily fooled at the evening coffee clutches.

I began shouting, "God damn it! I can't stand it. I can't stand the pain. I know what's happening. It's no use, I'm cross-programmed." He just continued looking at me. "Look, I'm the worm wiggling on the hook. I can't stand it. Give me something."

It almost seemed as if he understood what I was ranting and raving about. He seemed to be wavering, uncertain as to what to do. By this time, I was screaming, "I can't stand it! Do you want to see the wounds!?!" I started to rip my shirt off. I actually thought my body was covered with huge, bleeding welts.

He just swallowed, looking down at the floor. He looked quite ill. He gestured for me to stop, and then, with me waiting, doubled over in pain, he turned around and walked over to one of the large, metal cabinets. He came back with a little paper cup containing two large, brown pills.

I nodded a mute thanks, realizing I had been defeated, that I hadn't been able to hold out against the pain, that I hadn't been able to wait for my loved ones. I gulped down the pills and made my way back to the room. I flopped face down on the bed and waited for the pain to go away.

I began to drift off. After a short while, the young nurse came in to see me. I abstractly looked up at her. She stood next to the bed, a worried look on her face. "How do you feel?"

I heard myself answer, dimly from a distance, "I don't feel anything inside of me."

Eyes squinting through her large glasses, pinkish face screwed up, she exclaimed, "Oh, how terrible."

Terrible? Terrible! It was fantastic. The horrible, bone-crunching pain

Tuesday

was gone. I felt unbelievably good. It was as though I were a thin shell with nothing inside or outside of me except for an incredible, golden lightness. I felt like an empty eggshell, similar to those eggs which are hollowed out, painted, and used for decorations. Everything was so very beautiful. I was immersed in a gently, drifting sea of calm lightness. What was even better, I knew I was on something, and I didn't have to worry about my perceptions. I was on a drug. I had no pain, no worry, no analysis, no braining. There was just a calm, peaceful floating.

Lying on my stomach, head to the side, watching the nurse, she seemed to dissolve from the hips down, with the energy floating up, over, and into me like a genie's magic cloud. It happened. It was a drug happening. There was nothing to worry about. I'm reminded of a friend with whom I had tried to involve in a philosophical, head trip. A total womanizer, he had started shouting, "You know where my head is at? I'll tell you. It's up the ass of some chick, and I'm digging it." I guess he was talking about something else. The nurse's bottom covered me like a light shroud. I had a momentary, fleeting impulse to pull her into bed with me and merge energies. This quickly passed. At the same time, I also had a fleeting thought that this would be Bojangles' payment, the compromising of the nurse's aide and of myself. He would get a couple of extra points. They could have me as a crazy, then as an attempted escapee (although I did stop myself from running), and now as some kind of despoiler of young nurses or aides. These paranoid thoughts passed through my consciousness even more quickly than my momentary urge to merge with her. I felt too good and much too comfortable to move. Ignored, little Miss Glasses left.

I drifted. It was so good, so very peaceful and pleasant. The next several hours would be spent with me drifting in and out of a deep comfortable sleep while floating on magic clouds. In a dreamlike, dimly remembered awareness, everything was very good and beautiful, even fantastic.

I finally woke up. Getting up, wandering around, I was a little confused and disoriented. I then realized I was on something. Yes! Wow! I was speeding my guts out. Hey! Hey! Yippee! A speeding and a zipping

The Change Center

along life's merry way. It was soooo good. The energy just picked itself up and flowed into my bones. For once, I felt together and strong.

Everything had turned itself around. I was filled with joy, peace, and strength. I was on top of things, and I knew what was going on. Happy and energetic, I greedily scanned my environment. Occasionally, colors would get brighter and sounds clearer. Hey man, right on! I was in control, bright and bouncy. Forget the bullshit, forget the braining; I was on something. No longer a crybaby weakling, I wanted to hug and shout. It was so very sensational. Hey, c'mon everybody, let's get it ON.

It was like walking out of a thick, soupy fog into brilliant sunshine and just enjoying it. I began to really see the ward, noting all of the observation mirrors and other paraphernalia that had so freaked me. It was as if I were awake for the first time since I had been on the ward. I began enjoying the other patients and the staff, wishing only that they weren't such mopes and so very down. Supper was an experience, with the food tasted and savored. Filled with a new awareness and appreciation of my surroundings, I just let it all hang out, enjoying myself immensely. I felt clear, crisp, and strong.

By the time Liam and Linda got there, I was zippy, to be sure. What a relief. I would have someone to play with, someone who could understand and enjoy the experience with me. They, straggled in, all drawn and tired-looking, with circles around their eyes. Boy, what mopes.

I ran up to them like a whirlwind. "Hey, wow, come on, you two, stand up straight for goodness sakes. You both look worse than I do." They just kind of looked at me, too slow to react to this new version of me.

Undaunted, I pulled Liam aside, hugging him, moving quickly, not allowing him to catch up to where I was at. In mock seriousness, "Hey man, look, you need a rest. Look, this hospital deal isn't so bad. Look, you don't have to do any work, you have a nice clean bed, fantastic meals, all kinds of games and magazines and television to keep you amused and

Tuesday

drugs, hey man, there's all kinds of drugs you can get. I mean, screw this driving a cab nonsense."

I started putting the two of them on, surprising and shocking them. They began looking at me a little strangely. Could this be the weak shit of the previous night? Not waiting for them to figure it out, I told them about what had happened that afternoon, about the pain and the magic pills. They quickly began to understand. I got them laughing. Their energy level started to do a thing, climbing and almost catching mine. Whew. They were going to be okay. It was going to be a fun visit. Thank goodness, they were together enough, not to be caught in their dead-head moods.

Linda finally realized that this was, indeed, her man, all happy and manic. It was someone she could remember, someone with whom she had fallen completely in love. She just burst open, flowering into joy. She became irresistibly happy with her eyes crinkling, her mouth and lips only able to form big smiles, and her arms and hands continually hugging and squeezing me. She looked like she wanted to run and shout, crying out to the world that her man was back and everything, come hell or high water, was going to be just fine. Everything was going to be okay.

Liam just dug the happening. Suddenly serious, he leaned over to me and said, "But really, how do you feel?"

"Hey, look, man, I'm speeding my guts out. I feel so good, so strong, so together. The only bad thing is I have nothing to do. I could scrub down all of the floors, wash the walls, and do a whole number on this place. I feel great."

"Hey, great. Wow." He looked at me, beaming. Then, getting worried, "Hey, what happened to your hand?"

I looked down at my left hand. The top two knuckles were all bruised and swollen. Huh? I began getting psychedelic flashes of the previous night. What the? Had the energy door been real? Had I really run into it? I started to get into mind panic. Huh-uh. Nope. Not when I was so ON.

"Huh, nothing. I just ran into a door." I laughed to myself at my pun.

Yeah, I had just run into a door. I felt too good to be bothered about it. I straightened my arm, holding my hand out, flexing my fingers. The bruised knuckles went slightly psychedelic with the colors swirling and deepening. They seemed to get better before my eyes. "See, look, they're okay. There's nothing the matter with them."

We continued talking with the three of us, all happy and excited. Linda and Liam were overjoyed I was so ON and obviously so much better than I had been on their two previous visits. We were sitting in my hospital room. Mrs. U. came and chased us out. Visitors were not allowed in the rooms of patients. I started to protest, but Liam and Linda were on their feet and moving as soon as she asked us to move. I went along with them.

We sat down in the television room. It was crowded with patients and visitors. We sat at a table almost directly under the television. Liam sat facing me with his back to the television. Linda sat on my right, holding my hand, hugging and squeezing me.

I began painting an intricate mind fantasy for Liam. The night before, I had tried to tell them about my paranoia. I had not been very coherent. I had only been able to bring up bits and pieces, such as my brief interaction with Dr. D. when he had spoken Russian to me. Indeed, although I had rehearsed and tried to keep my perceptions somewhat logical, I hadn't really had any full-blown Change or Prisoner theory. Rather, it was something I popped into and out of. The only thing making any sense to Liam was when I explained to him about being so scattered.

Now I had more strength and was more coherent. I began detailing a prisoner fantasy. "Look, just suppose, that this and this were true. Now then..." As before, he listened and concentrated on what I was saying. The night before, he had remained open and non-judgmental, playing the role of a passive listener. With the new me, he was taking my word patterns, making extrapolations, forming his own concepts. We had done this many times together, talking on into the night.

Tuesday

The sitting room was crowded. The group at the next table began listening to me. I felt them, before I observed them listening in. I lowered my voice. They could still hear me. Liam and Linda seemed unaware. I began falling back into my scattered trepidation and hopelessness. Nope, not tonight; tonight, I was going to stay on. I felt too good. Time to lighten up.

Liam and I had been in deep conversation, both hunched over the table, looking into each other's eyes. I straightened up and began scanning the other people in the room, the room itself, and the television. The television. Oh shoot. Idly watching it, while still talking to Liam, I realized that the intricate mind fantasy I had been painting was patterned after the television program. When would my thoughts be my own?

We all mimic our environment. It has always irritated me, especially when I would find myself blindly repeating something I had just heard. That night, more in sync with my immediate environment, together with the heightened awareness of those magic pills, I realized my well-thought-out, serious head rap both paralleled and imitated the current television program. I may be easy, but not that easy. I cut the rap.

Liam, who had been drawn in and was attentively following my train of thought, was disappointed. "Hey, man, I was just getting into that."

"Yeah, I know, but it's all nonsense. Forget it."

Even though I realized my earth-shaking head trip was no more than a once removed interpretation of an ongoing television program, I didn't flip out. The hell with it was my only reaction. I was still too ON. I was together, a zipping and a spacing down life's merry way. Flow on, my boy. There's new action up ahead. Hang on but don't get hung up.

We all lightened up. They shared their news with me. I could even be interested in something other than my own situation. We talked and laughed. It was over too quickly; visiting hours were drawing to a close.

We walked back to my room in order to get their things. Away from the television room and its listeners, I quickly spaced back into my

The Change Center

"something strange is going on here" routine. I began trying to verbalize my fears of being a prisoner.

I had been too up and had appeared too normal for either Liam or Linda to worry or take me seriously. Liam, in mock seriousness, quickly came back with, "Hey man, don't you worry, if it comes to that, I'll come back with every head fit to walk. We'll bust this place wide open. We'll blow this place apart and get you the hell out of here." This was said with a conspiratorial wink.

What a pair. What good friends. They could even joke with me. Linda got into it. So, did I. On the way to the door, the three of us elaborated on how Liam would rescue me. We all made light of it, with them getting me to laugh at my paranoia. Seeing them out the door, I felt very good. They were so much fun and such reality inducers. They enabled me to recall a reality that was so much fun I just had to get myself together. Life was too good to spend on a closed ward.

I felt so good I didn't even mind the voice. For you see, while Liam and I were joking about my rescue, there was a voice screaming inside of my head, "The programming, the programming, what happened to the programming?" I guess a portion of me wanted to take the whole thing seriously. The television program had been about a desperate, trapped person trying to escape from some devious scheme. He had been trying to convince others of his plight. Oh yeah. Sure. In my peace, love and happiness days, the word had been, "Some people have dreams; we live ours." This had been great when the dreams and living had been of peace, love, happiness, nature, bliss, nirvana, and God. How had I fallen into being the goat of science fiction, spy thrillers, disintegration, and masochism?

I was still zippy after Liam and Linda left. The coffee clutch gathered. Like sitting around and getting stoned, I really enjoyed this one, as I was still higher than a kite. For the first time, I was an active participant. We talked about drugs, past experiences, and more. For the most part, I was on top of things. I had taken my regular medication and was starting to

Tuesday

feel nervous and hyper. I would occasionally drift out of the conversation, with my attention centered on my body. What was happening to me?

Instinctively, I was drinking grape juice after grape juice. Drinking it out of a small paper cup, I constantly got up, going to the refrigerator, and getting refills. I was even together enough to pour coffee for the others. The excess fluid and vitamin C would flush out my system and help counteract the drugs. It had been gospel in my trip days. Alcoholics need vitamin B. Other than actual physical damage such as to the liver, some of the side effects of excessive drinking such as Korsakoff's syndrome and delirium tremors can be avoided by taking vitamin B. Big drinkers going on benders do not eat well. Their mind-bending pink elephants are due to a vitamin deficiency. Druggies need vitamin C. A number of acidheads who I had known took huge quantities of vitamin C in order to recover from the drugs they had taken.

Talking with Lillian, I found out she was a registered nurse. She was self-committed because of severe migraines. Due to extreme nervousness, painful headaches, and a tense lifestyle, she had sought professional help several times. She could return to the outside world any time she thought she was ready for another go-around. I told her about the afternoon. She asked me to describe the pills I had taken.

"Why, I know what those are. They're…, a very strong tranquilizer."

Oh boy. Downers. I had never made the uppers and downers circuit. I distrusted drugs. I had rationalized taking psychoactive substances as a search for awareness, although they did become recreational. Some of our solid citizens, outraged by marijuana, seem to do okay when it comes to pep pills, caffeine, nicotine, sleeping pills, tranquilizers, and alcohol. The only time I had felt like this was on the speed found in most psychedelics. I had thought I had been given some kind of amphetamine. I was speeding, felt strong, alert, and energetic. And yet, I was on downers. The tranquilizers had woken me up, filling me with energy. This new information, combined with my regular medication, made me very jumpy. How would I get my system to stabilize?

Interacting with the patients and staff that night, I saw everything from a different perspective. It was fun. Everyone seemed increasingly normal, although it should be noted that Cynthia, Mrs. X, and other severely disturbed patients were not there. Observing the conversation, for once in on the jokes, I expanded on my musings of the previous night.

We can tell about people by what they are able to laugh at. Thoughts and ideas cascaded through my head. Per a remembered psychology book, laughter can be used to express latent hostility, such as our laughing at someone slipping on a banana peel or to identify incongruity such as the unexpected punch line of most jokes. My favorite joke: A drunk is leaning against a lamppost, walking around it. He turns to his equally drunk buddy and exclaims, "Oh my god, we're walled in."

The caretaker staff didn't seem to know when or where to laugh at the jokes the patients made. Certain jokes about being crazy or human frailty hit too close to home and would bring fear to the eyes of someone like Elaine. Jack would laugh at anything as long as he could release energy. Little kids many times don't know why their parents and other adults are laughing. The jokes are over their head. Teens, getting into off-color jokes could be the brunt of ridicule if they didn't understand a certain joke.

There, at the coffee clutch, my mind roamed over a whole series of insights into laughter and its significance. I was reminded of "laughing ourselves to death," "laughing our heads off," "he who laughs last, laughs best," and "the devil's laughter." I got into a whole mind game and began developing experimental approaches to measure the significance of laughter. It was a normal experience for me. Some call it thinking. I was getting better.

Zipping around, developing innocuous head trips, interacting first with Liam and Linda, and then with the other patients and staff, I felt good. Except for the ever-growing shakiness, I felt on top of things. There were still some strange things happening. I was still hearing voices, although now, the voice inside of my head was usually my own. While still having certain bizarre experiences, it was as though I could stand

Tuesday

back from them. I was no longer a total victim of my surroundings and perceptions.

It's a shame all of these new feelings, and heightened awareness only lasted a few hours. It was, however, a welcome change. By the time I was ready for bed, I was nervous, jumpy, and hyper. I was not tripping into any new mind or body problems. Even though I was shaky, I was able to burrow into my sheets and blankets, feeling good, remembering Liam's and Linda's visit, amused at some of our jokes. I fell asleep, feeling optimistic.

Thus ended my fourth day on the ward.

WEDNESDAY

I surfaced Wednesday. Still sick and horribly weak, I surfaced. Fragile and childlike, I was now walking ever so gingerly on solid turf.

Those first four days were and are a blur. Although a number of incidents from those first few days are bright and clear, still existing in small pockets of my memory, they are trip memories. The first two days are especially blurred. Saturday and Sunday had existed forever. While Monday and Tuesday seem more real, my memories were still those of an unreal, kaleidoscope-like experience. Those first four days had been spent underwater. Even the gusto and strength of my Tuesday tranquilizing had been spent buried. The air had been thick, with me covered by heavy layers of a limited, restricting environment.

If our journey through life is thought of as a ship sailing the seas or a boat making its way down a river, it can be seen that we are subject to both calm lulls and tempestuous storms, quick and slow currents, large and small waves. We stop at this and that shore, occasionally adrift in muddy reeds, sometimes racing across the water. At times, we have solid and sure handling of our craft, while at other times, there is an improper fudging of the controls. I had been shipwrecked.

First, I had been immersed in watery energy that reached my chin. Then I was underwater, going for that anchor of a hospital sign. With the shot of Thorazine acting as a catalyst, I had blacked out, waking to the world like a drowning swimmer attempting to move his or her mass through a thick, heavy, constricting liquid. Gulping for air, still able to cope after a fashion, I had eventually passed out. Somehow, I had miraculously reached the shore. Now, still horribly weak, I had finally

Wednesday

awakened. Not quite remembering how I had gotten so deep or why I had come so close to complete destruction, I was finally on solid ground.

I timidly approached the desk, asking the nurse on duty if I could borrow a razor. She looked at me quizzically, cocking her head. Finally, "Wait a minute. Come with me." I walked along with her, going to a part of the ward I didn't know existed. There were some lockers, probably off of the shower room. She opened one of the lockers. There, on a shelf, were all of my toilet articles. My razor, shaving cream, toothbrush (I had been using a ward issue one), and more were sitting there. Linda had brought them for me when I had first been admitted. I would no longer have to rely on Jack's supplies.

There was some bedding there. I found out that I could take some clean sheets and change my bed. Welcome news as most of my ward experience was spent in a sweating desperation.

My arms full, I made my way back to my room. I felt like a conquering hero with all kinds of booty or a child who had done well at Christmas. Making my bed was somewhat of an effort as my physical coordination was still not what it should be. It was good to feel useful, although it took me twice as long to make my bed, as it would usually take.

With my new haul of stuff, I was starting to accumulate quite a few things. Linda, on each of her visits, had brought me some more of my clothes as well as many surprises. Looking around the room, seeing it as if for the first time, I noticed Jack's area was severely depleted. He had had stacks of all kinds of things, including his guitar and sheet music. Although it had not been obvious to me, each day, he had taken more of his stuff to another room, probably the stereo room. His guitar had disappeared almost immediately after I had briefly used it. Although he had said he didn't mind my using it, it had been quickly gone. Gaining in strength, seeing my supplies grow in relationship to his, it was as though I were replacing him, pushing him off to somewhere else. I was becoming dominant. I felt a twinge of regret, perhaps even guilt.

The Change Center

I met Bill that morning. He was slow moving and slow talking. A severe hip injury greatly retarded his movements. Recently admitted, he appeared to be quite normal. He had a clear, good-looking face, black wavy hair, and a construction worker's body. He was on the ward because he had attempted suicide. To quiet the pain of his injured hip, he had gulped a bottle of sleeping pills. In pain, he had sought the nearest relief. He did not appear to be either psychotic or suicide-prone. I guessed him to be in his thirties. I would find out he was 28, about my age. His restricted mobility, together with the fatigue and pain lines in his face, made him look older.

We played gin. A carpenter, drinker, and card player, Bill was fun to be around. He was someone to whom I could talk. When we first sat down to play cards, I knew I loved playing cards, and I was good at various games, including gin. I had trouble holding and dealing the cards. Something new was happening. My physical coordination was getting worse. My strength and dexterity were on the wane. Confused, things became fuzzy. I had trouble concentrating, while Bill slowly explained the game. He seemed unconcerned with my bumbling.

Pop. I was back, knowing the game well. I had taken his slowness for stupidity and began holding back, as in the long-ago game with Bertha. I was wrong. Bill was good. I was forced to play as well as I could. Although I tended to win more hands, Bill tended to win the game, as he would get bigger scores when he went out. As with any good card player, he didn't worry about losing a hand; he just concentrated on winning the next one. With him, I didn't have to walk on eggshells, or worry about being too good or too sane. About my age, he was an equal in many ways. Spending time with him helped to pass the interminable day.

Now that I had surfaced and was no longer tripping my guts out, the scene had shifted. It was boring. Little was happening. Increasingly, the ward was becoming what it really was: a closed hospital corridor with a paucity of stimuli and a restricted mobility.

Something strange was continuing to happen. I was losing my physical coordination. My bones were filling with bubble gum. I was

Wednesday

becoming spastic. I retreated to my room. My thoughts wandered to Barbara's husband.

Mrs. B., the white day nurse who had helped me get my things that morning, looked incredibly like Barbara, a girl with whom I had grown up. Although Barbara and I had not been related except by the closeness of our two families, Barbara and I had been treated as cousins.

The nurse and Barbara had the same first name. I had told Mrs. B. all about Barbara. She listened, all sweet and attentive. She was very kind and understanding, just like Barbara would have been. As I told her the Barbara story, I was kind of hoping that finally, after I had given her enough clues, she would break out laughing, giving away the joke, and tell me what was going on. She didn't. After several days of observation, I would finally know that, indeed, she wasn't Barbara, just as I would realize Mrs. H. wasn't my prof's wife. For a while, though, even after I realized they weren't physically people out of my past, I would hold to a type of reincarnation theory or an astral cloning hypothesis.

Barbara was the daughter of one of my mother's closest friends. She was sweet and very religious, having almost become a nun. The two families had always hinted it would be nice if the two of us would get together, although the differences in our religions prohibited it. After various pitfalls, looking like she would never marry, Barbara had married a paraplegic, who was confined to a wheelchair.

He was one of the last Mind Control cases I had worked on. I had sent so very much love and energy, fighting in my mind to be able to picture him, able to stand up and function. I had thought I had been able to get through to him and may have been able to help him. Instead, he became worse. The marriage had eventually been annulled.

Now, lying in my room, I became increasingly debilitated. Although I didn't have the pain of the previous day, it was almost worse, as I became all rubbery, first losing my fine motor skills and then almost total control of my body. I fell into a feverish half-sleep.

Tossing and turning, I received strong mental pictures of Barbara's husband. It was as though I were merging with him, becoming him. That was it, then. I was to take his place as a hopeless cripple. Total fear. Total frustration. I could no longer control my body. I fell into a deep sleep.

Later, when I woke up, the head terror had passed. The rubbery weakness had not. I did have more control over my body. Depressed, feeling sorry for myself, unable to handle these relapses very well, I was able to finish the major piece of writing I did while on the ward. By this time, I realized I must have done something very wrong to be suffering so much. It started as a true confession to purge myself of sin.

True Confession

_____ *spent a year in bed with tuberculosis*

_____ *have been arrested twice*

_____ *have had almost all childhood diseases*

_____ *have done many bad things*

_____ *have been beaten, scared, tired,*

_____ *pushed my way through school studying into the night*

_____ *have sat spun out for months at a time--summer of xxxx*

_____ *have had zillions of shots and x-rays*

_____ *have watched people disintegrate before my eyes—stepfather,*
grandfather,

_____ *tried to be a saint*

_____ *tried to find the truth*

_____ *did/tried many things*

_____ *have been throughout the states, Mexico & Europe*

The last year or so have sent love to everything I came into contact with until the last 4 1/2 days I was at a place where I loved and appreciated everything and everyone I came into contact with I faked insanity and allowed myself to be committed

Wednesday

_____ *I die every time I go to sleep & am reborn each time I have an "aha!" insight or, in other words, wake up*

_____ *I have always felt compassion until*

_____ *I allowed myself to be put in here*

_____ *Everyone talks in riddles & sees & does things that I don't understand*

_____ *I am drained of love and can only try to do what I am told*

_____ *I have nothing against any minority or majority group since we all are, in essence, GOD*

_____ *People seem to think & do things of which I know not*

_____ *I want no visitors & if you're going to do it--do it quickly & cleanly*

_____ *I have no real desires except freedom*

_____ *If my ego-death can help someone please let me go quickly & cleanly*

Exhausted and starting to repeat myself, I stopped writing. On this level, I was just tired, confused, and in serious pain. Dropping back into thinking I was lost forever, a swift, clean death was preferable to this slow torture. The above starts with a, "Haven't I suffered enough?" introduction. Mentioning my travels was important, as the **enemy** would have a difficult time duplicating me. It was important to me to put down the bit about minority groups as I usually thought of the Master Controller as Japanese. I may have surfaced. I certainly wasn't well.

We had arts and crafts that afternoon. A nurse came and got me. Not feeling especially well, I had spent most of the day in my room. She led me to the kitchenette. A number of tables had been pushed together, covered with rolls of paper. Jack, Beth, Bill, and a couple of others were doing watercolors. Each of us was given a wooden plaque with a figure on it. The plaques were around 4" by 8". We could color them in. Everyone seemed intent on his or her painting. Even Jack was getting into it, and he was neither manic nor acting up.

I immediately experienced a testy moment. I couldn't open the paint bottles. Bill did it for me. My fingers were like large twigs. I had little strength and next to no dexterity. Bill took my plaque and showed me five

The Change Center

or six different ones we could color in. I chose a picture of a revolutionary soldier. I needed to hold the paintbrush in two hands. It took complete concentration. I worked for over an hour, losing myself in my task, trying to color within the lines, while I chain-smoked several cigarettes. I crudely colored in the soldier, leaving the background blank. On better days, I could have done a better job in some five or ten minutes.

The nurses were sympathetic to my condition. Their only advice was to keep moving and to continue to try and do things. Western medicine, with its getting sick in order to get better, can be a trying thing for its patients. I still did not connect these various physical maladies with my medication. Oh well, the medication did clear up my head.

I was quite proud of my unfinished painting. For the first time while on the ward, I thought of someone else. Linda. I would make her happy. I would give her a present. I scrawled, "To Linda, with all my LOVE," on the small plaque, signing and dating it. I found some thick, shocking pink, nearly fluorescent, corduroy-like yarn. I tied this cord around the plaque as if I were wrapping a package, finishing it off with a large bow. I have always loved giving people gifts, surprising them with small sentimental doodads. Taking my little plaque, I carefully put it aside. I was so excited by the prospect of giving it to her. To me, it was more important than the crown jewels. It had been a labor of love. Her man, slowly but surely, against impossible odds, was working his way back.

I saw Dr. D. that day. Briefly. We met in the hall. His, "How are you feeling?" was answered only by my, "Okay." I made no attempt to tell him about my pain of the previous day or the rubbery weakness, or the lack of coordination in my fingers today. He told me my mother and sister would be coming to see me on Saturday. He even hinted that if I were okay, I could be released in their custody. I took the news in a "matter of fact" manner, even lightly. It simply didn't register. It was too good to be true, too unreal, too much out of my sphere of comprehension. It hardly dented my awareness. I simply stood there, a subservient patient, shuffling my feet. I thanked him and mumbled something about how I was glad I was getting better. There were no cartwheels, no shouts of joy.

Wednesday

As I started walking back to my room, a thought crossed my consciousness. I stopped, turned and was able to catch him before he went into the sitting room to meet with another patient. "Sir, is it okay if I call one of my professors at the university?" His face tightened in a grimace. He didn't seem pleased.

When I mentioned Dr. Dwayne, he immediately lightened up. "Oh, yes. Of course, you can. I know him." I had finally remembered to ask for phone privileges. I had even gotten them.

He disappeared into the stereo sitting room. I wandered around in a daze. My family was coming. I could make a phone call to the outside world. This was too much. I couldn't lose it now. I began tightening myself against any head panic.

I slowly walked to the reception desk, timidly approaching the nurse stationed there. Addressing her, "The doctor says that I can make a phone call. He said I could call one of my professors at the university." No drum rolls. No excitement. No medal of achievement. She simply nodded toward the phone used for making outside phone calls. "Okay, there it is. Make your call." She went back to her work.

Small tears had started in my eyes. "I can't dial the phone." Her head jerked up with a sharp look of surprise on her face. In response to her glare, I said, "I have no strength in my fingers." Without questioning me about my disability, she looked the number up. Dialing it, getting an answer, she handed me the phone. She returned to her paperwork.

Talking to an outsider was exciting. Dr. Dwayne was surprised, but glad to hear from me. He had wondered what had happened to me. He stated that he knew that I wasn't irresponsible, and when I didn't show up for classes, he had wondered if I were ill. For the first time, I would tell another human being I had had a nervous breakdown. He showed sympathy and told me that he would visit me the next day. It was a short, but rewarding phone call.

I went back to my room, assured in the knowledge that people still remembered and liked me. My years of confinement and dread were,

The Change Center

after all, less than a week and two missed classes for Dr. Dwayne. It was difficult for me to grasp. Less than a week? I had been here less than a week?

With little or no control over my digital movements, together with an all-pervading elastic weakness, I realized what happiness is all about. Simply, it's being able to walk and talk at the same time. Going back to my room, I promised myself that if I ever became normal again, if I ever regained my physical strength and coordination, if I ever recovered my memory and intellectual skills, why then, I would never, ever, be unhappy again. Hah! What amazing, strange creatures we are.

Back in my room, I thought about it. They're coming, does that mean, is it possible, could it be, I mean... Caught up in my own life, I hadn't thought very much about either my mother or my sister. Certainly not at all, while I was on the ward. I had first been totally caught up in myself and had then focused somewhat on Liam and Linda. Now, I was filled with how much they both meant to me. My sister had married early and had moved to California. She and her family had moved back to Chicago when my stepfather and grandmother had died. She and her husband were busy raising five children. They lived in the house in which I had grown up. My widowed mother, in her sixties, lived alone in what was formerly my grandparents' house. They were coming to see me. They really were. It was hard to believe, virtually impossible, but maybe, just maybe, they were coming.

Over the next several hours, I was able to write several letters to them. With use, my fingers were improving. The letters, although written in a babyish scrawl, were still legible. I was still a little off in my time orientation and carefully dated them.

Wednesday

Date

Dear Mom & Sis

The doctor tells me that you are visiting me Saturday, x/xx/xx. Thank you very much. I love you both very much & don't want you to see me like this. However, I love you both so much that I do want to see both of you. If you think that it's okay and you both want to, I would really appreciate it.

I lived a lot of different ways & I guess you'll find out how deceiving I was. I'm sorry, but I have lied a lot.

When I got here, I thought I was dead (again) & tried to play everyone's games, but I didn't know the rules & have brought unhappiness to some people.

Like when I was a little boy, I was always shy. I'm still shy, and now some people are trying to play my game, but my only game is to try and be myself.

Please forgive me, but I want to be a big guy and play cards, mow lawns, fix houses & that kind of thing.

Don't let my troubles hurt you. I would like to come home and help things keep going again. Love, ----

I love you so much that I will try to be okay when you get here. Maybe the doctor will release me into your custody.

Love, ----

As you can see by these letters, I'm still a little disoriented. However, I am still a fast learner (memory & vocabulary). I have miraculously returned to my old self & I think people think that I was only fooling & that I am some kind of spy. You know I'm not. Sorry to cause you all of this grief. God bless us.

Thanks

I'm sorry I'm crazy. See you soon (maybe)

I was still fuzzy and weak. Going home to live with my widowed mother or with my sister and her five kids was so fantastic I couldn't even come right out and believe it could possibly be true. Turning 30, a former teacher, systems analyst, and project manager, working on a doctorate with a bachelor's and a master's degree, basically out of the nest since I went away to college at age 17, going home to momma was good beyond my most fantastic dreams. Sure. Why not?

By Wednesday, I was increasingly aware of my changing status. I had quickly gone from one of the most blown out, disabled patients to one of the most subservient and rational of those confined to the ward. Increasingly, I would take every opportunity to talk to the various authority figures, all those nurses who seemed together. Several of the patients, especially Jack, and some of the caretaker staff, would eye me suspiciously. Why was I always writing? What was I writing? What was I doing, always talking to those in charge? I became very sensitive to their stares and whispers.

Liam and Linda were late that night. My jumpiness had abated to some extent. Still weak, without complete control of my fine finger movements, the frustration of the afternoon had passed. I nervously waited for them. With the other visitors filing in, I began becoming quite despondent. Liam and Linda were my reality base, my contact with the outside world. To a certain extent, they were the carrot leading me off of the ward. I needed them. I began to worry they were not going to make it at all. I would start to shake, breaking out in perspiration. They had to make it. Please, God, let them be okay, let them be able to make it.

Unable to handle the television room, crowded with visitors, I attempted to stay in my room. It didn't work. I constantly walked to the reception desk to see what time it was. Ages spent waiting, but only minutes by the big, old clock on the wall. I began feeling fear. Maybe they weren't going to make it. Maybe they weren't okay. Maybe, just maybe, the hope of that afternoon was just a joke, just another way to break me. Maybe, Liam and Linda were...

And then they were there. They were only a half-hour or so late. They came in with a rush, both talking at once, both filled with energy. They apologized for being late. Liam, the town's first freak taxi cab driver, had had a last-minute call. Relief. They were here. They had made it. I was so very glad to see them.

Wednesday

As per usual, Linda brought me a bag of surprises. Cigarettes, candy, and some more clothes. What a wonder she was. While I went through the bags of gifts, we all tried to talk at once. They were at a much higher energy level than the night before. Perhaps due to the two of them racing to the hospital, knowing they were late. I was in much worse shape than the previous night. To their consternation, I began telling them about the afternoon, about my physical maladies. It must have been confusing for them. They remained basically the same; while I changed so radically each time, they saw me.

Opening their packages, telling them about the afternoon, I remembered Linda's gift. I jumped up, told them I would be right back and went to my room to get it. Returning with it, I felt a glow in my chest. Shyly, smiling to myself, I gave it to her, "Look honey, I know it's not much, but wow, if you knew how long it took for me to make this. Here." I gave it to her, waiting for the explosion of mirth and love.

It never happened. She took it, looked at it, didn't know what to say, put it in her purse, and forgot about it. Liam had started telling me about something. Linda just listened attentively to what he was saying, ignoring my gift. There may have been a brief, forced smile or a thank you, which I did not hear. I was the little kid, who had worked all afternoon on a butchered mother's day card. Coming home from school, presenting the scrawled atrocity to mom, knowing how pleased, even proud she would be, and I had been dismissed with a, "Thanks. Now go wash your hands and get ready for dinner." Oh, Linda. It was the first time she had ever hurt me. It was a sin of omission rather than one of intent.

As always, the visit with Linda and Liam was enjoyable and good for me. I hardly remember it, however. They were filled with telling me about their lives. Perhaps my high energy level of the previous night had inspired them to be up for me, to remember and rehearse anecdotes about what had been happening to them. Liam, for example, began telling cab stories, going on about his passengers and their idiosyncrasies. I listened with half an ear, smiling now and then. Linda got into it, amplifying his stories.

The Change Center

I wasn't quite ready for it. My world still began and ended with me. My thoughts could not go beyond my situation on the ward. They either didn't notice my weakness and fragile, self-centeredness, or they weren't able to switch gears. More importantly, I was still stunned. My love hadn't done cartwheels, hadn't exploded in joy over my gift of love and effort. Once again, I had failed.

For some time before my commitment, I had not known what failure was. It was not that I was a success; it was just that success and failure were out of my context. Sure, I failed. That had nothing to do with my being a failure. Each of us does what each of us does. I was concerned about out there, building search and psychic skills. I had a dream about more fully developing all of man's potential, of reaching the stars, of cutting through all of the self-deprecating bullshit, of actualizing myself and all of mankind into a rebirth of mutual love, respect, and understanding. My God was AWARENESS. I had perpetuated numerous atrocities on my body and soul, indulging in numerous perversions, getting lost in innumerable side trips of fear, depression, and trepidation. But it was all a game. All of my inadequacies and hang-ups, together with the nonsense I went through, were just part of the game. The bad things were just transitory, side trips, and false trails. Eventually, everything would be okay. It had to be.

The dream of being part of growing awareness and helping to develop human potential had been a good one. On the one hand, I fancied myself an explorer of inner space, delving into my mind, seeing how far I could go. What am I capable of? What are we capable of? With a background in psychology, education, and systems, I would first work on myself, building as much knowledge and as many skills as possible. I would then work on us. I had a dream of helping to develop optimal learning environments. What variables and structure are needed to more fully actualize each of us to our full potential?

If I lay torn and shriveled in my Chicago apartment, beset by horrible monsters and visions of a world gone mad, it was okay. I had screwed up. My mind was misinterpreting the wonder of it all. The wrong combination

Wednesday

of chemicals had brought on a bad trip. It was okay. That's it, ride with it, cry a little, go into yoga position 42B, that's it, it'll be okay. This, too, will pass. I'll get back on track.

Somehow, I had lost it. First, I had lost the dream and then the ability to do anything about it. The true horror of my ward experience may have begun that Wednesday evening. I was back, functioning in this world. For me, it was the second time around. In order to survive, I had been forced to bring back the old me, dredging the memories out of a buried-in-the-catastrophe, but still intact vaults of my mind. So many of the things I had learned as a child, as a teen, and as an adult, would have to be relearned. No longer a brave, fearless seeker of the unknown, no longer concerned with TRUTH, I was just a frightened weakling on a psychiatric ward, attempting to get well enough to escape a closed ward. Sure, I was back. But who or what was I? Needing to hold a paintbrush with two hands and not able to make my love happy. My feelings of failure would only get worse.

After a scattered visit, filled mostly with small talk, Liam and Linda left. Surprisingly, we hadn't talked much about the impending visit of my relatives. Linda did mention she had called my sister. I was still in no position to believe my family was actually coming and I would be able to leave the ward. It was still beyond my comprehension.

At the now habitual coffee clutch, although shaky and lethargic, I was able to enter into the group discussions with considerable gusto. I was talking to Lillian when someone mentioned Bill. Lillian said it was nice I had someone to play cards with. I replied, "Yeah, but he would much rather talk to you than play cards with me." At her surprise and pleasure, I continued, expanding on how he had kept on looking at her, liking what he saw. She took to shushing me with a, "Don't say that." I kept on. It was fun.

Lillian, only a little embarrassed and obviously pleased, began preening. In truth, Bill had been impressed by her and had asked about her. Later, whenever Bill was around, Lillian would always shoot me glances as if to say, "If you say anything, I'll brain you." I almost got into

The Change Center

it. I almost pulled a, "Ah Bill, come sit over here, I want you to meet this friend of mine." I was almost able to do it, but not quite. With practice, I could have been the ward matchmaker.

Bertha was at the coffee clutch. She kept on asking me questions about myself and about the two friends who always visited me. I began telling her about a day Linda and I had spent together while in Chicago. It started as a horror story, with me attempting to explain how I had begun completely spinning out. She became so engrossed, however, centering on the activities and antics of Linda and myself, that it became an adventure story. To a certain extent, both of our attention spans were too short to tell her an involved story with a punch line of growing dissolution.

I told her about how I had picked up Linda in mid-afternoon in Chicago's downtown section on the day before Christmas. She was able to get out of work early. We did some last-minute Christmas shopping. Linda was dressed to kill, as she worked in a somewhat fashionable Loop clothing store. Several weeks into my goodbye acid trip that didn't seem to want to end, I had on my parka and grubbies. Everything looked bright and different. I was stoned, manic, and happy. We had wandered through several State Street stores in downtown Chicago. Running in and out of these stores, I had pulled several bits, such as dancing with a floor mannequin until a security guard moved us along. At my bank, I had pretended to have a shoulder holster, fast drawing my trusty 45, not to get any money, but rather, to get some of the people out of line. At a very large, classy retail store, we had run up to three different salespeople, with me literally shouting, "Where are the toys for two-year-old kids?" We had received three different answers from the surprised, foreign-sounding, temporary Christmas help. As I ran around doing these various bits, Linda had constantly broken up, muffling her laughter. Nothing spectacular happened, but it was fun.

As I related these homely events, Bertha got into it. She kept on telling me, "What a dynamite feller you must be." She began asking me if she could touch me. She asked in a way that indicated I would flip out if she did. A portion of me wanted to kid with her, grab her and say, "What's

Wednesday

a little physical contact between consenting adults?" Another part of me cringed; I almost began screaming, "Don't touch me. Don't touch me." Lillian saved the day by saying, "Come on, Bertha, leave him alone, you're embarrassing him." Thankfully, Bertha did leave me alone, although she continued to eye me as though I were fresh meat.

I was beginning to like both Lillian and Bertha more and more. No longer the chief perpetuators of a sinister plot to change me, they were simply two nice women in their thirties or forties, who had adjusted well to life on the ward.

That night, the three of us laughed well and long. I enjoyed being the center of attention, recounting my past adventures. Prodded, I even began telling them about some of my first impressions of the ward. Before I got very far, Lillian remarked about how cute I had been, throwing all of my clothes into the garbage my first day on the ward. I weakly smiled and let it pass, as I had no idea what she was talking about, although a brief movie of my Mr. Clean routine traveled through my head. Before I could go on or get into any of my paranoia, Bertha asked me if I could remember my first night on the ward when we had played cards. I said, "Sure," but involuntarily shuddered. Although I could dimly recall playing cards with her, the episode had been too close and too psychedelic to remember well. I wasn't ready for another similar experience. She just got shy and remarked that I had been pretty well gone that night. We were even able to laugh about it.

It was getting late. The excitement of talking and laughing about the past was dwindling. The conversation was getting too close for comfort. Time to go to bed. I excused myself and left them there.

On the way to my room, I had a brief shock. They wheeled in a stretcher with a girl in her late teens on it. She appeared weak, helpless, crippled, and in pain. She wore glasses. Ah yes, of course. It was poor, little Miss Glasses. They had gotten her. It was a shame, as she had seemed nice enough. I wasn't able to dwell on it. The nurse quickly wheeled her by me, with the two of them disappearing into one of the rooms. Just as quickly, any thought of her was forgotten. I would find out the next

The Change Center

day that except for the glasses, the new patient did not look at all like the nurse I had dubbed Miss Glasses. There had been a microsecond of despair. I may be getting better, but I certainly wasn't well.

The end of my conversation with Bertha and Lillian, and seeing the new patient rolled by me, had been psychological shocks to my system. They were slight, brief shocks. Physically, I was experiencing a growing shakiness. Despite this, I was able to sleep well that night. My paranoia about the secret doings on the ward was slowly dissipating. My fantasy of being a helpless victim, subject to the dissolution and destruction of my identity by some hidden master or secret power, was abating. I was getting better.

Thus ended my fifth day on the ward.

THURSDAY

After breakfast and morning clean-up, I found several sports magazines and took them to my room. Lying in bed, I began reading them. Although a way to pass the time, it was more than that. I was actually reading them. No longer a helpless scanner of the written word, I was attempting to assimilate the new information. I was able to recall memories of teams and players, comparing my memories to the latest information. Oh, so and so is really on a hot streak. Rather than flipping out, I was able to accept that a given team or player was actually doing significantly better or worse than they had in the past. I went so far as to read the standings, go on to an article, and then, the magazine closed, try to recall which teams were in what place in the standings. I would then check my memory. I was slowly working myself back, regaining my lost recall and retention skills. I became totally absorbed in my reading.

She was a surprise, popping in on me. The social worker was back. During our first meeting, we had talked about insurance. I had told her I had an old hospitalization policy with a minimal daily benefit. It was even worse, as the benefit was about a third of what I thought it was. Having quit work to return to school, I did not have any regular health insurance. As I was getting better, the real world would begin to impinge upon my consciousness. Rather than paranoid fear, there would be a realistic worry. Paying for the hospital and doctor would put a serious dent in my savings.

She greeted me with a cheerful, "Hi. How are you?" She seemed to be glad to see me. I was certainly glad to see her. She had some forms and release papers for me to sign. She had caught me by surprise, while I was

Thursday

in deep concentration. It was a little difficult for me to switch gears. I half-heartedly attempted to scan the forms, while she explained to me what they were about. She indicated where I was supposed to sign the form. Dubious, unsure of myself, yet trusting her, I signed it in the indicated place.

"Okay. Good. Now then, you also have to sign it here."

Oooops. Oh no. I knew what was happening. I was signing away my identity. First, I had to sign the form for the old me. Now, I had to sign it for the new, still shaky me. I stopped. I began shouting, "I know what you're doing; I know what you're trying to do."

My sudden anger and shouting surprised her. Startled, she just looked at me, not knowing what to make of my angry resistance. She tried to reassure me. I would not have anything to do with it. On the one hand, I knew I was being squeezed. On the other hand, I also knew she didn't know anything about it. It was *them*. I began fighting with myself, trying to bring myself under control. She was so very nice. Our first meeting had been so very good. It had been a sane and rational rock in a sea of confusion and disorientation. Now, I was frightening her.

She mentioned my mother. It was either that they would notify her or my mother had agreed to something. My mother? Ah, here was something. They had slipped up. "The hospital has no way of knowing who my mother is. None of my identification has her name on it. Her last name's different than mine." Hah. Let them try to cover this error up.

I give her credit. Although new at the game, she did well. "Look, I'll get your mother's name from the reception desk." Huh? Have they gone this far? At the fear in my eyes, the social worker continued with, "Look, they probably got her name and address from your admittance forms. You have to put down your closest relative." I became uncertain, as I didn't remember doing anything like that. It didn't dawn on me that Linda had filled out my admittance forms or that Dr. D. and the hospital must have known who my mother was, if she was coming to visit me in a couple of days. I mutely nodded acceptance of the social worker's proposal.

The Change Center

She nervously hurried off to the reception desk, high heels clicking across the linoleum. Gawd, she had beautiful legs. More importantly, I noticed she was not yet wearing those special, restrictive shoes. Good for her. Maybe there was hope for her, after all. I felt sorry I had upset her. I hadn't meant to let her know I was not as normal as I had seemed at our first meeting.

She was back almost immediately. She had a small slip of white paper with my mother's name written on it in a fine hand. I reluctantly signed the necessary forms. "It's okay. I know what's happening. It's okay, though." She left, probably a little shaken and confused by my behavior. I simply dismissed the whole thing. They had done it again. I returned to my sports magazines.

Later, although still weak, I felt normal. A nurse came up to me and said I would have to have my chest x-ray retaken. The first one had not come out. Sure. Of course, it hadn't come out. I had purposely moved at the last moment to confuse the Master Controller. This time, I was able to wear my own clothes and walk, not ride in a wheelchair. What was this all about?

On the elevator, the nurse and I were silent. I waited for the horror to start, but it didn't. Once on the first floor, she led me to a new, more interior, x-ray room. We didn't go by the hospital's main entrance with its crowded waiting rooms. There was no motion or commotion. Once at the x-ray room, a slim, white nurse took my x-ray in a very matter-of-fact manner. It was over in a couple of minutes.

On the way back to the ward, still silent, I wondered what had really happened the first time I had been taken for an x-ray. I had no idea then, nor do I now. The glue holding my rational, cognitive self together was still too fresh to handle the pressure of dwelling on any of my ward experiences. Enough was enough. I let any musings about the first x-ray slip through my mind. It was time to think about other things.

Later that day, I had another bout with physical therapy. Jack refused to go, throwing a temper tantrum. It was a bad morning for him. He was

Thursday

completely hyper and especially manic. He would spend some time in the padded observation room I had never seen. Someone mentioned it was at his own request. He needed to let off some steam; the isolated room was a good place to yell and shout and pound walls without disturbing anyone.

I ended up going to the exercises with Beth, Cynthia, and Jane. Jane was the new person admitted the previous night. The one with glasses. She had made a remarkable recovery. She seemed very together and normal. She had had a bad drug reaction. Attempting to go to sleep, trying to come down from the speed of diet pills, she had either taken too many sleeping pills or else, the synergistic effect of taking both the barbiturates and diet pills had flipped her into a very bad state. She was young, maybe 19 or so, wore glasses, and although plump, she didn't seem fat enough to have to worry about diet pills. She spent her time on the ward reading paperback books. I had seen her earlier in the television room. It was only while on the elevator that I connected her with the weak, groggy, helpless, new patient of the previous night. She only slightly resembled Miss Glasses of my Tuesday episode.

Going to the therapy room, Jane was in an animated mood. She kept on asking us what it would be like. Beth, buoyed by Jane's amicable energy, did not seem as upset by the impending workout as she had been previously. Cynthia simply stared into space, although she did not seem to be as withdrawn as usual. She even seemed to be able to attend to some of what Jane was saying. She was still not able to speak, however. When Jane asked her a direct question, she simply switched her gaze to the floor. I mumbled a few things, letting Jane engage Beth in a question-and-answer period. I continued to regard her a little strangely, but no, this wasn't Miss Glasses. Hmm. My Change theory was not necessarily so.

Entering the physical therapy room, I made sure to take a look into the side room. Now, it only contained an empty bed. As the physical therapist began leading us in our exercises, I was struck by the irony of the situation. Here I was, male, near thirty, lying on the linoleum floor of the physical therapy room, doing exercises with three teenage girls. Rather than experiencing psychedelic alarm, I felt kind of silly. The therapist would say things like, "Now girls, this is a good one for slimming down your hips." Remembering me, she would stop, look at me sheepishly and say, "Well, it's good for everyone." She took to saying things like, "Now girls, and let's not forget the gentleman, this next exercise..."

I was still hypersensitive to my environment. On my back on the floor, doing leg spreads, I could feel the girls around me. Their energy seemed to reach across to me. Was this, indeed, some kind of scheme to feminize me? The thought quickly passed as I concentrated on the exercises. I enjoyed them. It was good to stretch my stiff, unused muscles. Girl Scout atmosphere aside, it was fun.

The session was over all too soon. On the elevator, as we returned to the ward, Jane and Beth were all bubbly, going back and forth in bright, alive chatter, talking about this and that. Cynthia's eyes tried to follow their conversation; she even smiled occasionally. I felt like I was with a group of girls after gym class. I held my peace, not attempting to join their discussion.

That afternoon, I was once again in severe pain. I had a truss with the devil, fighting some invisible entity who seemed to be trying to break my body and mind. The pain was a thick, pervading crunchiness that came from deep inside of me. In some ways, it was a combination of the pain of Tuesday and the rubbery weakness of the day before. Both aspects were less intense. I tossed and turned, struggling with this deep, inner wrenching. The pain came at me in waves from within, rising and falling in both strength and sharpness. At its ebb, it was like having a dull toothache that came from my very innards.

First, I would be totally at its mercy. Then, I would be on top, almost in control. But no, the pain was too strong, too severe. I bit my pillow, dug my fingernails into the palms of my hands, and tried to talk myself through it, anything to shut off this god-awful pain. I cursed and struggled against the pain, thinking of it as something tangible, something other than myself. Nearly delirious, I tossed and turned, praying for peace, for rest, for sleep. For over half an hour, I muttered and cursed, tossing and turning, not willing to give in. I was determined. There would be no

Thursday

magic pills this time. Finally, without really knowing when, I collapsed into a deep sleep, still fighting the demon within.

They woke me up. I had a visitor. Dr. Dwayne, one of my professors and a major reason for my returning to graduate school, was here to see me. I felt different, somehow. The screaming crunchiness was gone. It was as though I had won the battle with myself. Having had a number of serious illnesses throughout my life, I recognized the feeling. It was as though my fever had finally broken. Looking back, I feel this was my major turning point during my ward experience. Although I had surfaced the previous day, this was the first time I would really seem to be myself. After the restless struggle against the pain within, it would now be a downward slide into the real world.

I was still a little weak and groggy from having been awakened. They let Dr. Dwayne meet with me in my room. He sat on a chair at the foot of my bed. Other than Linda and Liam, this was my first interaction with someone who I knew from the outside world. He appeared to have his clinical hat on. Could he be one of them? No. This was Dwayne. He was too together, too himself.

Dwayne is one of the nicest human beings I have ever known. Both he and his wife are just plain, good people. He was in his fifties, with a muscular, stocky build going to a softer pudginess. He wore glasses and was completely bald with any fringe shaved off. He is a quiet, attentive man, passive and gentle almost to a fault. He sat there, studying me. He seemed accepting of my situation. I was still his student, friend, and near-peer.

How I liked this man. Although I had just returned to school the previous month, after a five-quarter absence, he had treated me as if I had just left the previous day. When I had expressed some problems and doubts about returning, he showed me some things I had written that first time around. I had been asked to assess the psychology program. I had made a number of recommendations. He had been very impressed. I was impressed that over a year later, he still had my paper and used it as a reference.

The Change Center

Talking to me in his typically soft-spoken manner, he asked me how I was doing. He told me Dr. D. was a good friend of his and an excellent doctor. Although I disagreed with his assessment, I had never really given Dr. D. a chance after our first, muddled interaction. Also, Dwayne tended to think highly of almost everybody. He mentioned his surprise at my missing those classes and also, my not showing up to administer some intelligence tests I had been scheduled to give. As in our brief phone conversation, he reiterated that he knew how responsible I was and not the sort of person who didn't fulfill my obligations.

I explained to him how I had just finished fighting the devil and how I thought I would be okay from here on out. He was very sympathetic to my condition. He urged me to write about my experiences, especially in light of my training and professional inclinations. We had a good talk. He mentioned that he would be out of town that weekend for a Reserve meeting; but that if I ever needed him for anything, I should be sure to look him up and feel free to ask for his assistance. He told me not to worry about trying to finish that quarter of school or about any other problems. I should spend my time and energy on getting well.

Jack, together with some of the other patients and some of the staff, continually eyeballed us. Who was this new visitor, allowed to meet with me in my room during non-visiting hours?

On the ward, this was an event. After wandering back and forth a couple of times in the hall, Jack barged in on us. Dwayne was polite and attentive to Jack's need for attention. Jack asked a few questions, and then started to dominate Dwayne's time, centering the attention on himself. Dwayne was good. Politely and without rancor, he got Jack out of the conversation and then, out of the room.

Dwayne did not seem at all concerned about my present circumstances or future competence. When I was ready to resume my academic training, there would be someone in my corner. He stayed for some 30 to 45 minutes. We ended up talking about the trivia of graduate school and daily life. By the time he left, I felt quite well and, for the first time while on the ward, even sure of myself. That far-away spark of hope was

Thursday

beginning to flicker too brightly for me to ignore. Maybe, just maybe, I was going to make it.

The rest of the day passed, as all must. For the most part, it was unremarkable. Time was spent in boredom and weakness. I played some cards with Bill. This brief interlude of activity was ended prematurely, as he had to quit in the middle of a game due to his hip hurting him too much. I watched some television, read a little, and talked to this patient and that nurse. I wandered around, thought a little (but not too much), and waited. There was always the waiting. Except for meals, the major ward activity was waiting.

In short, my time on the ward was degenerating into bored waiting. No longer tripping into mind-blowing panic, I was now able to put up with my diminishing physical pain, while slowly regaining my strength and memory. I was also learning some new things, namely, boredom and patience. The only real times, the only time of being completely in the here and now, was when Linda and Liam came to visit me.

Visiting hours finally approached. As always, the waiting increased in intensity. Linda and Liam were coming: my love and my compatriot. I would get to see them once again. Nervous anticipation. Uneven waiting. As the visitors flooded in, I anxiously looked for my two loved ones. Would they be late again?

Bojangles interrupted my anxious waiting. It was time for my medication. I had just finished taking it when they were there. It was so good to see them. Hugs and greetings accomplished, we looked for a place to sit down.

Feeling better, I wanted to share my loved ones with the other patients. This was a familiar behavioral pattern. I have always prided myself on having a large number of really interesting, diversified friends. I have always tried to get these quite different people together, hoping they would enjoy each other as much as I enjoyed each of them. It usually didn't work. This would prove to be especially true on the ward.

The Change Center

Come on. I'd like the two of you to meet some of the people I've met on the ward. We first went into the kitchenette. Elaine and her husband were there. There was a try at small talk. When I went to introduce Liam and Linda, I realized I didn't know Elaine's name. I don't think she knew my name. Patients didn't wear nametags. It was kind of sticky. Social amenities aside, we finally got all of the names straight. Liam, Linda, and I sat down with them. It was difficult making conversation, as we didn't really have anything in common. I realized my visit, the two hours of animated conversation with Linda and Liam, was being wasted.

We quickly excused ourselves and got out of there. The adjoining television sitting room was crowded with patients and visitors. We sat down at the one empty table. Beth was at a nearby table, playing scrabble with Jerry. She had not been getting any visitors lately. The previous night, at the coffee clutch, when Bertha had asked me about my two visitors, I had gone on and on about how great they were. Beth had been very downcast, saying she wished she had friends like that. I had told her I would have her meet my two friends. She had quickly cut off the conversation, "Oh no. That's okay. They're your friends." Now, seeing her, I tried to get her attention. When I finally caught her eye, she quickly looked away. She was too shy to meet them. I felt so bad for Beth, as she was so cute and fragile. I really felt a need to help her somehow.

I was still trying to get Beth's attention, when I found out from Linda that the incredible rumor was true. My mother and sister were indeed coming. She had talked to them. Depending on travel arrangements, they would either be there the next night or on Saturday. If everything went well, they would be able to visit me the next night. Although neither of us was able to come right out and definitely say I would be released into their custody, it did look as if I would be able to go home with them. The full importance and excitement of escaping the ward still didn't completely register on me. I was excited by the thought of my family's imminent arrival.

Our visit was a little scattered. I was still distracted by not having them meet Beth and by the aborted interaction with Elaine and her husband.

Thursday

Also, I was having a difficult time listening to Linda and absorbing the details of the impending visit. Who would pick them up at the airport? Where would they stay? This was beyond me. It was difficult enough to understand they were coming. My attempt at trying to follow all of this information was quickly put aside. Our meeting became centered in the immediate.

Simply, my face began pulling to the side. No longer attending to what Linda was saying, I tried to tell them about it. My face was bunching up on the left side in a spasm of muscle and nerve contraction. I could only speak, barely and with effort, through the right side of my mouth. I didn't have to tell them about it. They could see it. They looked at me with shocked dismay.

"Oh my god, are you okay? Has this happened before? What can we do for you?"

Liam was the first to get himself together. He told me to hold on. He ran and got Bojangles. Trying to tell Bo about it, Liam and Linda were both talking at once, babbling, "Look at this. Something's the matter with him. Look how his face is bunching to the side. What can we do about it?" Bo just looked at me, not knowing what to do. "Has this happened before? Does it hurt? How does it feel?"

Speaking out of the right side of my mouth, I was able to tell him this was the first time it happened, that it hurt, and I didn't know what to do. It must be the medication. He just continued to look at me, his mouth slightly open. With effort, using both my hands and my facial muscles, I was able to pull the bunching slightly back. It didn't get worse. With effort, I was able to hold it back somewhat. Bo just kept on looking at me. Finally, he came up with, "It should be okay. It should pass. Just keep trying to talk. It'll be okay." With this monumental advice, he left us sitting there.

The rest of my visit with Liam and Linda was spent in putting down Bojangles and the rest of the staff as well as ongoing concern about my frozen face. Liam was the most vocal. He flat out stated there was something wrong with some of the staff. They just seemed to act strange. Bojangles gave him the willies; Liam just plain didn't like him. He mentioned how some of the staff would watch the three of us, looking at us rather oddly. It was as though they were paranoid or hiding something. Plain and simple, they were just strange. Right on, brother.

My reality base was Liam; although not able to put his finger on it exactly, he also sensed something not exactly kosher, up to snuff, or on par with the staff. Although somewhat subtle, there was something in the actions of some of the staff, something in their behavior not quite right. Liam only reinforced my earlier impressions. Perhaps there had been more of a basis for my scattered self to indulge in all of those paranoid delusions than just my own projected fears.

Liam wouldn't let it go. He began putting Dr. D. down. "Ya know, your doctor is kind of strange too. Dr. D., the few times I've been able to talk to him, just insists you've been on drugs for a long time. I keep telling him that's not true, but he won't listen to me."

To my surprise, I found myself defending Dr. D. "Yeah, I know, Liam, but I did tell him I was on drugs. It seemed easier to explain my behavior. I guess I really was into some kind of acid residual or something."

"Yeah, I know, you mentioned that. He still acts kind of strange. I don't know about the staff here."

It's kind of funny, but Liam, during my ward stay, always seemed to have the right kind of words for me. Earlier, when I was so scattered, he had been able to listen to me. Then, he had been able to recast my paranoia and hallucinations into a world to which I could relate, to the occasional bad trips, and scattered vibes of my acid days. He had been able to join me and laugh with and at me when I had been high on those tranquillizers. Now, he was able to reinforce some of my suspicions about the staff.

Although I agreed with what he said, I also found myself defending some of the other staff, pointing out they were only human. After all, they were my staff.

Thursday

By the time Liam and Linda left, I was doing much better, although the left side of my face was still stiff and numb. As per usual, I would forget to mention it to Dr. D. the next day. I guess Bojangles just forgot about the incident, as it was never mentioned again. I was becoming increasingly suspicious of my medication.

The staff. I just don't know anymore. There were so many of them. Other than Dr. D., Liam only interacted with the after-hours night staff. I had originally thought of them to be interns. I believe they were aides. Perhaps they had little or no training. Maybe they were just slow people attempting to interact with us crazies.

The aides I remember include Bojangles, Danny, Mr. Sam, Jerry, and Miss Glasses (seen only on Tuesday). Bojangles and Danny were a little strange. Perhaps they were dipping into the medical supplies. In a way, they were ward bosses during their shifts and had more interaction with the patients than the professional staff did. I had had a dimly remembered interaction with Danny while almost totally spun out on one of those first days I spent on the ward. There were three of us standing at the reception desk. The third person wore glasses. Danny was playing with our heads. He had said something to the effect that we could probably all get off of the ward and could get that big, old ward door to just open, if we just had five eyes, or was it, "ayes?". I snapped to attention, as the number five was so important to me. I tried to figure out his riddle as there were three "ayes" and six or eight eyes, depending on whether or not you counted the glasses. He caught me counting and started in on me, "My, my, aren't we literal. Yes, sir, we're so literal I just guess we can't do it." Innocuous enough, perhaps. Except for the simple fact, I remember becoming disoriented, needing to get away from the desk as quickly as I could. What was going on?

Mr. Sam was affable enough, with his constant, "Mr. Blazek, sir." I always pictured him as slipping off to have a beer, although it was probably coffee. He loved to run errands and was always disappearing off of the ward. Jerry appeared deeply sensitive with intelligent eyes. Other than my catching him watching me, even staring at me in an odd manner, he seemed okay. My only remembered interaction with him was the first day I was on the ward.

Mrs. H. and Mrs. B. were two competent, white day nurses. They were only there from 9 to 5 on Monday through Friday. They seemed to be more wrapped up in the administrivia of ward life than any kind of patient interaction. Mrs. U. seemed nice enough, although other than her nicely rounded body and a couple of meaningful episodes, I only remember her with her head cocked in quizzical amazement. Mrs. S. had "head nurse" on her nametag. I would see her the next day. Other than that, I only remember her from the group therapy meeting earlier in the week and her being "programmed." I never spoke to her or interacted with her.

There were a plethora of black nurses. They seemed to come and go, with most of them weekend or odd-shift staff. Except for the very nice one who was always with Mrs. X and the heavy set one who had helped me by finding the Bible for me, I don't remember them.

The only doctor I remember seeing was Dr. D. While I don't think he could have been the doctor for all of the patients on the ward, I don't remember seeing any other doctors on the floor. Since they would probably meet with their patients in the stereo sitting room or the conference room across the hall from it, both of which were right by the ward entrance, it would have been easy for me to miss them.

On that first weekend, probably Sunday, there had been a group of important-looking men in suits and ties who visited the ward. I took them to be hospital administrators. They could have been doctors. Whatever the case, they had been given the grand tour with the staff deferring to them. One of them turned to me and asked me how I was being treated. In my most weakened, paranoid state, I had almost told him what an evil place this was and how he should run for his life, but I fell into a movie I had seen about women in prison. They had been horribly mistreated. A well-dressed visitor had approached a new prisoner. He had asked her how she was being treated. She had told him the truth about her terrible mistreatment. It turned out that he was one of the chief perpetuators of

Friday

the prisoners' mistreatment. Her situation became much worse after she tried to tell him about her predicament. In the moment that it took for me to answer him, I had raced through the entire movie and had ended up mumbling, "Okay, sir." Satisfied, he had gone on with the tour.

Actually, after that first weekend, I hadn't had much interaction with any of the staff. I was lucky. No one was cruel. The constant shift changes, together with the number of staff needed to cover the ward for 24 hours a day, resulted in a large number of dimly remembered people who always seemed to be coming and going. One sadist could have caused a considerable amount of damage to the other patients and me.

That night, I was a passive participant for only part of the coffee clutch. I sat around for a while. The stiffness in my face remained, so I was not up to talking very much. Thankfully, the bunching of tissue had stopped. Also, I was preoccupied with thoughts that I was going to go home. I listened to everyone for a while and then excused myself and went to bed early.

I was shaky and nervous. My body became incredibly tense, although no new horrors or head games appeared. I was simply intent on getting well, returning to the outside world and society. The stiffness in my face slowly dissipated.

Thus ended my sixth day on the ward.

FRIDAY

I woke up Friday morning feeling fine, feeling good, and feeling better than ever. Each day, I was becoming increasingly together. Although still shaky, with diminished faculties, I was now a person who I could remember, no longer living in a completely strange and alien world. In celebration, I wrote the following. It was the last piece of writing I did while confined to the ward.

Well, I'm back—just a little shaky. Thank you, Lord, for making me whole! Thank you forever & ever. God is good to those with the will to live. May I be okay & not continually screw up.

May life be good to my friends. God bless you Linda, & Liam. God bless mom & family. May I get better & better & may I be able to repay the good karma laid on me. Thank you.

Friday x/xx/xx

After breakfast, I sat chatting with Bertha. We filled out our menus. Each day, we would receive a small menu, making our food choices for dinner, supper, and the next day's breakfast. On my first day on the ward, the staff must have filled it out for me. On Sunday, I had simply stared at it. Bertha had filled it out for me. On the following days, I had filled it out with some difficulty. At first, I had had a fogged-in head, unable to concentrate on my choices. Choosing my meals had been a major decision-making process. Then, beset by physical difficulties, with little fine finger dexterity, I had some trouble making the correct entries. I remember the pain-staking slowness of trying to move the pencil to the correct boxes. On Friday, I quickly filled the menu out. It was no problem, whatsoever.

Friday

I joked with Bertha. "You know, up north, we call it lunch. Dinner is another word for supper. The only time you have dinner during the day is on Sunday." I crossed out the word "dinner," and wrote in "lunch." At the bottom of the menu, I wrote, "(us Northerners)." Bertha got a big kick out of it. She took our menus and gave them to one of the staff.

We continued to chat, waiting to go to another group therapy meeting. I told her about my reactions to the first one, about how, in order to liven things up, I had had an urge to jump up and shout, "I'm a CIA agent, and you're all under arrest for not complying with the Confession II Act." She got an even bigger kick out of that, going on about what a "dynamite feller" I was.

We walked to the group therapy meeting together, continuing to talk and joke. We were both in good moods. She would go home that night, and if the incredible rumors were true, I would go home the next day.

Sitting down in the conference room, I found myself watching the other patients. Jane was a new group member. Bill, with his aching hip, was not there. Neither Lillian nor Elaine was there. Lillian and Elaine had also missed the first session. Either participation was voluntary, or else, the meeting was only for Dr. D's patients.

We just sat around. Once again, not much was happening, and there were no great revelations. Bertha began talking. As she talked, she shot me sidelong glances, watching me out of the side of her face, eyeing me both shyly and slyly. She recounted my preparation of the day's menu, going into detail about how I had crossed out "dinner" and wrote in "lunch." This started both Dr. D. and Mrs. S., the chief nurse, talking. They brought up other north-south differences. Dr. D. watched me closely as he drawled out a couple of examples of regional differences, almost as if to say he could also follow this line of reasoning.

I squirmed in my seat, nodding politely as he and Mrs. S. talked. For the most part, the other patients sat passive and unimpressed. Although I usually liked being the center of attention, I always felt uncomfortable

The Change Center

around Dr. D. My only hope was I would appear sane and normal. He had my life in his hands.

North-south differences dismissed, everyone continued to sit around, waiting for someone to say something. Bertha had been a momentary hit. She once again assumed center stage. Having found her tongue, she began telling everyone how I wanted to play secret agent at the last group therapy session. She went into detail, repeating everything I had told her, going on and on, even embellishing the whole thing. I cringed.

I wanted to jump in and tell everyone it had only been a bit, a joke, something to break up the monotony. Look, Dr. D., I'm okay; I'm not really a paranoid schizophrenic. I just kept swallowing, looking at my feet, hoping she would run out of words and everything would be okay.

Dr. D. went professional, drawing himself up, saying, "I'm sure I've done nothing in which the CIA would take an interest." Ignoring Bertha, he kept staring at me. I just sat there, smiling weakly. Bertha, you're a dead woman. Please be quiet. Please shut up.

Although Dr. D. didn't seem at all amused, he thankfully didn't take it seriously enough to enter into some kind of discussion with me about paranoia. He still seemed bored in his matter-of-fact manner. I was starting to sweat and only hoped for all of this to be over. Soon.

Thank goodness for Jane. She started to talk. She was quite verbal, going into detail about how she hadn't been able to sleep and hadn't been eating well. This, combined with the sleeping pills she took, had caused her to flip out. She took over the session, with both Dr. D. and Mrs. S. appearing to be interested and supportive.

Relieved to no longer be the focus of the meeting, I missed most of it. I was thinking about other things, mostly humor. I had gone full circle so very quickly. As small children, learning so many new things, we are forced to focus on the immediate. As adults, many of us are distracted by the past or future, thinking about other things while going through the motions of living. I had realized the greater part of my adult life was spent in thinking, while I did other things. Dwelling on my thoughts, I would

Friday

put up with my environment, not particularly noticing what I was eating or otherwise doing. Drugs had changed that. The new perceptions had forced me to center my attention on the present. While living in the present is a desirable goal, my method of doing it had proven counterproductive.

While most of us are multi-channeled, able to hold more than one train of thought at a time, it's amazing what barren lives, so many of us trick ourselves into living. During conversations, we rehearse what we're going to say rather than really attending to and listening to what others say. And then, there is waiting. At work, we wait for lunch or quitting time. On weekdays, we wait for weekends. During our normal, day-to-day lives, we wait for vacations or special events. Finally, some of us realize we have spent a major portion of our lives not attending to what was really going on. We have spent our lives anticipating the future or worrying about both the past and future, without remembering to enjoy and live in the present.

While I can no longer recommend drugs of any kind (I still distrust aspirin), I have also spent a considerable amount of time learning meditation techniques and other disciplines to enable myself to center in the present. "If you live in the present, you live forever." To see the kingdom of heaven, each of us must become as a small child, absorbed in the moment with each experience a new source of wonder. If we attend to the moments of our lives, centered in the present, time becomes a myth.

Waking up on the ward, shattered, with no memory, I had been forced to live in a present I didn't understand. It had been a fearful hell, filled with sensory aberrations, physical pain, weakness, and disorientation. In self-defense, I had been forced to delve deep inside myself, resurrecting a former, more capable me. Gaining strength, I had been forced to continue to live in the present, as I did not have complete control of my thoughts or my body. Simple things required my complete attention. Now, in less than a week, I was able to go multi-channel, sitting in a group therapy session, half-listening, while attending to other things.

The pain of the ward experience taught me what so many of us exposed to pain and tragedy have learned: we may need screens to protect us from

The Change Center

the present. The ego defense mechanisms of Psychology 101 are valid and necessary. I had already gone a step further, falling into habitual modes of behavior, putting up with my environment while thinking about other things. Friday would be taken up in waiting for release. My eventual freedom would be a diminished one, restricted by haunting memories of the past. It would be quite some time before I would be able to center in a present filled with wonder.

I'm sure Jane's story was an interesting one, deserving of my attention. Instead, my head was filled with thoughts about humor. Expanding on my earlier insights, I began trying to develop a theory about humor and its role in helping psychotics and severe neurotics to cope with their worlds. I was reminded about how the aides never seemed to know when to laugh during the coffee clutches. I was tired of the overly serious professionals. A good joke would do wonders for all concerned. My thoughts and ideas about humor are somewhat inconsequential. They were never fully developed. The process or the way I began thinking, cannot be dismissed so easily. In less than a week, I was already becoming immersed in a familiar way of thinking. I was, indeed, getting better.

Dr. D. met with me after the group session. It was true. I was going to go home. My family would be there the next day. I agreed with Dr. D., that having experienced a brief but severe, disabling episode, it would be best for me to be released in their custody, and return to Chicago and my familiar surroundings. Although I would have agreed to anything to be released (yes, of course, I can walk on water), it did seem like a sensible solution.

I remained tight but calm with Dr. D., concentrating on his every word, nodding and agreeing with everything he said. I said, "Thank you," several times. Although a small portion of me started to bubble into manic joy, I just sat there, nodding, trying to absorb the wonder of it all. I was going home.

After meeting with him, I walked around in a daze. I was going to go home. For the most part, the rest of the day was spent waiting. The day was long. It went on forever. It was a nervous, hyper, anticipatory,

Friday

sweating like a pig, endless day of waiting. Yet, it was not the psychedelic infinity of the previous weekend.

Restless, I roamed the ward, talking to the nurses, to the patients, to anyone who could help pass the time. I ran into Lillian. She was able to share my excitement at going home. "See, and you kept on saying you were never going to leave; you would never be able to go home. Bertha is going home tonight. She's getting her hair done now. She'll be so excited you're going to go home." I had a passing thought of regret. The ward would be a different place for Lillian, with both Bertha and myself gone. It was a very passing thought I never verbalized. I was too excited. I was going home.

Lillian, and later, Bertha, were the only two patients I talked to about my being able to go home. I wanted to go around and shake hands with some of the others, especially Jack and Beth, say something witty, something with some closure to it. But what was there to say? I was going to go home; they weren't. Lillian and Bertha would mention it. "See, he's going home." The other patients would just space. There really wasn't anything to say. I remember Jack's, "I wish I could go home," and Beth's forlorn, "I'm just not ready to leave."

The anticipatory excitement of going home was almost too much for me, draining me of what little energy I had. It was difficult sitting around the television room. On the one hand, I couldn't sit still. On the other hand, I was filled with empathy for the other patients. I didn't know what to do for them, as they really couldn't share my joy. Growing weaker, I retreated to my room. I tried to read. I would do anything to pass the time. When would they be here? When could I leave?

I had a surprise visitor. Dr. Brian, another one of my professors, came to visit me. He was a welcome diversion. Brian was Sonia's husband. If I had been more together, I would have told him about Mrs. H., even introduced him to her. Maybe we could have compared a picture of his wife to her, to see if there was a resemblance. I was better, but still not well enough for those kinds of mental gymnastics.

The Change Center

Dr. Brian was nervous. Very. We met in my room with him sitting on a chair at the foot of my bed, just as Dwayne had done. While Dwayne had cloaked himself in his professional, clinical cloth of calm, passive acceptance, Brian kept on grinning, looking as though he wanted to break into wild laughter. As people went by in the hall, his head would jerk from side to side. He was a School Psychologist, with an emphasis on theories of learning. Not being a Clinical Psychologist, he was in a strange environment. How I appreciated his visit. It must have been a difficult thing for him to do.

Jack, never losing a chance, once again butted in on my visit. Brian became even more nervous, just smiling, and then, completely ignoring Jack. We both ignored Jack, with me finally asking him to leave. Brian went through all kinds of gyrations, cocking his head, screwing up his eyes, nodding after Jack as he left. I simply nodded, saying, "Yeah, Jack has some problems."

We talked mostly small talk. Brian was out of his depth. He had been the first person I had met when I had returned to campus for my second try at that elusive doctorate. I had seen him from a couple of blocks away and had yelled at him, running toward him, finally getting his attention. He had been surprised to see me and had asked me what I was doing there. When I told him, I was going to give graduate school another attempt, he became ebullient. He had said, "Okay. That's it. You don't deserve it, but you've got your fellowship back, as of now." I replied, "Hell, I didn't deserve it the first time, but I accept."

He had immediately tried to enlist me in some of his projects, telling me that with some work, I could catch my class by June. Even though I had been gone five quarters, he told me I was bright enough to do my thesis while taking courses, and there was even a chance I could graduate with the rest of my class. Hah. Little did he know I was no longer the wunderkind I was the first time I returned to graduate school. Later, he would show me a half-finished research project that could serve as my master's thesis. I became dizzy and disoriented. The notes he gave me were in my handwriting. Just as Dwayne had saved a file of my previous

Friday

work (a requested critique of the School Psychology program from a graduate student's point of view), Brian had also saved a file of mine. This file was regarding a research project I had started with some other graduate students for one of his classes. When I had left school the first time, I returned to a manager's position in Chicago. All of my files for the projects I had been working on over a year earlier had been neatly boxed and saved. First Chicago, then Dwayne, and then Brian ...

I began thinking it was my karma to go through life, forced to return to all of the places I had been, forced to complete all of the things I had started. Even today, I have such regret. How I wish I could have fulfilled Brian and Dwayne's expectations of me. How I wish I could have fulfilled my own expectations of myself.

Sitting there, Brian was wearing a fur-lined coat almost as out of place in Florida as my parka was. That's what I remember the most about his visit: Brian sitting there, too nervous to take his coat off, constantly smiling. It was good to visit with him, to talk about the other students and life in general. It was nice of him to come.

After he left, I thought about him. He was kind of a card. Liam and I had always joked about him. Still, he has given me two of my fondest memories. We had had a seminar on attribution theory. There was only a handful of us in the class. We met at his house, sitting in a circle on the floor. He had put a couple of six-packs of beer, a pitcher of lemonade, and some pretzels in the center of the circle. "Okay, help yourself. The purpose of this seminar is to explore how we think." Having left business as a senior analyst, forced to endure the low-life status of being a first-year graduate student, I was filled with thanks. I had finally arrived. This is what I had always imagined advanced study in psychology to be. A group of us, treated as adults, were going to explore the processes of the human mind.

My second memory is also related to how we think. Between classes, a group of us had been walking around campus. Brian's little daughter had been talking to some flowers and a tree, saying everything that came into her head. One of the other students had mused about what kind of

The Change Center

society we would have, if everyone did that, even as adults. Brian had replied, "Yeah. Some people call it thinking. We just don't do it out loud."

That afternoon, we had a special treat. There was an excursion to another part of the hospital. We were going to be able to go and see a movie. Well, sort of. Indicative of my new status and growing wellness, a nurse explained that my going with the group was optional. I quickly agreed to go. I would do anything to pass the time, anything to get off of the ward.

Mrs. S. and another nurse accompanied us. We were a motley crew. Dressed in the blue, ward outfits, not able to wear our street clothes, we all looked a little worse than normal, as we straggled through the halls. When we got to the showing room, we sat together, part of a larger group of staff and patients. People eyed us, quickly looking away. A young male and female were showing the films. I took them to be graduate students, probably getting advanced degrees in social work. They seemed nice enough, although they couldn't meet my eyes or those of the other ward patients. I guess they had been warned the crazies were coming.

The films were about Florida. They appeared to be "fun in the sun" promotional films. Once again, as with physical therapy, I was struck by the irony of my situation. I looked over the people in the room. The ward patients sat quietly, slumped and tired looking. The other viewers appeared to be aware of us, but avoided us by concentrating on the film. Mrs. S. and the other nurse were like mother hens, first herding us into our seats and then watching over us. The graduate student running the projector had some initial trouble getting it started. He explained what the film was about, avoiding our eyes as a couple of us turned and watched him.

My attention wandered back and forth, from the film of beautiful young people splashing in a swimming pool, to those of us watching it. A day or two earlier, I would have probably sat there softly crying, filled with an intense desire to get outside and join the people in the film. Now, knowing I was going home, I was struck by how different these young, healthy bodies appeared compared to us beaten down, slumped

Friday

over patients. And here I was, one of the beaten-down patients. Although I had cleaned up my act while on the ward, I was as low life as any other patient.

The rest of my attention was centered on my body. I was nervous and tense, still reacting to my medication. Neither the pain nor the rubbery feeling was as intense as the last few days. It was more as though emery cloth were being rubbed on the inside of my bones. Not sharp or anywhere near as painful as the bone-crunching of the last few days, it was still uncomfortable. I tensed myself against it, hoping only that it wouldn't get any worse and I wouldn't do anything which would embarrass me in front of all these people. I was too close to going home to go ballistic and appear abnormal.

The movies were finished without incident. None of us flipped out or otherwise made a commotion. We straggled back to the ward. How different we appeared, first contrasted to the other patients and then, even more so, to the bright, healthy people in the film.

I saw Bertha for the last time later that afternoon. She looked good. She was wearing a new dress and freshly applied makeup and sported a tightly coiffed, new hairdo. I told her how good she looked. She became even happier and started flirting with me, touching my arm and shoulder. Her game playing was okay. I was well enough that I didn't flinch at her touch. She was as happy for me as I was for her. We talked for a little bit; then, she rushed off to finish her packing.

It was time for supper. Just as I was going to get my tray, a nurse came up to me and told me someone was there to see me. Since it wasn't visiting hours, they wouldn't let him in to see me. I could say hello to him at the ward entrance. It was Ben. He was a fellow graduate student and a good friend. We had become close my first time around at graduate school. We had been the two old guys, my 27 to his 30, both of us redoing our lives to get a doctorate. After a rough start, almost not making it the first quarter (he received two "Cs," a third one, and he would have been dropped from the program), he had done well. He would go on to become

202

The Change Center

the first graduate student to receive a dual doctorate in School Psychology and in Clinical Psychology.

I had spent many hours tutoring him in statistics (he still received a C after all was said and done) and had argued on his behalf with the team of professors who taught the Advanced Learning class (they had averaged his grades on the three segments of the course two of which he had passed, treating them as a ratio scale which was a no-no, but they would not change his grade from a C). He barely scraped out a B on the second required course in statistics and was then home-free as the clinical work was easy for him. There had been my promise and his perseverance. Thankfully, one of us made it.

It was good to see him. He was a deeply serious, sensitive human being. His dad's emotional problems and breakdown had been a major reason for him to obtain a doctorate in the helping sciences. His wife was a treasure. I had thought she was one of the nurses at the emergency entrance when I was admitted. We talked quickly as I could only see him for a minute. We talked first through the partially open door and then, with an aide closing it, through a glass window. He wished me well and told me how surprised and sorry he had been when Dwayne had told him about what had happened to me.

Like the fool I was, caught up in only my own problems, I told him I now knew what his father had gone through. At the look of deep pain and sadness on his face, I immediately regretted my words. We talked for only a few minutes. I would never see him again.

I walked back to the television sitting room, feeling good about seeing him, but upset by my words and his reaction to them. I would have to stop my total self-absorption and begin to look beyond myself and remember the feelings of others.

My tray of food was waiting for me. It was overflowing. As a child, I had been admonished to eat all of my food and to clean my plate. Almost always, even when the food was mediocre, or an over-bearing hostess had forced too much on me, I would still try to finish whatever I have been

Friday

given. More than just childhood training, I believe food to be precious, even sacred. It certainly shouldn't be wasted. Jack, throwing a tantrum, or just in one of his ornery moods, would occasionally waste a whole plate of food. I would invariably cringe.

I stared at the food. Surely, I didn't order all of this. I looked around to see if anyone was playing a trick on me. No, all of the other patients had their own food and were intently eating. Oh, well. I dug in. Making a valiant effort, there was just too much. I ate most of it. I even tried to give a dessert or two away, although no one else wanted anything.

After supper, I sat there, stuffed. Lillian came by, a sneaky grin on her face. She asked me how my supper had been. I answered, "Fine," still not catching on. She kept on hanging around, kept on hinting about the food. Finally, it dawned on me. "Well, there was an awful lot of it. I couldn't finish it." She burst out laughing. Bertha had done it. That morning, she had changed my menu, adding all kinds of things.

Oh boy. Wait until I see her. I now owed her double. First of all, she had told all those stories about me at the group therapy meeting. Then, she had fooled around with my supper order. I had told her about my needing to finish my food and about how upset I would get when Jack would waste his. She had been too busy and distracted, too happy, for me to mention the group meeting when I had seen her before supper. Now, I would get even with her. Lillian told me I might still be able to catch her. I went looking for her. I missed her, though. She had already left.

When visiting hours finally arrived, Liam and Linda came in with a rush, all excited and happy. They looked good. Both of them were wearing clean clothes. Liam had carefully brushed his long, floppy hair. Linda, although she used it sparingly, had fresh makeup on. They looked as though they were going out some place.

Although I couldn't meet their high energy level, I felt good, just a little shaky. I had already taken my medication and was beginning to feel it. For some reason, early afternoon and mid-evening were my worst times regarding adverse reactions to the medication. While I have vivid

The Change Center

recollections of taking my medication in the early morning and right around visiting hours, I'm not sure if I also took it at midday. Although relatively mild, the evening reactions were immediate and noticeable. My early afternoon crunching (Tuesday, Wednesday, and to a lesser extent, Thursday) was either a delayed reaction, or else I was given medication three times a day, which seems more likely.

They had all kinds of news. Yes, my mother, sister, and brother-in-law were all coming. In fact, they would be there that night. Liam and Linda would have to leave early in order to pick them up at the airport. Yes, I was going to be released the following day. It was all arranged. My family would meet with Dr. D. on Saturday morning. I was definitely going home.

Oh boy. Excitement. And they were there to share it with me. Hugs and kisses. I was going home. Whew.

The three of us were all excited and bubbly. I kidded them about looking especially good for my family. They feigned surprise. "Hey, come on, we always look good." For the first time, the thought crossed my mind. I wondered at my mother's reaction to finding out Linda and I were living together. Oh well. We were adults. Both my mother and my sister thought Linda was the greatest. Hell, they must have already known about our living arrangements as Linda had been in constant phone contact with them.

Liam and Linda would probably take my family out to dinner. Everyone would probably stay at my apartment. It would all work out.

The rest of our visit was taken up with them asking about how I felt. No, the facial problems hadn't returned. I felt as good as I could under the circumstances.

The three of us kept on talking about anything which came to mind. We went over the impending visit, how I felt, and what Linda and Liam had been doing. It was a good time of shared happiness. It was as though they hated to leave. It was too good just to sit and talk and

Friday

touch. Surprisingly, I was the one who became worried about them being too late for the plane. I got up several times to check the clock over the reception desk as none of us wore watches. They kept on telling me not to worry about it. The airport was only some 10 or 15 minutes away, and planes were always late. I wasn't so sure.

Finally, I just let it go and settled down to enjoy their visit. All too soon, it was time for them to go. Time had switched on me. Instead of endless waiting for time to slowly pass, I now wanted every last possible second with them. Liam finally got caught up in not wanting to be late for the plane and said he and Linda had to go. I walked them to the exit. We all hugged each other one last time. And then, they were gone. With their departure, I was immediately let down. I was too excited just to sit around. The other patients still had visitors. I wandered around my room, quickly getting my things together. I didn't have much. Although Linda had constantly brought me something, the cigarettes and candy had been devoured. Most of my clothes had been used. It was simple enough to throw them in a bag. I carefully arranged my remaining clean clothes on one side of my closet. I arranged and accounted for all of my toilet articles. I even remembered to dig out the notes I had hidden. Well, there you have it. Five minutes of waiting were taken up in doing something. I did it a second time, burning up another couple of minutes.

Wander here. Sit there. Talk a bit. Join the coffee clutch as visiting hours ended. Tell Lillian about how I would be leaving the following day. I watched the other patients sit in their private worlds, spacing to who knows where, unable to share my joy. I felt some empathy with them and some sadness at getting better so quickly while they remained wherever they were.

But then I would space into the thrill of release. I could feel my growing nervousness and some discomfort. Disregard it. I was going home. I was leaving. No real closure. Who cares? I was going home. The hell with the present and all of this foolishness, I was going home. Come on, time, do a number. Let it be twelve hours later. Let me be free.

The Change Center

Eventually, it was time for sleep. Ah, sweet dreams. On the morrow, I would be out of here. Thank you all, each and everyone. May God bless us.

Thus ended my seventh and last day on the ward.

GETTING OUT

I was ready and waiting. My belongings were stacked neatly on my bed. I had gotten ready with care, shaving closely, brushing and combing my hair several times. I splashed cold water on my face more than once. There was nothing I could do about my deep, sunken eyes. Wandering around, I continually took deep breaths, remembering to breathe through my nose, trying my best to relax. I was sweating so badly after an hour of nervous pacing, I had to change my shirt. Linda and my family finally arrived. Linda was acting as a tour guide, leading the group. My sister followed her, holding my mother, helping her to walk. My brother-in-law, Tom, was in the background, bringing up the rear. Linda was the first to see me, exclaiming, "Oh, there he is. There he is."

Oh, how I remember the fearful look of concern and compassion in my mother's eyes. It's funny. Except for Linda and Liam, no one could look me in the eye. Now, I had trouble looking my family in the eye. I broke eye contact with my mother. My attention centered on her feet. I had forgotten. She had just had foot surgery on both of them. Her feet were wrapped in bandages, and she was wearing special, white, open shoes. She had trouble walking.

I was filled with a deep shame. My mother, in her sixties, only able to hobble, forced to come and rescue her young, healthy son. She, who had spent so much of her life living for my sister and me, was probably in greater pain than I was.

I was quickly across the corridor, hugging my mom. I then hugged my sister and awkwardly shook hands with Tom. Linda stood by my side, holding my hand, as we all exchanged "hellos" and asked, "How are you?" My mom was all concerned about me and kept asking me how I felt. There was nothing to say, except I was okay. I was more concerned about her feet than my condition. She looked a little drawn and in pain.

My family began telling me about their airplane ride and how Liam and Linda had picked them up at the airport. They had all gone out to eat, at one of those inexpensive steak places. My mom went on and on about how good the food had been. They had all stayed at our apartment, with my mom and Linda sleeping in our bed while Tom and Grace slept in the living room. Yes, the airplane ride had been okay, although there had been one stretch of turbulence. Yes, they all fit in the apartment. It had been fine. They had slept well after the adventure of getting here. Yes, they had eaten that morning. Linda had fried them some eggs.

They went on and on about their trip. It was easier for them to talk about themselves than it was for me to talk about myself. We were still standing in the hall. Very quickly, Dr. D. was there. A nurse came to tell us we were all to meet with him in the conference room. It was the one used for the group therapy sessions.

We trooped into the room. Everyone's attention immediately centered on Dr. D. My mother sat at rigid attention, totally concentrating on his every word. As he talked to us, explaining my condition, I listened with only half an ear. He explained I was being given some anti-psychotic medication to take home with me and to take it as directed. I should get a local doctor and see him periodically. He talked to them, not me. It gave me a chance to look my family over without making eye contact with them. How glad I was they were there. They all looked normal, the way I remembered them.

I was relieved. On the way to the conference room, walking across the hall, the light from the room had spilled across the floor in a light, golden-like orange path, highlighting my mother's feet. I had flinched, but no, this wasn't the time or place for hallucination #356A.

When the meeting was over, my family was very solicitous of me. They insisted on carrying my things. We went down to the first floor. The women went to the administration offices to check me out. Tom and I went outside to wait for them.

OUTSIDE! Oh my! Thank you, Lord. Thank you so very much. We stood there, looking off in the distance. It was humid, with a very light rain falling intermittently. It was warmish. It was northern Florida in February. I took deep breaths of the warm, humid air. It was incredibly fresh and beautiful. The ward had been clean and air-conditioned. The air on the ward, however, had been nothing like this. Even now, I can still smell the way the air was when I first got outside. It was so very good, so very beautiful. With deep thanks, I swore I would never ever screw up again. No one would ever again have any cause for putting me in a cage. Tom and I stood around, making small talk. Small talk. I could even chat about minor things. The life and death struggles were over. My strongest memory about my discharge was simply standing there, talking with Tom in the fresh air.

After quite some time, Linda, my mom, and my sister joined us, all talking at once about the endless red tape. Tom drove. There was some debate as to whether to make two trips as my Volkswagen beetle wasn't made for five adults. "No, no, we can make it in one trip." My mother and sister sat in the back holding my things while Linda sat on my lap in the front. Crowded, we slowly made it across town. Everything, including the streets, the houses, the cars, and the foliage, appeared to be bright and new. I loved it.

At the apartment, there was limited chaos. Things were scattered here and there. They had already started packing. Everyone immediately got business-like and busy, packing here, moving things there. No one would let me help. My only job was to get better. The plan was a simple one. Tom and Grace would drive my VW to Chicago. Linda and I would use their plane tickets and leave the next day with my mother. There was some question as to when Tom and Grace would leave, as he would have to work on Monday morning. It was about a 20-hour drive. It would depend on how soon the packing would be finished and how they felt.

My sister was scrubbing down the kitchen. My mother was helping

Getting OUT

Linda pack. Tom was moving and carrying things. I insisted on going and telling the building managers Linda and I would be moving out. Everyone said I shouldn't worry about anything and they would take care of it. Although weak, I couldn't just sit there. I insisted.

I went to the managers' apartment; proud I was free and able to do things independently. When I got to their apartment, there was a touch of Deja vu. As usual, the young, married pair was sprawled on the couch, watching television. It was my third or fourth time meeting with them. Each time, they had been in virtually the same position with the television going. I felt nervous and tense, not at my actions, but just in general. I had an urge to grate my teeth and found myself talking slightly out of the side of my mouth. Once again, in a minimal fashion, my medication was doing its thing.

I told them I had suffered a nervous breakdown, that I had been forced to drop out of school, that Linda and I would be leaving the next day, and any paperwork would be taken care of by my family. They seemed nonplussed, even bored. The wife just asked me to remember to return the keys. On the way back to my apartment, I was struck by how an eternity of hell to me had only been a brief week out of their lives. They probably didn't even know I had been gone.

Eventually, everything was taken care of. The VW was packed to overflowing. Tom and Grace would leave that evening, planning to drive all night. Before they left, we got a bucket of take-out chicken and several side orders. Liam and Bobby would come over and say goodbye.

Linda and I joked about the chicken. It was a pleasant memory. One evening we had eaten some eggs and were still hungry. We had ordered some chicken. We would always joke about it. "Which came first, the chicken or the egg? Why, the eggs, and then we ate the chicken."

Liam and I had no great words to say to each other. He and Bobby had come over, both looking a little stoned. I just hoped my mom wouldn't notice. Bobby was quiet and sat to the side. Liam and I did a lot of well-wishing. There wasn't much to say. We made plans for him to drive us to the airport the next day. He had to work and would use his cab.

Sleep was uneventful, although I tossed and turned in nervous anticipation of the next day. Strange dreams tried to impinge on my consciousness. I was too up to worry about them. They receded into the dim back corridors of my mind.

Going to the airport, getting on the plane, waving goodbye to Liam, a true friend, I was nervous and tense. I was beginning to come on to my medication and felt myself tensing against it. It had been a major question, discussed at length with Linda. Should I take my pills? Would something happen on the plane? We finally agreed it would be better if I took them. It turned out okay There were no flip-outs. There was just a little extra tension, but no mind-blowing pain or hallucinations.

Back in Chicago, Linda and I would stay with my mother. She would use my room, and I would sleep on the couch. Although I was still crippled with diminished faculties, we began making plans to get married.

I would go to a new doctor and receive a complete physical exam. He came highly recommended by Dr. D. He was a medical doctor, who worked with some people with a mental health condition, but he was not a psychiatrist. I was in good shape, except for nervous tension. I explained my various symptoms and told him I seemed to have several adverse physical reactions to my medication. He looked up my medicine in the *Physician Desk Reference*, a large thick book that included the typical side effects of the various prescription drugs. Most of the things I was complaining about were listed as possible side effects of the medication I was taking.

I seemed quite normal, although I still had severe problems with my fine motor dexterity. My hands were especially bad. I seemed so normal that he decided to put me on Librium (a light tranquilizer), telling me to decrease and then stop taking the antipsychotic medicine.

I began hallucinating once again. Without the antipsychotic medicine, I was still unstable. I never told anyone about it, not even my mother or Linda. The Librium and familiar surroundings helped me to put up with the sensory and perceptual aberrations. The ward had taught me well. No matter what was happening, no matter if I were hallucinating my guts out, I would never let anyone know. I would never spend another week on a closed ward.

Linda and I got married in May. We had a glorious honeymoon, borrowing Tom and Grace's camper truck, traveling to the West Coast and around the country for some six to eight weeks.

I would return to graduate school in Illinois in the fall. I was afraid to return to Florida. Both Linda and I agreed I could only be happy as a college teacher, doing research and writing. Taking the entrance exams, I had scored high. At the time, my scores were the best in the history of the department. I had always enjoyed taking standardized tests, sort of a test of will and capability. I prepared for them much like a gymnast or diver preparing for an athletic event. This time, when taking the graduate entrance exams, rather than being quick and facile, I had to dig my fingernails into the palms of my hands, bite my lips and curse the answers out of my memory banks. Taking a test was no longer the quick and easy task of my pre-ward days. I would receive a doctorate in Education, not Psychology. I did well enough, obtaining 10 A's and two B's in 12 courses. I completed a highly statistical dissertation on teaching effectiveness. My doctoral chairman said my comprehensive exams were the best he had ever read in more than ten years of advising doctoral candidates.

It would have been a good story, one of triumph, with me overcoming impossible odds. The bright student breaks down, rebuilds himself, and then comes back as a success. Hah. Trained to teach high school teachers how to teach, I obtained my doctorate at one of the few times in history when this country didn't need high school teachers, let alone someone to teach them. Not only did I not get a college teaching position, but I was not even able to obtain an interview.

It was the last straw. I would break up with Linda, leaving her with our meager possessions. I would go off in the distance, with no car, few possessions, and near penniless. Later, after finding work, I would try to reconcile with her. She would have none of it. She had found someone else, a loving, gentle high school teacher. Sort of the kind of guy I once thought I was.

It had been my hope to teach school (albeit college) and live in a college town with a white picket fence around the backyard, raising a couple of kids, and having a good life. To this end, I had gotten Linda out of the city, away from her druggie roommate, and had begun sharing with her what I thought would be a better life for both of us. It never happened, at least not for me. Except for one class, I would never teach college. I would never remarry or live the good life I had always imagined for myself.

While we had shared so much love and so many good things, I had also given Linda fear and pain, breaking into violence a couple of times during my recovery. The person she had loved so very much had been broken along the way. I would go on with my life as she would with hers.

It was only a week on a ward, such a short time. I may have gotten out, but I have never really left. While time has healed the sharpness of it, some of my demons still lurk beneath the layers of my rational mind. May the dear Lord forgive me my weakness. I can only hope.

AFTER IMAGES

I was certainly not well when I was released from the ward. For the next six months, I would rest and "get better." These are some random memories from my early time off of the ward. The rips in my consciousness would slowly abate. These after images have stayed with me. They are not necessarily in any order. Welcome to being schizoid.

• • •

Standing on my mother's porch in the crisp, Chicago winter, I bent over and scooped up some snow, methodically packing it into a hard, round ball. Straightening, I lobbed the missile at the metal clothes pole some 20 feet away. Ker bang. A hit. Curious, since I have never had an arm that could hit anything, I slowly fashioned another snowball and let it fly. Ker bang. Another hit. The arc was beautiful, the motion righteous. A vibrational plane had been eased out of the universe, across which an extension of myself (cleverly disguised as a ball of snow) unerringly traveled. Excited, I bent to the task, remembering to slow down and take a deep breath or two and then let another one fly. Ker bang. Oh my! Another hit. Easier than falling out of bed. Once again, the ease, the motion, and the symmetry were there.

Reruns began filling my head. There was Robin Hood hitting an arrow within an arrow to beat the bad guys. Zen archery: "Ah, sweet student, the key is concentration. Become as one with the target. Allow the arrow to move from self to self." Drumbeats and trumpets filled my head.

I fell away from wherever I had been. The next snowball fell into a neighbor's yard. Successive misses proved that the hitch in my arm was still there, my eye was still bad, and I really couldn't hit anything. If someone ever asks you why we settle for less than what we really are or can be, a simple reply of, "It's easier, somehow," will suffice.

• • •

Linda and I stood hugging each other. We were in the middle of a flat, empty, snow-covered field that was surrounded by frost-laden trees. It was a forest preserve, a few miles from my mother's house. Linda was facing south, I north with the moon (a pale silver in the light blue sky) directly east and the sun directly west. I was at the center of the only universe for which I had given everything that I had ever had. It seemed right, the terror of the ward was momentarily forgotten. Tears filled my eyes as memories of the pain and anguish of the ward and awareness of my broken head and body did not allow the embrace to continue.

• • •

It was a follow-up visit to my local doctor. He had discontinued my antipsychotic medicine due to my complaints about the physical problems it caused me. Now, I was only taking Librium, a light tranquilizer. Although everything was bright and I was edgy, I was maintaining.

As I approached the receptionist, I was startled. She was sitting behind a glass window with an open circle cut in the glass, enabling us to speak to each other. It appeared she was sitting in the dark, and the glass separating us was covered with frost. Yet, she did not appear to be cold. I held my tongue. This was obviously some kind of altered perception. She told me to take a seat and told me the doctor would be with me shortly. I sat quietly, reading a magazine, when I heard what I took to be a female patient screaming. It was a scream of absolute terror raising goose pimples on my arms. I nervously looked around, but the few other people in the waiting room were all acting normal. I ignored the screams and sat quietly, breathing through my nose. I would never ever be confined to a ward again. Thankfully, when I saw the doctor, it was only him and me, and there were no screaming patients. A lot of smiles and "I'm okay," and

The Change Center

I was out of there. Except for occasional blips, I was getting better. No one would ever know I was still having problems.

• • •

I was lying in bed, mom a room away and Linda two. I felt the labored, troubled sleep of my mother. My awareness reached for Linda. She was deeply asleep, many oceans away from wherever I was, untroubled, buried in herself. Shivering, I turned to the problem of trying to get some sleep.

I picked the car up a couple of blocks away. The radio was loud; it might as well have been pressed against my ear. Arggh!!! Ack! The sound filled my head, and then I was the radio, or rather, the radio was a subset of me. Energy coursed through my wires and transistors. It passed quickly, with me jerking back to the comforts of my bed.

Frightened and unable to sleep, I began lying on my back, arms at my side, assuming the "dead man" yoga position, dropping into passive, positive acceptance. It was then I felt him coming off of the walls, out of the blankets. I tried to allow it to happen ("flowing is," "this too shall pass," "non-attachment is the secret to enlightenment"), but it only became worse.

My grandfather, in his 80s, suffering much, confined to a nursing home, had come to visit me. My skin turned, shriveling, my teeth left, my gums hardened, and I became old, very old. Starting to resist, but remembering (oh dear, sweet Jesus, what did you mean by "do not resist evil") passive, positive acceptance, I allowed it to happen. I literally became a shrunken, old man, with the energy, youth, and vitality squeezing out of me. My breathing fell to my grandfather's half of a lung as I lay trembling, now curled in a fetal position, scared shitless. I fell into a deep sleep.

• • •

A few weeks after I got off the ward, Linda and I went to my bank located in downtown Chicago. It was connected to the Northwestern train station. We took the elevated (called the ell or subway as it went above and below the ground) downtown. It was a shaky trip with me all hyper and nervous. Everything looked bright and different, although these were my familiar surroundings which were supposed to help me stop hallucinating. I had no responsibilities other than remembering not to freak out. Although the whole ride was testy, we made it to the bank without incident. It was there the trouble began.

I was standing in line. Linda was off somewhere. The two gentlemen standing ahead of me in line were talking to each other in some foreign language (German?). Hard to explain, but I had the illusion I was able to understand what they were saying while also knowing I did not know what language they were speaking. It appeared they began arguing about what day it was, and then, oops, I was back on the ward. Time travelers? The exact day became quite important. I smelled a powerful, dangerous, drugging gas, with both of them becoming less substantial. I became dizzy and altered; Linda came over and joined me. I turned to her, whimpering that we had to get out of there (a small portion of my mind was aware that after 10-15 minutes of waiting, I was almost next in line—I was getting better). She showed no surprise, not arguing with me, taking me by the arm, and getting both of us out of there.

We stopped and sat down in the breezeway connecting the bank and some stores to the train station. There was room to sit along the sides of the breezeway. Having worked downtown, I had traveled this route many times. We sat there, with me all sweating and hyper and with Linda holding on to me, ready to hug me, to listen to me, or do whatever I needed.

An elderly woman, white-haired and feeble, came walking slowly toward us hunched over her cane. Inadvertently, I began staring at her. Oh no. She began dissolving, coming apart at the seams. My world went tilt. She became, for all practical purposes, an amoeba. I began screaming, "oh no!" in my head. Only in my head, however, as nothing that ever happened to me again, no matter how outrageous, would ever give anyone an excuse for locking me up, not even melting people. If nothing else, I could hold my tongue. I began blinking furiously. The third or fourth blink was magic; I was able to see her as an old lady once

The Change Center

again. Linda knew something had happened, what with me going rigid and all. A look at my face even brought fear to her eyes. I buried my head in my hands and mumbled, "Let's get out of here." We did.

• • •

Drugs gave me visuals and audios (increased sensitivity and/or hallucinations); it took insanity to provide me with a full-blown olfactory. My nephew needed to take driving lessons to either get car insurance or obtain it at reduced rates. It was something like that. Driving along, I spotted a sign announcing free driving lessons for teenagers. Curious, I stopped to investigate.

The office was closed, and the door was locked. Peering inside, I could make out the dim lines of what appeared to be large embroidered traffic signs (stop, yield, and so forth). Amazed, I thought this was a childish way to teach teenagers and commented to myself, "This looks fishy." Oooops. My nostrils were filled with the pungent odor of fish; it was as though I were standing in an open fish market. Talk about easy. Shaken, I left.

• • •

One of the most courageous things I would do in those early days off of the ward is to walk four blocks to the neighborhood drug store to buy cigarettes. At the time, my only duty in life was to drive Linda to work and get better. Lying around the house, "getting better," trying to figure things out, attempting to minimize my paranoia and sensory aberrations, write (impossible), watch daytime television (difficult), read (hard to do for more than a few minutes), I would occasionally get myself together and take a walk for the daily paper or cigarettes.

Inevitably, I would do this when there was a tinge of suspense and danger connected with this simple act. When I was on the verge, so to speak. I had big mountains to weary over such as a couple of dogs whose barking would startle me, the possibility of kids getting out of school with their nervous energy and quick movements allowing me to almost lose it, and of course, there was always the problem of maybe having to have to talk to someone.

Additionally, "change" and "matches," both connected with buying cigarettes, were standbys in my altered state of awareness. For example, the woman behind the counter would say, "Here's your <u>matches</u>," and flip me a <u>match</u>book. The covers were red, white, and blue, with a picture of an enlisted man and the legend, "Save our Prisoners of War." Oh sure. Match. P.O.W. My match. My world would go tilt, and I'd be back on the ward doing P.O.W. , Or instead of flipping out over the matches, I would be doing some nightmare in my head, imagining myself becoming all kinds of terrible, wasted things, and she would say, "Here's your CHANGE." I, of course, connected her words to what was going on in my head. Sure. Why not?

On one occasion, I stopped to browse through the paperbacks at the drugstore. I picked up one about a woman breaking a heroin habit. She talked of a gentle giant who protected her and who granted her bliss, but who eventually turned into a bone-crushing force satisfied only by more junk. Reading a few pages about her experiences, I did that move-over transition and began living her delusion, seeing and feeling her giant. The effect was similar to the oranges and reds of the knockout shot I had received in the emergency ward. Complete fear. I realized I was experiencing what she was describing. Would I become a heroin addict? I didn't bother buying the book.

• • •

And then there was Linda. How it turned. In the weeks preceding my breakdown, she had seemed to have been such a mystical being. She had been so "right on." Synchronous. If I were thinking dark thoughts, her look, touch, and words were just what I needed to bring me to a better present. If I were into something good, she would simply join me, sharing it with me. This harmony became totally discordant.

For example, on one occasion, she was at the front door, getting the paper, while we were talking about something. I had been momentarily rational, but then I slipped away and began doing mind terror. I fell into

The Change Center

an anti-war movie, *Johnny,* or was it *Johnny goes to War?* It was about a conscious being who is completely paralyzed due to an injury during World War I. He has no arms or legs and is just a head and a torso. Everyone thinks he's an unknowing vegetable and acts accordingly, with him lying there for years. Having no lip movement, his mind screams over and over again, "Kill me. Kill me." And then I was there, from small talk with Linda to remembering the movie, to becoming Johnny. I became a lump of cortex, screaming in my head, "Kill me. Kill me."

I began surfacing from this experience, shaken and dizzy with a voice in my head still screaming, "Kill me." Only seconds had passed. Linda, who had simply walked across the room, while I did eons of mind time, turned and brought me back to the here and now by replying to a statement I had previously made. Her simple, "Yes, I think you're right," only brought me more fear. In the pre-breakdown days, it would have been a, "Oh, don't be silly!" as if she knew what I had been thinking, or she would have seen my glazed eyes and quickly cleared them with a hug.

I became dependent on Linda. She could enter the room, and I would need to touch her, need to hug her. Too often, rationality would drain out of me. I would melt, merging with her clothing, then her, then with a version of her she will probably never know, becoming a mindless, clinging, vibrational parasite. I could feel a tangible energy flooding out of me as I filled her with my love and essence. She always grooved on it; while the dependent infant I had become repulsed me.

I began seeing a different her. She had been my OTHER; some mystical being who was my mirror image, my female side, my complement, and the yin to my yang. Now, I saw an everyday her, magnified by my childlike sensitivity. I would pick her up from work (at this time, she sold clothes at a suburban plaza near my mother's house), and she would sit in the car, legs crossed, bouncing a knee, chewing gum (goddesses don't chew gum, even I knew that), talking about what had happened at coffee break, about customers, ad infinitum.

In my delusion, I was still doing life and death battles, living on the edge, fighting portions of myself that still didn't work. In addition to the

After Images

jagged, oddly spliced films which continually tried to bubble up from my subconscious, there was the more immediate problem of getting my hands to work. I was not interested in what happened during her coffee break.

• • •

In those days, weeks, and months following my release from the ward, I was certainly not well. In addition to the mental and physical disabilities, there was also occasional rage which broke to the surface.

Several weeks after my release from the hospital, I received a supplemental bill for my x-ray. There was no mention of the spot on my lung (obvious, if anyone had read the x-ray as I had had tuberculosis as a child and take an abnormal chest x-ray to this day, let alone so many years ago while on the ward).

As I stared at the bill, dim recollections of my god-awful x-ray trip while on the ward ripped through my consciousness. Staring at the bill, I was seized with an uncontrollable rage. I crumpled it into a ball, threw it across the room, and began screaming, totally upset and frightening both Linda and my mother. I was finally able to control my anger and tell them why I was so very upset. Although they listened to me and tried to comfort me, the fear in their eyes had nothing to do with the x-ray bill.

• • •

My search for truth and understanding was forgotten as I worked on survival. One brief sojourn into trying to get to the bottom of what happened still haunts me.

I had driven Linda to work and had started home. It was mid-morning of a gray, overcast day. I felt very tense, more nervous than usual. I was slightly altered and felt very stoned. I also felt expectant, as though something very important was going to happen. I really didn't want to go home. As I drove along, I turned here, then there, and then, back another way. I found myself crisscrossing Chicago's north side and adjoining suburbs. I drove and drove, aimlessly turning this way and that.

I began thinking, "This is it. This is it." Although not as strong and certainly not with the determination and energy which occurred when I committed myself, I began feeling as if some confrontation, some climax, or catharsis was about to take place. I continued to drive and then felt myself being drawn in a certain direction. Memories of the ward flooded my awareness. I continued, feeling relatively safe in my car, driving through more or less familiar neighborhoods. Pre-ward, I had gotten stoned many times, wandering aimlessly into "happenings." It was something like that, with me operating on close to a remote control. I began driving with a purpose, feeling this, indeed, would be a moment of truth.

I ended up on Chicago's north side, somewhere around north Clark Street. It felt right, with me almost tugged toward some destination. I parked the car and realized I was heading for some kind of shop or store. The cloud cover had disappeared. In the bright sun, I started across the street.

As I reached the center of the street, my foot on the dividing line, I looked up. There was an empty lot next to the building. To the right of the store at the back of the empty lot there was a large wooden fence, painted a dark green. Scrawled across the fence with what looked to be white paint was a large graffiti, "Linda and Howie?" I stopped, momentarily stunned.

My attention shifted to the shop. Just where was I going? I took another step. What was that in the window? It was some kind of a demon's head or witch mask. I could now read the writing on the door. Oh, shoot. It was an occult shop. Better a Buddhist temple or an ice cream store.

I stopped, cursing under my breath. Enough was enough. I turned around and began walking back to my car. Back on the sidewalk, walking along with my head down, there was some writing etched in the cement walk. "Linda and Don." Linda had been going out with someone named Don when I had met her. He had been quickly forgotten as we were swept away in ecstasy.

I shook my head, continued to my car, and drove home. Enough was more than enough. My mind tried to make much ado of the whole incident. Was it a message from God or the devil's laughter? Probably just another coincidence in a life filled with the improbable. Years later, curious, I would not be able to find the shop, the fence, or the sidewalk.

• • •

Worst of all, was the fall from grace. I still believe. There *are* beings who <u>do</u> identify with *spirit*, who can control brain waves and bodily illnesses, who can project essence through time and space, who can travel through the many levels of this universe of ours. There *are* people, who through the grace of God and the law of karma, do *know*. Okay, there must be. I no longer know as I no longer travel in those circles.

Perhaps vainglorious and stupid, I still feel I had come so close to something very wonderful. I had lost control, shattering myself along the way. Broken, I had been forced to be reborn in the only real world I have ever known, a material world of rationalism and dualism, ignorance and confusion. If only I would have known, I would have done everything in my power to avoid spending a week on a ward.

• • •

Ray was a good friend of mine who I had known for some dozen years before my week on the ward. Linda and I visited him and his wife on the west coast during our honeymoon. We spent several days with them. Ray, of all of the straight people I knew, probably understood what I had been trying to do the best.

Ray: I don't know. You seem the same.

Me: Yes. Thank you. I feel the same.

Ray: I mean, you're just like the old you. You act like you always did. You still like to drink beer and shoot pool. You seem the same.

Me: Yes.

Ray: I mean, I think you wanted to be different. But you seem the same.

Me: Yes, of course.

FINAL WORD

And there you have it. I escaped the Change Center after a week of confinement. Rather than reborn or transformed, I believe I was reprocessed. I was glued back together with broken, jagged pieces of my head still needing to be healed. I left the ward as a patched-up version of myself.

It took months after my release from the ward for me to heal. I stopped hallucinating, could use my hands again, and successfully finished a doctorate in Education. However, it would take years before some of the monsters lurking in my subconscious mind were put to rest.

Writing this book helped to heal me. I hope that reading it was interesting and valuable for you. I would hope that some of you have experienced the following:

- A sense of wonder at the incredible range of human experience
- A sense of hope at this celebration of human resiliency
- Gratitude (oh my goodness, you may be able to walk and talk, love and dream, and go outside)

For those of you who are interested in mental health:

- Visitors are the lifeline of confined mental patients (too many patients are warehoused with few or no visitors)
- Other patients are the strongest influence on a confined patient (then comes caretaker staff, aides, nurses, social workers, physical therapists, and finally, the doctor in charge of their care)
- Mental patients may be moving mentally at different speeds than

Final Word

you, may have distorted audio and visual perceptions, and may be delusional when interpreting their reality

I hope you noticed how my hallucinations changed and then mostly dissipated. From "huh?" to pain brought on by the medication to boredom. I am grateful for the benign setting. The ward was clean and modern, with plentiful staff, good food, and no violent patients.

I am very thankful. I survived the Change Center. In closing, I would like to share my daily affirmation with you:

Today, I choose to be healthy and happy. May I be filled with gratitude, love, and kindness for all. May I be generous with my time and resources.

APPENDIX

This was originally written as a stand-alone piece a few years after it happened. It occurred about six months before my hospitalization.

This is the most outrageous thing that has ever happened to me. It was not included in the original publication of this book. I thought it was too close to fantasy and science fiction, although it is an accurate description of what happened to me. I did not want to detract from the actual week I spent on a closed psychiatric ward. In retrospect, I think it aids the reader to see the overall picture of what happened to me.

The major purpose of this book has been fulfilled: Self-healing. I view my story as one of hope and resiliency. I am very grateful I can walk and talk at the same time. Thank you for reading it.

Note: There is some overlap with the body of *The Change Center*.

DEAD LIKE HIM

As William Shakespeare wrote in *Hamlet*:

Horatio: O day and night, but this is wondrous strange!

Hamlet: And therefore, as a stranger give it welcome.

> There are more things in heaven and earth, Horatio,
>
> Than are dreamt of in your philosophy.

The *Illusory Nature of the World* from the Buddha as quoted in *The Essential Mystics* by Andrew Harvey:

Know all things to be like this:

A mirage, a cloud castle,

A dream, an apparition,

Without essence, but with qualities that can be seen.

Know all things to be like this:

As the moon in a bright sky

In some clear lake reflected,

Though to that lake the moon has never moved.

Know all things to be like this:

As an echo that derives

From music, sounds, and weeping,

Yet in that echo there is no melody.

Know all things to be like this:

As a magician makes illusions

Of horses, oxen, carts, and other things,

Nothing is as it appears.

From W. Clement Stone:

Whatever the mind can conceive and believe, the mind can achieve.

From me:

The experiential possibilities of any single human being are without limit.

The Change Center

This is the story of how I got mixed up with a dead person. At least that's my story. You can make up your own mind.

It was a crazy time in my life.

A year earlier, I had returned to grad school while I was in my late 20s. At the time, I drank and smoked too much and had acquired a beer belly. School would be my holy grail and save me from myself. Or so I thought.

It started out well. I made grades and became acclimated to being the old one at grad school (one of the three oldest out of 52 first year graduate students in psychology), although I was only 27. Dating a 19 year old, living in a house on a lake, delving into yoga and grass, I let my hair grow to my shoulders and lost around 35 lb., including four inches off of my waist.

I then discovered acid (the LSD of movie, book, and era fame) and took my first acid trip on my 28th birthday. My world changed. I returned to Chicago a few months later like a spanked puppy with my tail between my legs. My few months as a hippie and a trip head had turned from total wonder and astonishment to fear and paranoia. First, we heard of busts, then we knew of busts, and then friends were getting busted. Then the people who had been over the night before partying like there was no tomorrow had been busted. I was gripped with irrational fear and returned home at the end of the summer quarter. I had somehow made grades for four successive quarters although, I did not remember attending classes for several months.

I returned to my previous job, where I had worked as a manual systems analyst for a large Midwestern railroad. I actually returned with a raise and a promotion to project manager. I cut my hair, wore a suit and tie, and made it to work each day. After nearly a year of doing work and getting high on weekends, my personality started its split. I would be totally straight during workdays and then become a road warrior on weekends. From just smoking pot, I had also sunk back into bourbon and cigarettes.

Dead Like Him

In June of the year following my return from college, I dropped some pure acid and did Lincoln Park in Chicago. In the middle of my trip, ending my walk through Lincoln Park (both the park and the zoo), I came across some Hare Krishna monks chanting and beating drums. I was drawn to them. Actually, they drew me in like a magnet draws stray metal. As I watched them, I got caught up in their movements and chanting. They became rubbery and started to melt. Realizing I was tripping, I shrugged away from the melting monks and continued my walk in the park. About 20 feet away from them, I ran into their energy circle. It was as though a circumference of energy had been drawn around them, about 20-30 feet away from them. It was felt, but not seen. It stopped me. My head drifted into the clouds surrounded by chanting monks and beating drums. As I began to lose it and become completely caught up in the reverie, a jazz combo started a couple of hundred yards away.

The music of the small black jazz group caught me, and I stood transfixed between the two worlds. In trying to describe my day in the park, I would write something similar to the following: "As my head was caught up in the clouds surrounded by the chanting monks and beating drums, the music of the jazz combo snaked across the grass like a silver serpent, wrapping itself around my right leg. I stood transfixed, caught between the two worlds."

The thing is, tripping on some good LSD, I saw (or thought I saw or imagined I saw or made up I saw) a band of silver energy zipping across the park lawn, going from the jazz combo to me, wrapping itself around my leg. Okay, it did not take the shape of a snake, although I'm sure it could have if the thought would have entered my mind. Ever since, and this happened decades ago, whenever I read picturesque authors who use a lot of imagery and symbols, I wonder what they saw or experienced. Did Blake really see those angels and demons he wrote about? Or was it just his imagination? Was he describing images he had seen in his head, or did he just create them out of words? Or did he see these images as real things in a dream or vision, knowing they were not real? Or was he just hallucinating his guts out?

The Change Center

Another thing of note occurred earlier in the trip as I was coming on to the drug. I was in no self (that is, I was just walking, not self-conscious, not thinking, just being) when my consciousness became caught up in something. It happened very quickly. I became an unknowing, terrified being pressed up against an anchor fence. The fear, actually terror, was all consuming. I was totally witless, only knowing some powerful force was confronting me and scaring the zip out of me. A split second later, I was back in my own body, somewhat confused and dazed. I looked around me, and there was what appeared to be a retarded boy pressed up against a wire fence. His wide, terrified eyes held no thought other than total fear. A large person, probably his father, was screaming at him. I was going to intervene and then fell away from the whole thing, forgetting what I was doing. I continued my walk in the park.

I have always given lip service to "we are all connected," "we are all one," "what each of us does affects all of us," and so on. Ever since this event, I know that at least once, for a very short while, I was literally this mentally disabled child, unknowing and terrified, pressed up against a fence. This and other trip experiences have led me to a pantheistic view of the universe. We are connected. We really are different patterns and combinations of the same energy. Or so it seems.

Not much changed in my life after my trip in the park. I continued. Something was missing in my life. Where were the wonder and promise? I began being drawn to the esoteric. I saw an ad and went to a meeting at a downtown hotel featuring some natural psychics. I went with a buddy of mine, which was surprising as he ridiculed anything out of the ordinary, including psychic abilities, astrology, and the like. He went to laugh. I went to learn. I think both of us did some of each.

This panel of natural psychics was kind of freaky. They were strange— literally. They reminded me of a carnival sideshow. A black, non-psychic male led the group. He acted as an emcee and was very dynamic, waving his arms around, talking eloquently and forcefully. He reminded me of a carnival pitchman. Maybe the circus was in town. The most normal-looking of the psychics was a slightly heavy white woman who showed

Dead Like Him

good cleavage. She appeared to be the leader's woman. My friend and I had gotten very stoned. He found most of what was happening to be hilarious nonsense. I thought I could see how they seemed to affect each other nonverbally with invisible energy waves. We got out of there after some demos and some laughs.

A couple of weeks later, there was a large poster in the window of the bar next door to my apartment building, announcing there would be a demonstration of psychic abilities on the coming Friday night. I lived in Chicago's Old Town at the time. Curious, I made a mental note to go to the demonstration. As it turned out, the small bar had a huge meeting room in the back, located behind some closed doors. I hadn't known it was there. Surprise. It was the same group of natural psychics I had seen downtown, just as edgy now as they were then. I left early but picked up a pamphlet from a pile I had seen one of the spectator's place on a table of literature.

The brochure advertised a class, purporting to train one in Mind Control, which included the development of psychic abilities. Training consisted of two weekends, actually four 12-hour days. The class would start the next morning at a small hotel a couple of blocks from where I lived. I made a mental note to check it out.

I got up early for a Saturday, making it out of bed by ten or so. With a start, I realized I was already too late for the class. I decided, however, to go and see what was happening. Not rushing, figuring at best that I would have to wait for another class, I got to the hotel late morning.

I was able to find what appeared to be a small classroom in an area filled with meeting rooms. Someone was writing on the board in front of the room. It was a small room and empty except for the male in his late 30s or early 40s, covering a board with bullet points. It was the same person from the previous night, who had left the pamphlets at the meeting. When he noticed me, he came over with a bright smile, vigorously shaking my hand, "Hi. I'm Bill. I'm a trained psychic. Welcome."

He explained that the class was at an early lunch, and he would have usually gone with them, but he wanted to have all of his notes and points ready. He said with a twinkle in his eye, "What a coincidence that I chose to stay here during the break, and that's when you arrived!" I would find out "coincidences" were an "in" joke in Mind Control.

I had discovered Mind Control. It was pretty amazing stuff. Simply, it involved self-programming using a slower level of brain waves. Imagine an upside-down pyramid. We live on the large, top surface (beta waves). Moving downward or inward, as it were, there was the dream state where the programming took place. What we programmed at the alpha or dream level would affect our conscious or normal state of being. For example, we could imagine ourselves quitting smoking or losing weight, or getting a promotion. Our programmed minds would drive us in that direction. It was sort of like self-hypnosis at a deep level of mind, using slower brain waves than our normal, waking state.

While the alpha or dream state (subconscious) affected the beta or conscious state, the next level down is the theta state (deep subconscious), where creative imagery took place, and then, the delta state, analogous to the unconscious state. Although a little oversimplified, I knew something of brain waves and accepted what the two instructors said (the second instructor had gone to lunch with the half dozen or so students). Although I had missed the morning session, I ended up joining the class.

The result of four 12-hour training days (two weekends) was that you could work a person given the name, address, sex and age. You were trained to be able to go to your level (alpha waves). In the laboratory of your mind, you could picture the person and identify bodily, mental, or emotional problems. It was amazing. It was even unbelievable. Once you saw what was wrong, you could visualize them as okay and send energy to them to help them. The energy did not come from you; it was as though you were tapping some incredible source and directing it to the person you were working. I have no real evidence I helped anyone. Diagnostically, however, Mind Control was astonishing. I saw, felt, and experienced things which still dazzle my imagination and make me wonder about the glory of it all.

Dead Like Him

I worked everyone, including family, friends, and just about anyone I came into contact with for any extended period. For example, in the crowded rush hour bus going back and forth to work each day, I would go to my level, scan for any problems that anyone on the bus may have had and send energy to all.

Okay. Is this, or is it not preposterous? I mean, come on, here I was, in my late 20s with four whole days of training, and I was a trained psychic, a faith healer, someone who could work and maybe even heal a person not physically present. Are you kidding me? It's some kind of joke, right? Well, let me back up for a moment.

During the last day of class, big Joe, a large, overweight guy who collected tolls at a highway toll booth, became belligerent, making a lot of noise that it was a great class and seemed helpful in a lot of ways but that it should be called Creative Imagery or some such thing as it had nothing to do with psychic abilities:

"Okay, there were some great memory techniques, some relaxation techniques, some good visualization, but I'm no trained psychic. This course should be called some kind of Visual or Creative Imagery course, but shouldn't have anything to do with being psychic."

The instructors assured everyone that everything was okay and that we would be working on health cases by the end of the day. A couple of hours later, I led Joe through his first case. We were asked to choose someone who needed help. I chose my aunt. She had polycythemia, a relatively rare blood disease where there are too great a proportion of red blood cells. In my aunt's case, her bone marrow produced too many red cells, and she had to receive periodic blood transfusions. I wrote my aunt's age and location on a 4x6 card, as well as her condition. Joe went to his level and seemed to be describing a combination of my aunt and my mother (her sister). With some prompting from me, he seemed to be able to describe my aunt accurately. There was nothing very psychic going on here, or was there? As Joe worked my aunt, he said something like the following:

The Change Center

"Well, the big thing is there are all these purplish blood cells. They outnumber and seem to be fighting the white cells. It seems really wrong. I don't know what this is called, but I'm going to send her some help."

Well, there you have it. You could have knocked me out of my chair with the proverbial feather. I remember the 4x6 card trembling in my hand. No one had seen it except me, and I'm sure Joe didn't know what polycythemia was, even if he would have seen it.

I was hooked. How could this be? As it turned out, I could work health cases. Surprisingly, there didn't seem to be any carryover into traditional areas like telepathy or telekinesis or any type of paranormal abilities. For example, at a graduate meeting, we tried all kinds of things including using those cards that contained a star, wavy lines, etc., which are used in paranormal experiments. The other graduates and I, proved to be as non-psychic as you can be (I seemed to do even worse than chance; maybe I was a reverse psychic), except for the ability to work health cases. Diagnostically, MC was scary accurate regarding health cases.

I learned quickly not to tell others about Mind Control. For example, at work, I was on the way to my first coffee of the morning: and walked by the secretary who I shared with my boss and his boss (I got about 10% of her time). She looked stressed and strained, and without thinking, I told her that her ulcers were just starting up, and if she kept to a bland diet and avoided stress, she would be fine. When I came back from getting my coffee, she had her head in her hands. I asked her if she was okay. She asked me how I could possibly know about her ulcers as she was just diagnosed a couple of days ago, and no one knew about them. I joked that I was psychic; we never talked about it again.

I tried to tell my boss about Mind Control (I had worked him and the secretary the previous night) and he asked me about himself. I told him he was really healthy, but his knee seemed to bother him (as it turned out, he had had a football injury way back), and it seemed to give him some leg problems. He asked me which knee was bad, and I quickly recalled working him, scanned the screen in my head, and said his left one. He relaxed, smiled, and said he would have believed me, but it was the right one. I then realized that when you are looking at a person facing you, the right knee is on the left (I may have been psychic, but I never claimed to be all that quick or clever.)

The few people I knew in the Chicago area who smoked pot or otherwise did drugs would not listen to anything about Mind Control. The only two people who seemed open to hearing about it were my mom and her lady friend. They had started going to a Unitarian church and appeared open and accepting of the cryptic.

MC could be comical. I was working family members and scanned my cousin's wife. There was an incredible whitish-gold light pouring forth from her belly. I knew from training and other cases she was pregnant. Excited, I called my mom and asked her to guess: Who in the family was pregnant? She guessed just about every woman in the family except for my cousin's wife. Finally, exasperated, I told her who it was. She said, "Oh my. My son, the trained psychic. She's seven months pregnant, and everyone in the family knows about it."

At the same time, it could be very serious. One of my instructors had asked all of us to work his aunt, who was failing and seemed resistant to his help. A few days later, when I worked her, it was mind blowing. I went to my level, and my mind pictured her standing on the deck of what looked to be a Spanish galleon, sailing slowly off into the distance. She was very calm, very peaceful, and stood alone on the deck, gently waving goodbye to a shore I could not see. Everything was covered in a bright red with an orange tinge, which I had learned to associate with cancer. I called my instructor to tell him that I had worked his aunt and before I could say anything, he said that yes, she had passed away, but at least it was a peaceful death. And yes, she had died of cancer, although I may have known she had cancer before I worked her.

We had been programmed not to hurt anyone and to be only able to benefit the human race. Additionally, I would always say a small prayer, asking that my actions be in accordance with God's will and that I would not be allowed to hurt anyone. I had been astounded by the psychedelics and realized there was much in this world beyond my understanding.

The Change Center

MC seemed like an incredible tool which could be used to help others. If nothing else, by continually going inside myself, and generating alpha waves, I became calmer. I also became clearer. The clutter usually filling my head seemed to recede. My focus, concentration, and memory all improved. After all, I was a trained psychic. And so, my life continued.

It was a Thursday evening. I was home from work. It was still summer and still light out. I was in a half-lotus meditating. Even in my youth, I could not do a full lotus, had some trouble holding a half-lotus for any length of time, and usually sat in an easy position, which just requires you to sit cross-legged. I had run into some really good pot a few days before. Maybe that's what all this is about, just another drug trip; yeah, right.

To some extent, the pot had fogged my head, and I felt the need to be clear. I never worked cases if I had smoked pot or drank alcohol, as it was too serious, and also, stimulants tended to throw me off. I was meditating, trying to quiet myself. I had not smoked, taken, or drank anything.

While meditating, I slipped into something by accident. I spontaneously and without volition experienced something I had never felt before. I'll only mention the results. It was as though something deep in the center of my head opened as four aspects of me opened to the four directions. It came and went very quickly. Were these four faces of me or something imposed on me? Looking back, I am not sure. Basically, there was a "me" (or some other entity) facing forward, one to the right, one to the back, and one to the left.

I opened my eyes in surprise and noticed a record album cover (Judy Collins in her heyday) had gone semi-psychedelic, becoming brighter and 3-dimensional. I closed my eyes and went back to trying to meditate. An X formed in my head, horizontal to the floor I was sitting on. It began spinning. Energy trails formed on the ends of the X. The swirling X in my head became a swastika.

Ack. Movies of Hitler, marching soldiers, bombed cities, and concentration camps poured through my head. Hitler ranting and raving, soldiers marching . These movies were in black and white and looked like those newsreels they used to play in movie shows in the 1950s. I think my mind was just associating the swastika with films of Nazis I had seen as a child. It may have been more than that, but I doubt it. I finally stopped trying to meditate and lay in a semi-fetal position. I did not want to watch marching Nazis or a shouting Hitler.

Later that night, as I was falling asleep, I could hear their jackboots slapping the cement as the Nazi soldiers marched through the courtyard outside my window. I think the image of the swastika had tripped me into my version of Anne Frank. I seemed to be hiding from the marching soldiers. Okay, I was not transported back in time or space, and I knew with at least part of my brain I was in Chicago, and there were no soldiers. It only got stranger.

That night, I woke up out of a deep sleep and was a little disoriented. There was a shadowy figure bent over my clock radio. At first, I was frightened, and then I realized he could not sense I was there. Whatever he was doing was very, very important. I knew that much. I had to remember what he was doing. It was important. It was the figure of an older man. He bent to his task fully focused, with total concentration. Occasionally, he would also furtively look around as if trying to see if someone was trying to see what he was doing. It was as though we were in different dimensions, as I knew he could not see me.

Okay. I was either still asleep and dreaming I was awake, or I was awake and hallucinating my guts out. Either way, it was an eerily real experience. It was almost as if we were in parallel universes or some such. It was as though I were watching him from a different realm or from behind one of those mirrors where I could see the other side, but people on the other side could not see me.

The next day I made it to work. I guess I was pretty hyper. One of the straightest looking men on the floor, in his 40s, bald with thick glasses, stopped by my office; he asked me if I wanted some downers. I looked at him in shock, and he explained what downers were and said he had some tranquilizers if I needed some. I shook my head no. Although I had

The Change Center

smoked marijuana and taken a handful of psychedelic trips, I never did uppers or downers unless you include alcohol. In later years, I would even eliminate caffeine from my diet. I was unsure why my coworker had been concerned about me, but I did feel nervous and restless.

My boss took me out to lunch. I think he thought taking a walk in the fresh air and sunshine would calm me down. We walked around the west end of downtown (technically west of the loop as we were outside the ell tracks) along the Chicago River. Everything was bright, strange, and hectic. We ended up eating sandwiches at a standup deli in the train station. We met a friend of his while eating. The friend had a red, florid face and seemed nice enough, although I kept spacing out of the conversation. He kept talking, and my boss kept listening, and I was relieved I did not have to contribute anything as my mind was wandering. We got through lunch without incident.

Back outside, my boss and I stood on a bridge overlooking some train tracks. Three black kids about a block away were climbing over some obstacles and coming toward us. I stiffened in horror. My boss noticed me stiffen and tried to joke about it, "Hey, for a moment there, it looked like they were coming right for us, ready to attack us." He didn't understand. My world had gone two-dimensional. To me, it looked as though these three black kids were climbing out of a painting.

On the walk back to the office, I zeroed in on a person with his foot in a soft cast. It was as though I was looking at him through the wrong end of a telescope from a couple of hundred feet in the air. I felt a momentary burden of despair. How could I possibly help everyone who needed healing?

The rest of the day is lost to me. That evening, restless, unable to stay at home, I stopped in the tavern next to my apartment. While living in Chicago's Old Town for nearly a year, it was only my third or fourth time in the bar, the same one that had hosted the psychic demonstrations. There were two women sitting at the near end of the bar, talking to the bartender. Otherwise, the place was empty. They seemed to know me (an obscure part of my brain remembered meeting them or at least saying hi to them a few days earlier), and I sat down next to the woman on the right. I kept spacing in and out of the conversation the two of them were having with the bartender.

I think most males become horny around puberty and remain that way until they're put in the ground. There is an urban myth that if you're in need and want to get laid, all you have to do is stand on a busy, crowded street corner and ask the first hundred acceptable women if they want to have sex. The odds are that at least one will say yes or so the myth goes. I have heard that story from several different guys in many settings, so if you're horny, stand on a busy corner, and keep asking until someone says yes. Other than the dangers of sleeping with strangers, I always imagined myself getting slapped or arrested.

My self-image, carried over from high school, was of a shy, intelligent introvert, a semi-nerd, if you will. Although I have been fortunate enough in this life to be close with a handful of women, I have usually been shy with women, and did the following for the first and only time in my life. It is totally out of character for me.

Sitting at the bar, I kept spacing in and out. I turned to the woman next to me, made eye contact and asked her, "Do you want to f_ _ _?"

She looked startled and gave me a, "W-what?" I repeated my question.

After she recovered somewhat, she said, "What about my girlfriend?"

I knew all about girlfriends. Having been in the Chicago bar scene for a few years, I knew most women used other women to get out of pickups and passes. Either the one you were trying to pick up had driven, so the girlfriend had no way to get home, or the girlfriend couldn't be left alone or whatever. I decided to make a joke of it, although spacing in and out, I do not think I was good at making jokes.

"I'm not sure I can handle both of you." Space.

Realizing I had not been very flattering, when I came back, I said, "Besides, I would rather be alone with you." Space.

I was dimly aware of her talking to her girlfriend in whispers. I noticed she gulped her screwdriver and ordered another one. She went through

The Change Center

four or five drinks in the next 20-30 minutes. I was more gone than there and sipped a beer or two.

Finally, she turned to me, bumping my leg with hers and with our legs pressed together, she asked me, "Your place or mine?" It was my turn to be startled.

"I live next door."

We finished our drinks and got up to leave. As we were leaving the bar, I was still holding the door for her, and she had just passed me and gone out on the sidewalk, when the bartender came running from behind the bar and grabbed me. In low, furtive tones, he said, "The other night after closing, she and her girlfriend and me had quite a time on the pool table in the back. They're great."

I just grinned and followed my lady out into the night. Ah yes, the trained psychic, I knew all about girlfriends. Sure I did. Just as well, as a threesome may have killed me.

It started out okay, even really good. She was warm and passionate and really liked sex. I had a huge member and the strength of 10,000. Although we were forced to stop a few times to catch our breath, we had intercourse forever. We went from passionate lovemaking to aerobic exercise to exhaustion. Finally, she stopped me and said she had to get some sleep. I was still wired and could have probably run around the block a few times.

It turned out she was a nurse. She gave me some Valium. She told me to take one now, wait 20 minutes and take another one if I still needed it to go to sleep. She also gave me an extra pill or two, just in case. She lay down on her back and almost instantly fell asleep. This time I did not pass on the tranquilizers. I gulped all of the pills down without water.

As I watched her sleeping, her features changed. She became my dead stepfather. He had had a heart operation some five years earlier and never came out of a coma after the operation. Her face had changed and now she appeared as he had when he was lying in a coma after the operation from which he had never awoken. Although it was realistic and eerie, I

Dead Like Him

knew it was not really my Dad (just another hallucination) lying there on my living room floor.

The next day is lost to me, but I did get her home. I was able to drive? I do remember a large ceramic Buddha in the corner of her bedroom. It made me feel ill at ease. I slept, and we made out some more.

That night (Saturday), I found myself wandering on foot through an unfamiliar neighborhood. It was an area in the city with shops and bars. I was approached by a very old, bent over gypsy woman. I had read where certain yogis could look at a person and see them as very young and as very old. In effect, they could take a person through his or her stages of life. As the gypsy pitched me about reading my fortune or some such, I looked into her eyes. Her features started changing, first softening and then becoming younger and younger. She became strikingly beautiful. She was perhaps more beautiful than anyone or anything I had ever seen. I ignored what she was saying and when she appeared to be about 20, I told her she was a very beautiful woman. This stopped her for a moment. I shrugged out of wherever I was and got out of there.

Okay, the events from Thursday evening to this point on Saturday are mentioned to show how jumbled I was after my altered experience with the swastika. It was sort of as though I were "tripping" on a psychedelic, although except for the Valium the previous night, I had not taken anything. On the other hand, I guess there are always flashbacks. The following is totally out of the realm of my trip experiences, and I have no explanation or rationalization to explain it.

I continued wandering and was attracted to a large green neon sign in the distance. It pulled me to it like a bright light attracts moths on a summer night. It turned out to be a corner bar, an old fashioned type of place. I went in. It had very high ceilings, a large wooden bar, booths along the windows, and tables filling any empty space. It was crowded, filled with laughter and energy. It was Saturday night, and this was one of the places to be. People at the nearby tables were animated with spirited conversations and waving of hands as points were made. There was a lot of smoke (this was back in the days when one could still smoke in Chicago

246

The Change Center

bars), but it wasn't too bad as the smoke drifted upward toward the high ceilings.

What happened next is the most improbable thing to ever happen to me. It is why I'm writing this, why I have let these buried memories surface from the deep, closed vaults within my mind. As I stood there, I suddenly realized there was no sound. I looked around, and everything was frozen in time and place. It was like in those Star Trek episodes where crewmembers were on a holodeck, and the captain would say, "Computer, freeze program." I idly noticed the bartender's hand was frozen some eight inches above an open cash drawer. No one was moving. The smoke had stopped rising. I realized I could do or take whatever I wanted. I remember having the thought while looking at the open cash register drawer, "It's a good thing I'm not a thief."

Bzzzzz. There was a noise, and everything started up again and became my normal. The bartender finished ringing up the sale, people were laughing and having intense conversations, smoke was rising, and there you have it. Over the next day or so, a bright flash would turn my perceptual world into a still life, and a loud buzzing noise would set everything back in motion. It is perhaps the strangest thing to ever happen to me and quite different than anything I ever experienced on psychedelics.

Memories of the rest of that night and the next day are too scattered and bizarre to try and reproduce as had been most of Saturday. In addition to my world sporadically standing still, another strange thing that occasionally happened was as though something more real or at least something very important seemed to be going on at right angles to what I could see or hear. Hard to explain, but I could never quite see around the corner. I'm reminded of Buddhist texts comparing our view of reality to looking at the reflection of the moon on a still lake or of Plato saying we are looking at shadows on a cave wall made by those walking past the entrance of the cave and mistaking their shadows for reality. Somehow, it seemed something more real was just around the corner. I could not, however, see what was going on at right angles to my world.

Dead Like Him

On Sunday, early evening, still light outside, I found myself back in the bar next to my apartment building. For a very short time, I guess it was my hangout place. There were a couple of guys talking with the bartender. They were all talking in loud voices, and I could hear what they were saying as I spaced in and out. They were talking about the dead guy who was found in the apartment building next door.

At first, I thought they were talking about me. Too many strange things were happening and I hadn't taken anything since the Valium on Friday night. For all I knew, I was lying dead in my apartment next door.

It seems a man was found dead in the kitchen of his apartment. It was on the third floor. I lived on the second floor. His apartment was right above mine. Both apartments were laid out the same. Going in the front way, I had a small foyer with a closet, then a large room with windows overlooking the courtyard; this room served as my living room and bedroom. A hallway led from the front room to the kitchen. The bathroom was off to the right in the middle of the hallway. The kitchen was large; to the left was another window overlooking the courtyard and room for a small table. I guess it was my dining room. To the right were the appliances, sink, back door, and another window. The back door was wood, solid on the bottom, and a latticed window on the top. It opened to the wooden back stairs and ran along the outside of the building, which was brick.

Someone walking by on the back stairs noticed a man lying on the kitchen floor in the apartment above me. As it turned out, he had been dead several days. (Could it have been since Thursday night? What do you think?) When they broke a pane of glass in the door to open it, a terrible odor and gases from the decaying body rushed out. One of the guys in the bar had talked to the person who found the body and emphasized how terrible the stink and fumes were.

When I reached home, everything seemed normal. My apartment, at least the kitchen, was closed uptight, and nothing seemed out of the ordinary. Later that evening, I went to the toilet and reached for the book on the bathroom floor. I would usually read while doing my business. It

The Change Center

was the *Tibetan Book of the Dead*. I had been to Barbara's bookstore in Old Town a few weeks earlier. I picked it up as well as *Alice in Wonderland*, Nietzsche's *Zarathustra*, and the latest Mike Hammer thriller. Although eclectic in my tastes, it sounds now like I was just another ex-hippie male in his late 20s.

The front cover of this trade paperback had a diagram on it that stopped me. It was a blueprint of what I had experienced Thursday night during my meditation. There was a swastika surrounded by a Jewish star, surrounded by a circle, surrounded by four crowns. If you viewed the meditating me from the ceiling, the symbol showed what I had experienced, although I do not remember a Jewish star or circle.

Through the years, I have thought the four crowns symbolized the four aspects of the Hindu deity (Brahma the creator, Vishnu the preserver, Brahma the created, and Shiva the destroyer). Recently, I read an excerpt on a website describing a similar symbol with the four crowns representing four types of Buddha hood and the swastika being a good luck symbol representing eternal life. I like the four faces of the Hindu deity as a better explanation and do not buy the good luck symbol. I had grown to think of the swastika similar to those handles on a hatch on a submarine. They're in an x shape and you turn the handle with both hands. In other words, I viewed the swastika as something used to open or close something as though it were a torque wrench.

According to a footnote, this symbol or diagram represented a dorje, a seal or portal between universes. I had not read the book at all, as it had been bound incorrectly. Neither the pages nor sections were in the correct order. As I understand the book of the dead, however, a holy person reads instructions to a dying or newly dead person, helping the person avoid pitfalls of the afterlife and reach a desired place or goal. In effect, the book is a funerary, containing instructions to lead a person through the Bardo (which literally means "in-between") from one life to another. I opened the book to the middle. I think the part I started to read was part of the appendix, the actual instructions to the dead person, rather than any narrative explaining the theory or philosophy of the ritual.

The paragraph started, "Now that you are dead, you will . . . "I skimmed the paragraph. It described some of the things I had been experiencing. I stopped reading it and dropped the book on the floor. I was still too kinetic to think about it.

[Okay, I had not looked at the book for decades when I wrote this brief description of my experience. I then found it after I finished writing this text. The symbol was on the front cover but much smaller than I had remembered it. I also could not find the above quote and may have just imagined it.]

That night, I slept surprisingly well. It was probably my first really good night of sleep after three troubled ones. I felt as though I had had a weird, off-the-wall kind of dream or some kind of bad trip. It was good to be back.

It was Monday morning, and I started to get ready to go to work. The shower and shave went fine. I was in my underwear and feeling good. I went into the kitchen and got some orange juice, and stood there looking out the back window. There was an office building in the near distance. I idly watched a couple workers on an upper floor. I remember thinking they looked like statues. Oh no. They weren't moving; they were just sitting or standing there, frozen in time and space. What was happening to me? When would it end?

To this point, I had been relatively sane. My perceptual world had been out of whack compared to my normal one. Still, my actions were just reactions to circumstances with little or no paranoia or aberrant behavior. After tripping and being exposed to Mind Control, I could handle these altered states of awareness or consciousness. They were strange, but "this too will pass." Now, nearly back, I went a little goofy. First of all, I realized "they" were after me. I had no idea who "they" were or why they would be after me. I masked my conscious thoughts and continued dressing for work as if everything were okay. I was just a regular guy dressing for work. Everything was okay. At the same time, my mind was working quickly on how I could end this perceptual nightmare.

The Change Center

Ah hah! It was my grandfather. I would have to confront him. My maternal grandparents were from Romania. My grandmother was from a village in farm country, and my grandfather was from the foothills of Transylvania. Both my sister and I had prominent eyeteeth, and there were always family jokes about vampires. My grandfather was a wiry man who had worked hard all of his life. I always remember his gnarled hands. I liked him very much; however, he was taciturn and still spoke broken English after over 50 years in this country. Our longest conversation was something to the effect of "Ah, you are a good boy. You work long hours, and you make a lot of money. This is good. Work is good." The first time he told me this, I tried to explain to him I was salaried, and I worked long because this is what my job required, and I was trying to work my way up the corporate ladder. He didn't get it. I then gave up, and whenever I got home late from work, he would say something similar to how hard I was working and how much money I was making, and I would smile. We didn't talk much. Now, I had the sudden inspiration I must confront him, that he was the source of these strange experiences.

I continued to mask my thoughts and pretend I was going to work. I finished dressing and started off. Instead of going to the bus stop, however, I began walking to my grandfather's house. My grandmother and stepfather were both dead; my sister was living in the family house where she and I grew up. Now, she had a husband and five children. My mother was staying with my grandfather in what had been my grandparents' house. So, there I was, dressed in a business suit, white shirt and tie, wearing my dress shoes, walking to my grandfather's house. The problem was a simple one. It was 10 to 15 miles away.

It took me quite a while to get there. It was late summer, and I was sweaty. My feet hurt. But this had to be done. I had to confront my grandfather. I had to find out what was happening to me. He and my mother lived in a small house, almost a cottage, in the back of a city lot. The house sat up against the alley. It had a very large, fenced-in front lawn and no backyard. As I opened the front gate, I was very tense and keyed up. This would be the ultimate confrontation.

Dead Like Him

Surprise. My grandfather was not at home. My mother was. She was in bedclothes and a robe, too ill to go to work. It was late morning by this time. She was surprised to see me, but did not comment on my suit or disheveled appearance. She looked at me with concern, asking if I was okay.

"Mom, I'm dead."

"Honey, what's the matter?"

"Mom, I'm dead. Really."

"Do you want some chicken soup?"

Yes, of course. Chicken soup. Next to my deceased grandmother, my mother made the best chicken soup in the world. It was to die for (sorry about my sick humor). I had a couple of bowls of this wonderful concoction. I then went to sleep, tucked in by my mom. I was still her little boy, even though I had a couple of college degrees by this time in my life.

I slept and slept and slept. On Tuesday morning, I felt much better. I walked to my sister's, which was a couple of miles away. I think I just needed to see her and her kids. I remember being entranced by their aquarium. I had lunch there and started to leave early afternoon. For whatever reason, my youngest nephew, who was 10 or 11 at the time, stopped me with an "Unc." I guess he had heard me talking with his mother. He said, "Unc, take the bus home. It's easier than walking."

I took his advice. I had to take three buses to get back to Old Town, but I was walked out. On the Milwaukee Avenue bus, I passed Schurz high school about the time classes were getting out. It was about halfway home. I remember the kinetic energy of the teenagers and all of their loud talk and rapid movements. Although I was a little nervous and tense, nothing happened. They totally ignored me, an old man in his late 20s in their midst. I made it home.

When I went into my apartment, I had one last burst of fear. Everything seemed okay and normal, although it was a little stuffy, as the apartment had been closed up for a couple of days. When I walked

The Change Center

into the kitchen, the screen for the window overlooking the courtyard was covered with hundreds and hundreds of flies. I was taken aback. There were also a lot of flies on the back window and door, although not as many. Instead of hiding or having anything psychedelic happen, I quickly rationalized that it must have something to do with the dead person they had found upstairs. Perhaps the gases of the decaying body had drawn them. Maybe I had some garbage in the kitchen keeping them here. Whatever. I dismissed them from my mind and did not worry about them. They were gone the next day.

Well, that's it. Over the years, I have come to believe more and more strongly that my consciousness or awareness (vibrations, if you will) got mixed up with those of the dead man upstairs. Whatever the case, it was a long weekend of fantasy and adventure. I would go on with my life. It would take a long time to reconstruct the laboratory of my mind and be able to work health cases once again. It would make no difference, however, as in a few months I would end my Mind Control days forever as certain areas of my brain seemed damaged by my experience on the ward.

You know, it's funny, but every once in a while (not very often at all), my world tilts sideways, and I feel some fear. For a moment or two, I wonder, really wonder, if maybe, just maybe, I'm dead like him.

Epilogue

I would have thought I would have studied the *Tibetan Book of the Dead*, maybe even seek out a teacher, some monk who knew English. I would sit at his feet and learn about this mystical symbol and the reality it represented, and figure out what had happened to me. I would grow in spiritual development, and experience an awakening, nirvana, or the like.

Hah. Some months later, I decided to return to graduate school for the winter quarter. I would try one more time for that elusive doctorate. It may have worked out if not for my ongoing weakness. The first time, I had been feted and wished well by all. This time, my boss, fearful for me, tried to talk me out of it.

On the night before I was going to leave for Florida, a friend came over. I thought he was going to bring his girlfriend. Instead, he brought her roommate. He asked me if I wanted to do some windowpane (LSD) as a goodbye trip to Chicago. It was December, and my last trip had been the previous June. I said, "Sure." As I took it, the woman (my wife-to-be) said, "Let's put our heads together." Although she didn't do drugs, my friend and I put our heads on each side of hers. And so it began. I would never come down.

It was as though I had stopped for a drink on the way home from work and had one too many. Slightly tipsy, I would never sober up even though I would never have anything more to drink.

After a couple of months of almost continually being high (at least altered) without taking anything, I thought I was going to hurt her (we were living together while I was doing graduate school in Florida) and turned myself into a local hospital.

The Change Center

They would give me a shot of Thorazine, and I would wake up in a hospital bed on a closed psychiatric ward, not knowing who I was or where I was, or why I was there.

Although I was only hospitalized for a week, it would take me months to regain my cognitive abilities and almost six months to have full use of my hands. I would never do Mind Control again, with whole areas of my brain still in chaos for a very long time. I would go back to school one last time.

Completing a doctorate in Education at a Midwestern university instead of a doctorate in School Psychology in Florida, I received 10 A's and 2 B's and did a highly technical dissertation. My dissertation chairman told me he had been advising doctoral candidates for over ten years and my doctoral comprehensives (a full day of testing) were the best he ever read.

It's funny. I have never felt very smart since my hospitalization, certainly not compared to my Mind Control days. I was not especially clearheaded nor insightful. I occasionally remember how clear and wonderful things had seemed when I was working cases, but they are dim memories.

When I started writing this, a woman asked me if I believed in ghosts. I thought long and hard and finally answered her truthfully, "I don't know." That is, I do not even know if I believe in ghosts or not.

And there you have it. As I stand on the brink of old age, I realize I do not really know anything. All of the hundreds (okay, thousands) of books I have read, the three college degrees, the extensive travel, even my meditation and seeking after the truth are as ashes scattered to the wind. Did my awareness really get mixed up with that of a dead person? Maybe. And then again, maybe not. Who knows? Who can help me understand?

I have started practicing a type of yoga emphasizing the elimination of stress from our minds and bodies. As I work toward health and being well, attempting to discard the stress and discordant energy of a life of ennui, my past continues to surface. If I were in AA, I think this story

Epilogue

would be part of a 12-step program, something I would have to do to go forward.

I'm reminded of a friend who also chased his tail for much of his life. He had discovered "truth" while tripping and called me from the west coast to tell me his latest insight. "Don't you get it? Don't you understand? It's all a joke. Everything is a joke. And you know what? The joke is on us."

Printed in the USA
CPSIA information can be obtained
at www.ICGtesting.com
LVHW010349280923
759473LV00005B/138